CAPITAL PUNISHMENT

CAPITAL PUNISHMENT

A Reader

edited by Glen H. Stassen

The Pilgrim Library of Ethics

THE PILGRIM PRESS, *Cleveland, Ohio*

The Pilgrim Press, Cleveland, Ohio 44115
© 1998 by Glen H. Stassen

All rights reserved. Published 1998

Printed in the United States of America on acid-free paper

03   02   01   99   98   5   4   3   2   1

Library of Congress Cataloging-in-Publication Data

Capital punishment : a reader / edited by Glen H. Stassen.
        p.   cm. — (Pilgrim library of ethics)
    Includes bibliographical references (p.   ).
    ISBN 0-8298-1178-8 (pbk. : alk. paper)
    1. Capital punishment—Moral and ethical aspects.   2. Capital
punishment—Religious aspects.   3. Capital punishment—Biblical
teaching.   4. Criminal justice, Administration of.   I. Stassen,
Glen Harold, 1936– .   II. Series.
    HV8694.C285   1998
    364.66—dc21   98-38356
                                                                    CIP

Contents

PART THREE
Justice as Fairness and Equal Treatment before the Law

PART FOUR
Scriptural Guidance on Capital Punishment

PART FIVE
The Consistent Ethic of the Sacredness of Human Life

PART SIX
Society's Violent Spirit and the Need for Restoring Just Order

PART SEVEN
The Role of Religion and the Practices of Faith Communities

Acknowledgments

I OWE SINCERE THANKS TO the helpful students in the computer lab of Southern Baptist Theological Seminary, who scanned most of the chapters; and to Ja-Rhonda Staples and Beth Beauchamp, who performed the initial smoothing out of bumps in several of the chapters as they emerged from the scanner. I am grateful to James Megivern, who pointed me to the chapter by Mohammed Arkoun. I owe profound thanks to Michael Westmoreland-White, who has read extensively in the ethical literature on capital punishment, found many of the chapters that are included here, and joined with me in stimulating conversation about the issues and the literature.

Introduction: Beyond the Pro–Con Debate

FEW ISSUES OF OUR TIME stir more emotions or provoke more side-taking than capital punishment. *Capital Punishment: A Reader,* as you would expect, presents a vigorous pro–con debate on this critical issue. But it also does much more than that. It clarifies key variables that make the difference in different approaches to religious ethics, for example, by shedding light on contrasting understandings of justice as a crucial variable in ethics. It demonstrates different ways of interpreting scriptures and different understandings of God, as foundational for religious ethics. It illustrates different understandings of causes of what is wrong—in this case, crime and injustice—and identifies some constructive actions that are effective in reducing the number of homicides. It points to various practices of churches and other faith communities. It uses the debate about capital punishment as a magnifying glass to detect clues to what is wrong in our society and what we need to ensure a more just and peaceful social order.

The overwhelming majority of articles in the broad sweep of ethical, religious, and social science journals oppose the death penalty, as do the statements of the major church bodies. I have chosen the essays in this book for their interest, and because they represent different dimensions and different variables in the ethical debate. I have avoided reducing the debate to two simple positions, pro and con, although I have sought to include strong voices in favor of the death penalty as well as against it. I see this debate as an excellent device for teaching the crucial dimensions of ethical practice.

My goal was to make *Capital Punishment: A Reader* useful not only to individuals and groups, but also in courses that wish to compare different ways of making ethical arguments, on this or any issue. The debate about capital punishment illustrates these different ways of doing ethics especially clearly.

Justice

The contents of the volume illustrate different understandings of justice nicely. In Mary Sue Penn's chapter, Marietta Jaeger argues that "God's idea of justice is

1

not punishment but restoration." She labels the death penalty a "gut level, bloodthirsty desire for revenge" that leaves family members of victims "empty and unsatisfied and unhealed." Walter Berns counters, arguing for justice as retribution, payback, angry revenge. Justice, he asserts, should demonstrate that we care enough about moral and legal community to be angry and to give the death penalty to heinous murderers who undermine that community. Howard Zehr argues for justice as restoration: it should empower victims, make offenders accountable, and seek to identify needs and obligations so that things can be made as right as possible. William Bowers and Benjamin Steiner relate justice as restoration to public opinion surveys.

Stephen Nathanson reasons that equal treatment before the law is an essential dimension of justice. The understanding of justice that shapes Ernest van den Haag's argument is justice as what a person deserves; he rejects justice as equality and lumps it together with justice as equal treatment. Hugo Adam Bedau advocates equal treatment before the law, but assumes that desert is also an important dimension, arguing that discrimination causes the death penalty to be applied to persons who do not deserve it. Alexander Williams Jr. calls for procedural justice, and for a pragmatic or realistic concept of justice that recognizes the state's right to protect itself from the reality of dangerous criminals; the reality that we do not today live in a utopia; and the reality that Williams, a state's attorney, would lose his job and his ability to effect justice if he did not support the death penalty.

In the chapter on deterrence, van den Haag argues from a utilitarian concept of justice as the greatest good for the greatest number, though he indicates that this concept does not represent his full interest—as we see in his other chapter in this volume, which focuses on justice as fairness.

On deterrence, I have also included what I believe to be the best statistical study available. Brian Forst uses the method of multiple regression, which can measure the impact of numerous likely influences on the homicide rate—exactly what van den Haag says no study that he has seen has been able to do. Forst includes comparisons across the states as well as over time, and comparisons of *how much* each variable has changed rather than simply *whether* it has increased or decreased. He focuses on the crucial 1960s, when the use of the death penalty was changing in different ways in different states, and when the homicide rate began increasing dramatically starting in 1963 as the Vietnam War commenced. (As I document in my own chapter, homicide rates regularly jump when nations engage in war. When governments appear to justify killing, murder rates increase. This may explain what others have pointed out: that after capital executions make the news, homicide rates in the news area increase.) There have been numerous statistical studies of the impact of the death penalty on homicide rates, which in turn have been analyzed and checked by other researchers, and the large preponderance of results points in the same direction as Forst's study does. Hence van den Haag, conceding that "we have no proof of the positive deterrence of the penalty," discounts statistical research and argues instead on the basis of his own general understanding.

Essays written prior to 1991 often say the murder rate is increasing, as then it was. But since 1991 the murder rate has been decreasing steadily and significantly (at least through 1998, the time of this writing). This may indicate that we are learning some effective ways to get at the causes of the high murder rate, and are at long last beginning to act on what we are learning. Several of the chapters point in the direction of shifting the argument from a simple pro–con about the death penalty to paying attention to what will work to reduce the number of murders.

The "seamless garment" argument for a consistent pro-life position on all matters of life and death, including abortion, war, nuclear proliferation, euthanasia, world hunger, violence, and capital punishment, is a relatively recent development. This is justice as promoting the sacredness of human life.

Other concepts of justice may be recognized in other chapters.

God

Besides having different understandings of justice, the contributors demonstrate different understandings of God. Mary Sue Penn writes, "So Pelke started to pray for God to give him love and compassion for Paula and her family. He decided then and there to write Paula and share his grandmother's faith with her." Jacob Vellenga makes his pivotal passage God's statement in Genesis 9:4–6: "Whoever sheds the blood of man, by man shall his blood be shed; for God made man in his own image." He argues that "the Holy God does not show mercy contrary to his righteousness but in harmony with it. This is why the awful Cross was necessary and a righteous Christ had to hang on it." And he identifies God's will closely with the law and authority of society: "The whole trend is that the Church leave matters of justice and law enforcement to the government in power." Walter Berns does not mention God explicitly in his chapter, but instead sees societal authority as functioning in a similar way. Robert Young's research shows how forcefully these understandings of authority and compassion affect people's ethics.

Howard Zehr writes that "when confronted with wrongdoing, God is described as exceedingly angry. . . . But the story does not stop there. God is angry at wrongdoing, but nevertheless does not give up! That is the whole story of the people of God: they do terrible things, richly deserving of wrath, but ultimately God does not give up. God is a God of wrath but ultimately of restoration."

You are encouraged to search out and detect other understandings of God's character, action, and will in the various chapters, and to examine how those beliefs help shape the arguments. Analyzing and comparing these pivotal assumptions helps sort out the debate on this or any ethical issue, and helps clarify one's own ethics.

The Threat, or the Cause of What's Going Wrong

The understanding of the threat, that is, the cause of what's going wrong, is also a key variable that shapes one's ethics. How one understands the threat usually correlates with how one understands human nature, human dignity, and human sin. I encourage readers to compare the assumptions about the threat in the various chapters.

Penn's chapter sees the threat as a vindictive mind-set in which family members of one who has been murdered allow themselves to become in a sense the killer's next victims by remaining bitter and tormented, filled with hatred and unhappiness.

Walter Berns writes that murder undermines moral and legal community by attacking the trust required for community; "and if we do not care enough to be angry, then we do not care for community and we undermine it as well. . . . A nation of simple self-interested men will soon enough perish from the earth."

The other chapters suggest different understandings of the threat, different causes of murder, and different kinds of unjust discrimination. Different diagnoses of the threat shape the kinds of corrective action that we take.

Scripture

All four chapters on Scripture advocate careful attention to the context of the passages in order to interpret their meaning accurately, rather than merely lining up scriptural quotes out of context on one or another side of the issue. It is instructive to ask what contexts these four chapters pay attention to, and how well they do in fact consider the original social, linguistic, ethical, and theological contexts, as well as the best biblical scholarship on the meaning of the passages in the original languages and contexts (while making some allowance for the limited space of this volume). It is also interesting to ask what assumptions about God, justice, and the threat inform their scriptural interpretation.

Robert Young's sociological study began with his experience that Christians on opposite sides of the issue frequently cite the Bible as their authority. He wanted to research what loyalties seem to shape our reading of the Scriptures. His insights shed light on the biblical interpretations in this book.

Gerald Blidstein's chapter is a sensitive and thoughtful discussion of the teaching of the Hebrew Scriptures on killing killers and the discussion of the meaning of killing in rabbinic literature as it illuminates that question. This is not simply an argument for or against capital punishment, but a deepening of our understanding. With some hesitation I have included my own essay because it was endorsed by all recent presidents of the Society of Christian Ethics as well as by all but one member of the society who read it and responded; hence it seems to generally represent what most Christian ethicists judge to be true. I chose Jacob Vellenga's chapter to represent a somewhat opposing viewpoint, which it does succinctly and well. Several other chapters besides those in the section on scriptural guidance also present insightful biblical interpretation, illustrating different ways of understanding scripture. To readers seeking a straight pro—con debate about what the Bible teaches on capital punishment, and a lengthier discussion than we have space for here, I recommend H. Wayne House and John Howard Yoder, *The Death Penalty Debate* (Dallas: Word Publishing, 1991).

Social Change: Healing Our Violence

I am struck by how many of these chapters revolve around the function of capital punishment in the social order and the need for change in that order. Advocates of retribution argue that this severe penalty is needed to restore social order after a severe crime. Advocates of justice as fairness argue that capital punishment's biases against the poor, the uneducated, and persons of color spread cynicism and disrespect for law and justice. James McBride's chapter, based on René Girard's scapegoat theory, which is rapidly gaining influence, asserts that execution is a form of ritual sacrifice intended to redeem the body politic. John Langan cites Mark Tushnet's chapter, which suggests that we are not ready to abolish the death penalty because our society is too committed to violence. Advocates of society's need for reducing the number of homicides argue that capital punishment diverts passion away from effective measures that do reduce homicides. All agree that our social order is in trouble, is too violent, and needs healing. All want us to direct our attention to effective ways to reduce murder and violence in our society, and to begin to turn our society away from violence and toward mutual respect and the dignity of human life. This is the direction, I believe, in which these different chapters point the debate.

This means we should conclude with effective practices for healing ourselves and our society—initiatives we can take that help transform our violent society by bringing community-restoring justice. In fact the book has already pointed in that direction, arguing for practices shown to be effective in chapters by Zehr, Forst, Stassen, Bernardin, and Langan. But two other chapters drive the point home—those by Young and Westmoreland-White. These writers point to practices within faith communities that can make a difference. An important trend within ethics, and especially Christian ethics, emphasizes that we should not only discuss where we stand on issues, as if having a position were the most effective and faithful thing we could do, but should also focus on community practices that we can initiate or participate in that are faithful to biblical revelation and that shape community and persons in ways that can make a difference. So the concluding chapter points to practices that show evidence of making religious community more faithful, decreasing homicides, and giving hope for a society with less violence. But the concluding chapter is incomplete, because this is a new, growing edge of the debate. It needs to grow even more: You, the reader, can help it grow. You can read all the chapters carefully, not only those in the concluding section, looking for clues about what kinds of practices will be effective and faithful and will fit your sense of responsibility and initiative to bring the changes we need. You can join in—not only in the debate, but in the practices of healing.

PART ONE

JUSTICE AS RETRIBUTION VERSUS JUSTICE AS RESTORATION

[1]

Leaven of Forgiveness: Murder Victims' Families Stand against the Death Penalty

Mary Sue Penn

BILL PELKE HAD COME A LONG WAY from the day he had a vision of his murdered grandmother while atop his crane at a Portage, Indiana, steel mill to the day he told his story to a Gary, Indiana, high school classroom seven years later. He had traveled the distance between a desire for revenge and the need for reconciliation. It remains an unfathomable gap to some, including his close family members.

When Pelke finished telling the Lew Wallace High School class how he had come to forgive—and even love—a former student of their school who had brutally killed his grandmother, some shook their heads. Some gasped. "You must have a big heart," one girl said. Pelke replied, "I have a big God."

"I believe in God, too," the student said, "but I believe nobody has the authority to take anybody else's life."

Pelke's response: Exactly. And that "nobody" includes the State of Indiana. That is why he ended up fighting the death sentence handed down July 11, 1986, against 16-year-old Paula Cooper, who had pleaded guilty to killing his grandmother. Cooper's sentence was commuted to 60 years, meaning she'll serve 30 if given the standard half-time for good behavior.

SOURCE: From Mary Sue Penn, "Leaven of Forgiveness: Murder Victims' Families Stand against the Death Penalty," *Sojourners* 24, no. 2 (May–June 1995). Reprinted with permission from *Sojourners*.

Pelke, along with Marietta Jaeger, whose daughter was snatched out of her tent on a camping trip, are two of the 1,500 members of Murder Victims Families for Reconciliation, a group of people who have experienced the murder of a loved one but who oppose the death penalty. MVFR works like a leaven of forgiveness and nonviolence in a culture prone to revenge and retribution.

Bill Pelke

Pelke's Lew Wallace High School visit, part of a series of MVFR-sponsored events in 1994 called the Journey of Hope, took on deep personal significance. Pelke's public stand against the death penalty initially caused tension between him and his father, who favored capital punishment for Paula Cooper. The bloodied body of Bill's grandmother, 78-year-old Ruth Pelke, was found by Bill's father.

"He's got scars from what he saw that he'll have to live with for the rest of his life," Bill Pelke says. "And my father testified in court that it would be a travesty of justice if she did not get the death penalty. I knew he was going to have some problems with what I was doing."

Bill says the relationship has since healed; they simply avoid talking to each other about Paula Cooper or the death penalty. Still, opposition came from many corners. Pelke's wife, Judy, thought he was crazy for forgiving Paula, and even his best friend questioned his actions. One of Pelke's cousins who sought Paula's execution continues to speak publicly of the pain he feels when Pelke rallies against the death penalty.

On the other hand, another cousin, Judy Weyhe, belongs to MVFR. She tearfully presented a plaque in memory of her murdered grandmother to Lew Wallace High School in a gesture of reconciliation. The plaque carries the phrase "in the spirit of love, compassion, and forgiveness." Nowadays Bill Pelke recites the last four words like a mantra. But it wasn't always like that.

On May 14, 1985, four high school girls wanted money to play the arcades. One suggested they see Ruth Pelke, a well-respected resident of her community. Pretending to seek Bible lessons, the girls were let in. When they came out, they stole Ruth Pelke's car, leaving her repeatedly stabbed body on the dining room floor.

A year later a judge sentenced Paula Cooper, considered the dominating force in the murder, to death. Her three accomplices got jail time. Pelke recalls having "no problem" with Cooper's death sentence.

But his views took a U-turn four months later when, distraught over having just broken up with Judy, the steelworker began to pray from up on his crane.

In tears, he questioned the events in his life, his stint in Vietnam, a divorce followed by bankruptcy.

"And it was at that point where I began to picture somebody with a whole lot more problems than I had. I pictured Paula Cooper slumped in the corner of her cell with tears in her eyes, saying, 'What have I done, what have I done?'"

Pelke recalled that on the day of her sentencing, when it became clear the judge was about to order the death penalty, Paula's grandfather cried out, "They're going to kill my baby, they're going to kill my baby." The grandfather was ordered out of the courtroom and Pelke remembers the tears in the man's eyes, and the tears running down Paula's cheeks, staining her light blue dress as she was led off to death row.

Then suddenly he pictured his grandmother, the way she looked in a photo run in a newspaper with each story about the murder and court proceedings. "It was a very beautiful picture of her taken several years before she was killed," Pelke says. But this time Pelke saw tears coming down her cheeks. "There was no doubt in my mind that they were tears of love and compassion for Paula and for her family. I was convinced that she wanted someone in our family to have that same love and compassion.

"At that point I started thinking about forgiveness and how I was raised and what the Bible had to say. I recalled how Christ was crucified, nailed in his hands and his feet, with a crown of thorns in his brow, and he looked up to heaven and said, 'Father, forgive them, they know not what they're doing.' I basically thought that's where Paula fit in, I mean she didn't know what she was doing—that was a crazy act that took place in my grandmother's house."

So Pelke started to pray for God to give him love and compassion for Paula and her family. He decided then and there to write Paula and share his grandmother's faith with her. "I knew immediately that I no longer wanted her to die and I no longer had to try to forgive her—forgiveness at that point was automatic."

He has since exchanged more than two hundred letters with her. He has learned that Paula Cooper, a victim of child abuse who attended ten different schools by the time of her arrest, has received the equivalent of a high school diploma while in prison and has been taking college correspondence courses. She has told Pelke she feels remorse for the pain she caused him and his family. She knows she'll have to live with her past actions. She wants to help young people avoid the pitfalls she experienced.

Forgiveness changed everything. All of a sudden it didn't make sense to Pelke to hold a grudge against someone who had called him a name ten years ago. He quit getting drunk from time to time. Forgiveness helped him heal his relationship with Judy.

And it gave him the strength to plant a crab apple tree in front of Lew Wallace High School, a few blocks from where his grandmother lived, as a sign of healing. A circle of students and death penalty abolitionists looked on as the tree was placed in a hole and students and MVFR members took turns shoveling dirt over its roots. Someone started singing "We Shall Overcome," and the circle picked up the tune. Bill Pelke laid one of the last shovelfuls of dirt around the tree. His face twisting with emotion, he said, "I think my grandmother has a smile on her face today. It's very, very rewarding."

Marietta Jaeger

Like Pelke, Marietta Jaeger says she is the one who benefits from the God-given ability to forgive. She has seen what can happen to people who, like her, have lost a loved one to the violent act of another human being.

Family members who maintain a "vindictive mind-set" allow themselves to become in a sense the killer's next victims because the quality of their life diminishes, Jaeger says. They remain bitter and tormented, filled with hatred and unhappiness. Jaeger, a Detroit writer, says she struggled with the same feelings after a man kidnapped her seven-year-old daughter, Susie, from a tent in the middle of the night during their family vacation in Montana in June 1973.

"I'd had a real wrestling match with God shortly after my little girl disappeared. I had to get eye to eye with God and get down to the absolute basics. But after a nightlong struggle, I said to God I would be willing to forgive this man. That was hard for me to say, because initially I would have been happy to take his life with my own bare hands. But I said to God, I give you permission to change my heart. I can't do it alone."

At that point, not knowing where or how Susie was, Jaeger, the mother of five children, said the only way she could cooperate with God was to listen to the calling of her Catholic faith. It told her that the kidnapper was "just as precious as my little Susie" in God's eyes. She reminded herself that the kidnapper was a "son of God and Jesus had died for him too. Therefore he had dignity. And so, pragmatically I had to try to think and speak of him with respect and not use derogatory terms. And I asked other people if they would speak of him with respect, at least in my presence."

Thus began a yearlong spiritual journey. Jaeger constantly prayed for the unknown kidnapper, willing that at least one good thing would happen to him everyday. "And you know what happens when we start praying for somebody— God changes our own hearts. The more I prayed for him, the more I realized how very important it was for this man to experience the love of God."

On the year-to-the-minute anniversary of the kidnapping, the man called.

He had seen a newspaper article that said Jaeger felt concern for him and wanted to talk to him. He called to taunt her. "To my own amazement, as I was hearing his voice in my ears, I was filled with genuine feelings of concern and compassion for him. No one was more surprised than I. But that's the miracle that God had worked in my heart."

Also taken aback, the kidnapper stayed on the line, letting down his guard and inadvertently revealing so much about himself that the FBI was able to identify and arrest him. Jaeger learned that he had murdered her daughter.

She says she struggled with forgiveness. She questioned whether she would be betraying her daughter if she were to forgive someone who had done such terrible things to her. But she says God kept calling her beyond that. "Though initially I ran the gamut of outraged reaction, I have come to believe that the only whole and healthy and happy and holy way that we can respond to a hopeless situation like that is to forgive."

The penalty for murder and kidnap in Montana was death. Jaeger notes that this had had no deterrent effect on the kidnapper. "By this time I had finally come to understand that God's idea of justice is not punishment but restoration." She asked the FBI to offer him life imprisonment and a chance for psychiatric care. He confessed to Susie's murder and that of two boys and a teenage girl.

Jaeger says the death penalty does not accomplish what society thinks it will. She labels it a "gut level, bloodthirsty desire for revenge" that leaves family members of victims "empty and unsatisfied and unhealed." Capital punishment has the same ill effect on society as it does on individuals, she believes.

"Believe me, there are no amount of retaliatory acts that will compensate for the loss of my little girl or restore her to my arms. Even to say that the death of one malfunctioning person is going to be just retribution is an insult to her immeasurable worth to me. My little girl was a gift of beauty and sweetness and goodness in my life. To kill somebody in her name is really to violate her and profane her. I'd rather honor her life by saying that all of life is sacred and all of life is worthy of preservation from the very beginning of conception till the end when we die."

MVFR's abolitionist perspective is all the more relevant and urgent as politicians striving for a tough-on-crime image try to make it easier to be executed, and more and more of the executed have serious questions arise as to their guilt or turn out to have been innocent. Members proclaim their message at rallies and in churches, in front of prisons and through their newspaper, *The Voice*. They have found a way out of their personal hell through love, compassion, and forgiveness.

[2]

The Morality of Anger

Walter Berns

UNTIL RECENTLY, MY BUSINESS did not require me to think about the punishment of criminals in general or the legitimacy and efficacy of capital punishment in particular. In a vague way, I was aware of the disagreement among professionals concerning the purpose of punishment—whether it was intended to deter others, to rehabilitate the criminal, or to pay him back—but like most laymen I had no particular reason to decide which purpose was right or to what extent they may all have been right. I did know that retribution was held in ill repute among criminologists and jurists—to them, retribution was a fancy name for revenge, and revenge was barbaric—and, of course, I knew that capital punishment had the support only of policemen, prison guards, and some local politicians, the sort of people Arthur Koestler calls "hanghards" (Philadelphia's Mayor Rizzo comes to mind). The intellectual community denounced it as both unnecessary and immoral. It was the phenomenon of Simon Wiesenthal that allowed me to understand why the intellectuals were wrong and why the police, the politicians, and the majority of the voters were right: We punish criminals principally in order to pay them back, and we execute the worst of them out of moral necessity. Anyone who respects Wiesenthal's mission will be driven to the same conclusion.

SOURCE: From Walter Berns, "The Morality of Anger," in *For Capital Punishment: Crime and the Morality of the Death Penalty* (New York: Basic Books, 1979). © 1979 by Walter Berns. Reprinted by permission of the author.

Of course, not everyone will respect that mission. It will strike the busy man—I mean the sort of man who sees things only in the light cast by a concern for his own interests—as somewhat bizarre. Why should anyone devote his life—more than thirty years of it!—exclusively to the task of hunting down the Nazi war criminals who survived World War II and escaped punishment? Wiesenthal says his conscience forces him "to bring the guilty ones to trial." But why punish them? What do we hope to accomplish now by punishing SS Obersturmbannführer Adolf Eichmann or SS Obersturmbannführer Franz Stangl or someday—who knows?—Reichsleiter Martin Bormann? We surely don't expect to rehabilitate them, and it would be foolish to think that by punishing them we might thereby deter others. The answer, I think, is clear: We want to punish them in order to pay them back. We think they must be made to pay for their crimes with their lives, and we think that we, the survivors of the world they violated, may legitimately exact that payment because we, too, are their victims. By punishing them, we demonstrate that there are laws that bind men across generations as well as across (and within) nations, that we are not simply isolated individuals, each pursuing his selfish interests and connected with others by a mere contract to live and let live. To state it simply, Wiesenthal allows us to see that it is right, morally right, to be angry with criminals and to express that anger publicly, officially, and in an appropriate manner, which may require the worst of them to be executed.

Modern civil-libertarian opponents of capital punishment do not understand this. They say that to execute a criminal is to deny his human dignity; they also say that the death penalty is not useful, that nothing useful is accomplished by executing anyone. Being utilitarians, they are essentially selfish men, distrustful of passion, who do not understand the connection between anger and justice, and between anger and human dignity.

Anger is expressed or manifested on those occasions when someone has acted in a manner that is thought to be unjust, and one of its origins is the opinion that men are responsible, and should be held responsible, for what they do. Thus, as Aristotle teaches us, anger is accompanied not only by the pain caused by the one who is the object of anger, but by the pleasure arising from the expectation of inflicting revenge on someone who is thought to deserve it. We can become angry with an inanimate object (the door we run into and then kick in return) only by foolishly attributing responsibility to it, and we cannot do that for long, which is why we do not think of returning later to revenge ourselves on the door. For the same reason, we cannot be more than momentarily angry with any one creature other than man; only a fool and worse would dream of taking revenge on a dog. And, finally, we tend to pity rather than to be angry with men who—because they are insane, for example—are not responsible for their acts. Anger, then, is a very human passion not only because only a human being can be angry, but also because anger acknowledges the humanity of its objects: it holds them accountable for what they do. And in holding particular men responsible, it pays them the respect that is due them as men.

Anger recognizes that only men have the capacity to be moral beings and, in so doing, acknowledges the dignity of human beings. Anger is somehow connected with justice, and it is this that modern penology has not understood; it tends, on the whole, to regard anger as a selfish indulgence.

Anger can, of course, be that; and if someone does not become angry with an insult or an injury suffered unjustly, we tend to think he does not think much of himself. But it need not be selfish, not in the sense of being provoked only by an injury suffered by oneself. There were many angry men in America when President Kennedy was killed; one of them—Jack Ruby—took it upon himself to exact the punishment that, if indeed deserved, ought to have been exacted by the law. There were perhaps even angrier men when Martin Luther King Jr. was killed, for King, more than anyone else at the time, embodied a people's quest for justice; the anger—more, the "black rage"—expressed on that occasion was simply a manifestation of the great change that had occurred among black men in America, a change wrought in large part by King and his associates in the civil-rights movement; the servility and fear of the past had been replaced by pride and anger, and the treatment that had formerly been accepted as a matter of course or as if it were deserved was now seen for what it was, unjust and unacceptable. King preached love, but the movement he led depended on anger as well as love, and that anger was not despicable, being neither selfish nor unjustified. On the contrary, it was a reflection of what was called solidarity and may more accurately be called a profound caring for others, black for other blacks, white for blacks, and, in the world King was trying to build, American for other Americans. If men are not saddened when someone else suffers, or angry when someone else suffers unjustly, the implication is that they do not care for anyone other than themselves or that they lack some quality that befits a man. When we criticize them for this, we acknowledge that they ought to care for others. If men are not angry when a neighbor suffers at the hands of a criminal, the implication is that their moral faculties have been corrupted, that they are not good citizens.

Criminals are properly the objects of anger, and the perpetrators of terrible crimes—for example, Lee Harvey Oswald and James Earl Ray—are properly the objects of great anger. They have done more than inflict an injury on an isolated individual; they have violated the foundations of trust and friendship, the necessary elements of a moral community, the only community worth living in. A moral community, unlike a hive of bees or a hill of ants, is one whose members are expected freely to obey the laws and, unlike those in a tyranny, are trusted to obey the laws. The criminal has violated that trust, and in so doing has injured not merely his immediate victim but the community as such. He has called into question the very possibility of that community by suggesting that men cannot be trusted to respect freely the property, the person, and the dignity of those with whom they are associated. If, then, men are not angry when someone else is robbed, raped, or murdered, the implication is that no moral community exists, because those men do not care for anyone other than themselves. Anger is an expression of that caring, and society needs men who care for one another, who share their pleasures and their pains, and do so for the sake of the others. It is the passion that can cause us to act for reasons having nothing to do with selfish or mean calculation; indeed, when educated, it can become a generous passion, the passion that protects the community or country by demanding punishment for its enemies. It is the stuff from which heroes are made.

A moral community is not possible without anger and the moral indignation that accompanies it. Thus the most powerful attack on capital punishment was written by a man, Albert Camus, who denied the legitimacy of anger and moral indignation by denying the very possibility of a moral community in our time. The anger expressed in our world, he said, is nothing but hypocrisy. His novel *L'Étranger* (variously translated as *The Stranger* or *The Outsider*) is a brilliant portrayal of what Camus insisted is our world, a world deprived of God, as he put it. It is a world we would not choose to live in and one that Camus, the hero of the French Resistance, disdained. Nevertheless, the novel is a modern masterpiece, and Meursault, its antihero (for a world without anger can have no heroes), is a murderer.

He is a murderer whose crime is excused, even as his lack of hypocrisy is praised, because the universe, we are told, is "benignly indifferent" to how we live or what we do. Of course, the law is not indifferent; the law punished Meursault and it threatens to punish us if we do as he did. But Camus the novelist teaches us that the law is simply a collection of arbitrary conceits. The people around Meursault apparently were not indifferent; they expressed dismay at his lack of attachment to his mother and disapprobation of his crime. But Camus the novelist teaches us that other people are hypocrites. They pretend not to know what Camus the opponent of capital punishment tells: namely, that "our civilization has lost the only values that, in a certain way, can justify that penalty... [the existence of] a truth or a principle that is superior to man." There is no basis for friendship and no moral law; therefore, no one, not even a murderer, can violate the terms of friendship or break that law; and there is no basis for the anger that we express when someone breaks that law. The only thing we share as men, the only thing that connects us one to another, is a "solidarity against death," and a judgment of capital punishment "upsets" that solidarity. The purpose of human life is to stay alive.

Like Meursault, Macbeth was a murderer, and like *L'Étranger*, Shakespeare's *Macbeth* is the story of a murder, but there the similarity ends. As Lincoln said, "Nothing equals *Macbeth*." He was comparing it with the other Shakespearean plays he knew, the plays he had "gone over perhaps as frequently as any unprofessional reader... *Lear, Richard Third, Henry Eighth, Hamlet*"; but I think he meant to say more than that none of these equals *Macbeth*. I think he meant that no other literary work equals it. "It is wonderful," he said. *Macbeth* is wonderful because, to say nothing more here, it teaches us the awesomeness of the commandment "Thou shalt not kill."

What can a dramatic poet tell us about murder? More, probably, than anyone else, if he is a poet worthy of consideration, and yet nothing that does not inhere in the act itself. In *Macbeth* Shakespeare shows us murders committed in a political world by a man so driven by ambition to rule that world that he becomes a tyrant. He shows us also the consequences, which were terrible, worse even than Macbeth feared. The cosmos rebelled, turned into chaos by his deeds. He shows a world that was not "benignly indifferent" to what we call crimes and especially to murder, a world constituted by laws divine as well as human, and Macbeth violated the most awful of those laws. Because the world was so constituted, Macbeth suffered the torments of the great and the damned, torments far beyond the "practice" of any physician. He had known glory and had deserved the respect and affection of king, countrymen, army, friends, and wife; and he lost it all. At the end he was reduced to saying that life "is a tale told by an idiot, full of sound and fury, signifying nothing"; yet, in spite of the horrors provoked in us by his acts, he excites no anger in us. We pity him; even so, we understand the anger of his countrymen and the dramatic necessity of his death. Macbeth is a play about ambition, murder, tyranny; about horror, anger, vengeance, and perhaps more than any other of Shakespeare's plays, justice. Because of justice, Macbeth has to die, not by his own hand—he will not "play the Roman fool, and die on [his] sword"—but at the hand of the avenging Macduff. The dramatic necessity of his death would appear to rest on its moral necessity. Is that right? Does this play conform to our sense of what a murder means? Lincoln thought it was "wonderful."

Surely Shakespeare's is a truer account of murder than the one provided by Camus, and by truer I mean truer to our moral sense of what a murder is and what the consequences that attend it must be. Shakespeare shows us vengeful men because there is something in the souls of men—then and now—that requires such crimes to be avenged. Can we imagine a world that does not take its revenge on the man who kills Macduff's wife and children? (Can we imagine the play in which Macbeth does not die?) Can we imagine a people that does not hate murderers? (Can we imagine a world where Meursault is an outsider only because he does not pretend to be outraged by murder?) Shakespeare's poetry could not have been written out of the moral sense that the death penalty's opponents insist we ought to have. Indeed, the issue of capital punishment can be said to turn on whether Shakespeare's or Camus's is the more telling account of murder.

There is a sense in which punishment may be likened to dramatic poetry. Dramatic poetry depicts men's actions because men are revealed in, or make themselves known through, their actions; and the essence of a human action, according to Aristotle, consists in its being virtuous or vicious. Only a ruler or a contender for rule can act with the freedom and on a scale that allows the virtuousness or viciousness of human deeds to be fully displayed. Macbeth was such a man, and in his fall, brought about by his own acts, and in the consequent suffering he endured, is revealed the meaning of morality. In *Macbeth* the majesty of the moral law is demonstrated to us; as I said, it teaches us the awesomeness of the commandment Thou shalt not kill. In a similar fashion, the punishments imposed by the legal order remind us of the reign of the moral order; not only do they remind us of it, but by enforcing its prescriptions, they enhance the dignity of the legal order in the eyes of moral men, in the eyes of those decent citizens who cry out "for gods who will avenge injustice." That is especially important in a self-governing community, a community that gives laws to itself.

If the laws were understood to be divinely inspired or, in the extreme case, divinely given, they would enjoy all the dignity that the opinions of men can grant and all the dignity they require to ensure their being obeyed by most of the men living under them. Like Duncan in the opinion of Macduff, the laws would be "the Lord's anointed," and would be obeyed even as Macduff obeyed the laws of the Scottish kingdom. Only a Macbeth would challenge them, and only a Meursault would ignore them. But the laws of the United States are not of this description; in fact, among the proposed amendments that became the Bill of Rights was one declaring, not that all power comes from God, but rather "that all power is originally vested in, and consequently derives from the people"; and this proposal was dropped only because it was thought to be redundant: the Constitution's preamble said essentially the same thing, and what we know as the Tenth Amendment reiterated it. So Madison proposed to make the Constitution venerable in the minds of the people, and Lincoln, in an early speech, went so far as to say that a "political religion" should be made of it. They did not doubt that the Constitution and the laws made pursuant to it would be supported by "enlightened reason," but fearing that enlightened reason would be in short supply, they sought to augment it. The laws of the United States would be obeyed by some men because they could hear and understand "the voice of enlightened reason," and by other men because they would regard the laws with that "veneration which time bestows on everything."

Supreme Court justices have occasionally complained of our habit of making "constitutionality synonymous with wisdom." But the extent to which the Constitution is venerated and its authority accepted depends on the compatibility of its rules with our moral sensibilities; despite its venerable character, the Constitution is not the only source of these moral sensibilities. There was even a period, before slavery was abolished by the Thirteenth Amendment, when the Constitution was regarded by some very moral men as an abomination. Garrison called it "a covenant with death and an agreement with Hell," and there were honorable men holding important political offices and judicial appointments who refused to enforce the Fugitive Slave Law even though its constitutionality had been affirmed. In time this opinion spread far beyond the ranks of the original abolitionists until those who held it composed a constitutional majority of the people, and slavery was abolished.

But Lincoln knew that more than amendments were required to make the Constitution once more worthy of the veneration of moral men. That is why, in the Gettysburg Address, he made the principle of the Constitution an inheritance from "our fathers." That it should be so esteemed is especially important in a self-governing nation that gives laws to itself, because it is only a short step from the principle that the laws are merely a product of one's own will to the opinion that the only consideration that informs the law is self-interest; and this opinion is only one remove from lawlessness. A nation of simple self-interested men will soon enough perish from the earth.

It was not an accident that Lincoln spoke as he did at Gettysburg or that he chose as the occasion for his words the dedication of a cemetery built on a portion of the most significant battlefield of the Civil War. Two and a half years earlier, in his first inaugural address, he had said that Americans, north and south, were not and must not be enemies, but friends. Passion had strained but must not be allowed to break the bonds of affection that tied them one to another. He closed by saying this: "The mystic chords of memory, stretching from every battlefield, and patriot grave, to every living heart and hearthstone, all over this broad land, will yet swell the chorus of the Union, when again touched, as surely they will be, by the better angels of our nature." The chords of memory that would swell the chorus of the Union could be touched, even by a man of Lincoln's stature, only on the most solemn occasions, and in the life of a nation no occasion is more solemn than the burial of the patriots who have died defending it on the field of battle. War is surely an evil, but as Hegel said, it is not an "absolute evil." It exacts the supreme sacrifice, but precisely because of that it can call forth such sublime rhetoric as Lincoln's. His words at Gettysburg serve to remind Americans in particular of what Hegel said people in general needed to know, and could be made to know by means of war and the sacrifices demanded of them in wars: namely, that their country is something more than a "civil society" the purpose of which is simply the protection of individual and selfish interests.

Capital punishment, like Shakespeare's dramatic and Lincoln's political poetry (and it is surely that, and was understood by him to be that), serves to remind us of the majesty of the moral order that is embodied in our law, and of the terrible consequences of its breach. The law must not be understood to be merely a statute that we enact or repeal at our will, and obey or disobey at our convenience—especially not the criminal law. Wherever law is regarded as merely statutory, men will soon enough disobey it, and will learn how to do so without any inconvenience to themselves. The criminal law must possess a dignity far beyond that possessed by mere statutory enactment or utilitarian and self-interested calculations. The most powerful means we have to give it that dignity is to authorize it to impose the ultimate penalty. The criminal law must be made awful, by which I mean inspiring, or commanding "profound respect or reverential fear." It must remind us of the moral order by which alone we can live as human beings, and in America, now that the Supreme Court has outlawed banishment, the only punishment that can do this is capital punishment.

The founder of modern criminology, the eighteenth-century Italian Cesare Beccaria, opposed both banishment and capital punishment because he understood that both were inconsistent with the principle of self-interest, and self-interest was the basis of the political order he favored. If a man's first or only duty is to himself, of course he will prefer his money to his country, he will also prefer his money to his brother. In fact, he will prefer his brother's money to his brother, and a people of this description, or a country that understands itself in this Beccarian manner, can put the mark of Cain on no one. For the same reason, such a country can have no legitimate reason to execute its criminals, or, indeed, to punish them in any manner. What would be accomplished by punishment in such a place? Punishment arises out of the demand for justice, and justice is demanded by angry, morally indignant men; its purpose is to satisfy that moral indignation and thereby promote the law-abidingness that, it is assumed, accompanies it. But the principle of self-interest denies the moral basis of that indignation.

Not only will a country based solely on self-interest have no legitimate reason to punish; it may have no need to punish. It may be able to solve what we call the crime problem by substituting a law of contracts for a law of crimes. According to Beccaria's social contract, men agree to yield their natural freedom to the "sovereign" in exchange for his promise to keep the peace. As it becomes more difficult for the sovereign to fulfill his part of the contract, there is a demand that he be made to pay for his nonperformance. From this comes compensation or insurance schemes embodied in statutes whereby the sovereign (or state), being unable to keep the peace by punishing criminals, agrees to compensate its contractual partners for injuries suffered at the hands of criminals, injuries the police are unable to prevent. The insurance policy takes the place of law enforcement and the *posse comitatus,* and John Wayne and Gary Cooper give way to Mutual of Omaha. There is no anger in this kind of law, and none (or no reason for any) in the society. The principle can be carried further still. If we ignore the victim (and nothing we do can restore his life anyway), there would appear to be no reason why—the worth of a man being his price, as Beccaria's teacher, Thomas Hobbes, put it—coverage should not be extended to the losses incurred in a murder. If we ignore the victim's sensibilities (and what are they but absurd vanities?), there would appear to be no reason why—the worth of a woman being her price—coverage should not be extended to the losses incurred in a rape. Other examples will no doubt suggest themselves.

This might appear to be an almost perfect solution to what we persist in calling the crime problem, achieved without risking the terrible things sometimes done by an angry people. A people that is not angry with criminals will not be able to deter crime, but a people fully covered by insurance has no need to deter crime: they will be insured against all the losses they can, in principle, suffer. What is now called crime can be expected to increase in volume, of course, and this will cause an increase in the premiums paid, directly or in the form of taxes. But it will no longer be necessary to apprehend, try, and punish criminals, which now costs Americans more than $1.5 billion a month (and is increasing at an annual rate of about 15 percent), and one can buy a lot of insurance for $1.5 billion. There is this difficulty, as Rousseau put it: To exclude anger from the human community is to concentrate all the passions in a "self-interest of the meanest sort," and such a place would not be fit for human habitation.

When, in 1976, the Supreme Court declared death to be a constitutional penalty, it decided that the United States was not that sort of country; most of us, I think, can appreciate that judgment. We want to live among people who do not value their possessions more than their citizenship, who do not think exclusively or even primarily of their own rights, people whom we can depend on even as they exercise their rights, and whom we can trust, which is to say, people who, even in the absence of a policeman, will not assault our bodies or steal our possessions, and might even come to our assistance when we need it, and who stand ready, when the occasion demands it, to risk their lives in defense of their country. If we are of the opinion that the United States may rightly ask of its citizens this awful sacrifice, then we are also of the opinion that it may rightly impose the most awful penalty; if it may rightly honor its heroes, it may rightly execute the worst of its criminals. By doing so, it will remind its citizens that it is a country worthy of heroes.

[3]

Restoring Justice

Howard Zehr

WHAT LAWS HAVE BEEN broken? Who "done" it? What does the offender deserve? In spite of its breathtaking sophistication and complexity, the Western criminal justice process boils down to these three simple questions.

Note that there is nothing in those questions which refers to the primary stakeholder in a crime: the victim. Is it surprising, then, that victims and their loved ones so often feel neglected and victimized by justice?

Over ten million Americans are victims of violent crime each year. More than twenty thousand American families lose a loved one to homicide annually. This is not some insignificant minority of people: we're talking here about a sizable number of neighbors and communities who experience serious trauma every year as a result of crime. The impact ripples out throughout our world.

Victimization is a truly devastating experience that affects many areas of a person's life—not only the direct victim but also those close to victims (sometimes called secondary victims or "co-victims"). Seemingly minor offenses, including property crimes, can be deeply traumatic, even life-altering. Bruce Shapiro, editor of *The Nation*, victim of a vicious knife attack, describes this disorder as "a profoundly political state in which the world has gone wrong, in

SOURCE: Howard Zehr adapted his essay, "Retributive Justice, Restorative Justice," from *New Perspectives on Crime and Justice* (MCC U.S. Office of Criminal Justice and MCC Canada Victim Offender Ministries, 1985), for the present book. Used by permission of the author.

which you feel isolated from the broader community by the inarticulable extremity of experience." This captures well the sense of disorder, the sense of isolation, the feeling of being out of control and cut off from others who have not shared the experience.

Victimization usually triggers feelings of extreme fear and vulnerability. Guilt, self-blame, myriad questions come with it. So does tremendous anger: anger at the offender but also anger at oneself, at the system, at one's loved ones, even at God. A sense of isolation and disconnection from friends and families is common. One may come to doubt everything and everyone he or she has believed in. The experience affects most areas of life—work, play, sleep, marriage—leaving one isolated, full of doubt, questioning his or her own memories, perceptions, and interpretations. Unnerving dreams, unfathomable mood swings, overwhelming and seemingly unending grief, an oscillation between emotional numbness and emotional overload—these are among the many ramifications of crime.

In short, the crisis of victimization is comprehensive. It can be described as three overlapping circles: a crisis of self-image (who am I really?), a crisis of meaning (what do I believe?), and a crisis of relationship (whom can I trust?).

Judith Lewis Herman, in her important book *Trauma and Recovery,* notes that crime destroys fundamental assumptions about the safety and predictability of the world, the positive value of the self, and the meaningful order of creation. Complex systems of self-protection, meaning, control, and connection are torn apart, leaving victims isolated and confused.

Out of the trauma of victims' experiences come many needs. Some of these have to be met by victims themselves and their intimates. But some of their needs should be addressed by the larger society, especially the justice process.

Most immediate, perhaps, is the need for the creation of a safe place physically, symbolically, and emotionally. Those who have been victimized want to know that it will not recur to them or to others.

Beyond that, they need to feel safe space to mourn what has happened. The descent into mourning, says Herman, is one of the most dreaded tasks but it is essential to reconstruction. This requires an act of courage on the part of the victim as well as support from her or his loved ones, but public acknowledgment of the trauma—in biblical terms, *lament*—is also important.

Victims badly need what might be called somewhat ambiguously an "experience of justice." This has many dimensions. Often it is assumed that vengeance is part of this need but various studies suggest that this is not necessarily so, that the need for vengeance often may be the result of justice denied. Herman notes that the "fantasy of revenge" is often a mirror image of the traumatic memory but with the roles of victim and offender reversed. It reflects a wish for catharsis, and victims or co-victims often imagine it will bring relief, but in fact it often increases the torment.

The experience of justice seems to include public assurance that what happened to the victim was wrong, that it was unfair, that it was undeserved. Victims need to know that something is being done to make sure that the offense does not happen again. Often they feel the need for some repayment of losses, in part because of the statement of responsibility that is implied. So restitution and apologies from an offender can play an important role in the experience of justice; so too can public condemnation of the act and exoneration of the victim.

Victims also need answers; in fact, studies in several countries show that crime victims often rate the need for answers above needs for compensation. Why me? What could I have done differently? What kind of person did this and why? These are just a few of the questions that haunt victims. Without answers, it can be very difficult to restore a sense of order and therefore to heal.

Another area is sometimes called "truth-telling"—opportunities to tell their stories and to vent their feelings, often repeatedly, to people that matter: to friends, to law enforcement people, perhaps even to those who caused this pain. Only by expressing their anger and by repeatedly telling their stories can they integrate this terrible experience into their own stories, their own identities. Until this happens, the experience, the offender, will control their lives. Only when they have integrated the experience, which includes answering key questions, will they regain the sense of personal autonomy and order that is essential to wholeness.

Also important is the need for empowerment. In the crime, an offender has taken power over victims' lives—not only of their body and or property during the incident itself, but over their subsequent emotions, dreams, and reality. Indeed, many victims find that, at least for a while, the offense and the offender are in control of their psyche. That is profoundly unnerving. Without an experience of justice and healing, this too can last a lifetime.

Herman notes that fundamental to crime is the experience of disempowerment and disconnection, so recovery requires empowerment and creation of new connections. While there is individual work that victims must do, recovery can only happen in relationship. The community, through the justice system, has an important responsibility in this healing journey.

But justice as we usually know it ignores victims and their needs. All too often they discover that they are at most a footnote in the process, recognized only if they are needed as witnesses. The point was made graphically by a woman who once told me of being totally left out of two cases where she was victim. She was the prosecuting attorney in that district, and her own staff had considered it unnecessary to keep her as the victim informed! In one murder case in which I was involved, the surviving family members had to fight for the "privilege" of talking to the prosecutor to let her know their perspective on the case.

The legal process tends to ignore victims, then reinterprets their experience in foreign legal terms until it hardly sounds like their own. It steals their experience; it denies them the participation and meaning that is so crucial to recovery. What socially legitimate channels are left for their anger? What alternatives are there to fears and stereotypes about offenders? Who can be surprised that victims are so dissatisfied? Herman concludes that "if one set out to design a system for provoking intrusive post-traumatic symptoms, one could not do better than a court of law." And this trauma is amplified in death-penalty cases, which often drag out over years due to frequent—and often necessary—appeals and other legal proceedings.

The system we call "criminal justice" does not work. Certainly, at least, it does not work for victims.

But it is not working for offenders either. It is not preventing offenders from committing crimes, as we know well from recidivism figures. And it is not healing them. On the contrary, the experience of punishment and of imprisonment is deeply damaging, often encouraging rather than discouraging criminal behavior. Nor is the justice system holding offenders accountable. Genuine accountability means, first of all, that when you offend, you need to understand and take responsibility for what you did. Offenders need to be encouraged to understand the real human consequences of their actions. But accountability has a second component as well; offenders need to be encouraged to take responsibility for making things right, for righting the wrong.

Unfortunately, though, our legal process does not encourage such accountability on the part of offenders. Nowhere in the process are offenders given the opportunity to understand the implications of what they have done.

Justice as we know it doesn't serve victims' needs well, but neither does it address the real needs of offenders. What some have termed the "new retributivism" has greatly increased the numbers in prison and on death row. This increase in punishment has been promoted in the language of accountability, but ironically, criminal justice in the Western world has very little to do with real accountability. What does it mean to have your house burglarized, to be assaulted, to have a loved one murdered? Little in the justice process encourages offenders to understand the consequences of their actions or to empathize with victims. On the contrary, the adversarial game requires offenders to look out for themselves. Offenders are discouraged from acknowledging their responsibility and are given little opportunity to act on this responsibility in concrete ways. The "neutralizing strategies"—the stereotypes and rationalizations that offenders use to distance themselves from the people they hurt—are never challenged. The sense of alienation from society felt by many offenders is only heightened by the legal process and the prison experience. For many young men in urban America, in fact, the prison experience is a rite of passage, an important credential for life on the streets. Is there any wonder that the system's "client loyalty" is so high?

Wrongful acts must, of course, be denounced. Society must draw lines between acceptable and unacceptable behavior, and punishment is often justified in these terms. Unfortunately, though, punishment is a poor teacher, and often teaches the wrong lesson. This may help explain why America has the world's highest imprisonment rate and yet crime rates—including murder rates—are so high.

Just why this punishment fails is beyond the scope of this essay but here are two suggestions. One has to do with the way we stigmatize those who offend, making it difficult for them to rejoin (or join!) society. This has been described well by Australian criminologist John Braithwaite. In his pioneering book, Braithwaite notes that one of the most powerful forms of social control is shame, but there are two kinds of shame: stigmatizing shame, and reintegrative shame.

Reintegrative shame denounces the offense but not the offender and in addition offers a way back. Through steps such as acknowledgment of the wrong and actions to make things right, self-respect and acceptance into the community become possible. Such shame uses wrongdoing as an opportunity to build character and community.

The Western criminal justice approach, however, embodies stigmatizing shame. It sends the message that not only are your behaviors bad, but you are bad and there is really nothing that you can do which will make up for it. It becomes very difficult, therefore, to be reintegrated into society. So people who offend feel permanently labeled as offenders and begin to seek out other deviant people, thus giving rise to gangs and other groupings of "outsiders."

Another factor, according to Canadian criminologist Ezzat Fattah, is the oft-overlooked reality that most violence is an expression of grievance, a reaction to some sort of victimization. Most victimizers have also been victims, Fattah suggests, so it is easy to understand why punishment fails. For offenders who have been victimized—or at least see themselves as victims—punishment can only be seen as an added victimization. What punishment models is not that victimizing others is wrong, but that it is acceptable to victimize those who victimize you. This may be one explanation for the pattern some have observed of rising murder rates immediately following an execution.

These failures suggest that the problem of justice is more fundamental than a few programs. Unfortunately, though, the debate throughout the history of criminology has tended to be about theories of punishment rather than concepts of justice generally. Yet it is our justice paradigm itself—our assumptions, our definitions of crime and justice—that are at the root of our failure to provide justice to victims, to offenders, to the community. The "lens" through which we view crime and justice is itself flawed; this "lens" is the reason that victims are ignored, that offenders are not held accountable, that the community has no role, that reforms so often end up failures.

The prevailing paradigm or lens of justice, which I call the retributive paradigm, might be characterized like this:

Crime
   is a violation of the law,
   and the state is the victim.
The aim of justice
   is to establish blame (guilt)
   and administer pain (punishment).
The process of justice
   is a conflict between adversaries
   in which offender is pitted against state,
   rules and intentions outweigh outcomes,
   and one side wins while the other loses.

It can be put more simply: Crime is breaking the rules. The state, not the individual, is the primary victim. Justice is establishing blame and giving out pain through a contest between the offender and the state.

In fact, as suggested in the opening paragraph of this essay, justice can almost be reduced to three questions: What laws were broken? Who done it? What do they deserve?

This retributive lens or paradigm helps to explain why victims are so neglected: they are not part of the definition at all! Preoccupied with blame and pain, retributive justice is primarily negative and backward-looking. Retributive justice does not consider causes and does not aim at solutions. Instead it stigmatizes offenders for past actions, making social reintegration nearly impossible. Moreover, the process of administering blame and pain is so technical that victims and offenders are forced to rely on experts and to redefine their perceptions and experiences in terms that are foreign to them. Alienation is the inevitable result.

As a value system, the retributive understanding of justice is primarily negative and contains no inherent reason to treat people in caring ways. There is no built-in motive, within the retributive ethical system, to be humane. If the goal is to deliver pain, there are no inherent self-limits on how much pain we deliver. So we have to impose limits and guidelines from outside the ethical system. Not surprisingly, such outside guidelines are often ineffective.

Today it seems natural and commonsensical to view justice this way. But this set of assumptions, this "lens," is not inevitable: other options are possible.

In fact, other options are found in our own histories. Throughout most of Western history, for example, little differentiation was made between crimes and other harms. Crime was a violation of people and of community. Such wrongs create obligations: justice called for things to be made right. The options of vengeance or courts existed but were largely backups for when negotiation and restitution did not work. The aim was to restore. Crime was not a monopoly of the state; even when victims and offenders resorted to courts, they retained power to settle when they wished.

But then a legal revolution occurred which defined crime as categorically different than other wrongs, deserving of special procedures in which punishment was the normal outcome. Public interests were elevated above private and the state assumed the responsibility—indeed, a monopoly—of response.

This legal revolution needed justification and here the church weighed in, providing a theological rationale. Unfortunately, there occurred what Dutch scholar Herman Bianchi has termed a "short-circuit." Certain biblical concepts were taken from their context and grafted onto foreign Greco-Roman principles. The Bible was then reinterpreted through a hybrid lens that viewed God as a punitive and legalistic judge. The result: an obsession in the West with the retributive theme in the Bible.

In reality the Bible presents a different lens for viewing wrongdoing. This may come as a shock to those who think of biblical justice as "an eye for an eye." "An eye for an eye" is not what it seems. In a society unused to the rule of law, it was intended as a limit on, rather than a command to do, violence. It established a rule of proportion which laid the basis for restitution. Interestingly, the statement of this rule in the book of Leviticus is followed immediately by an injunction to treat strangers as oneself; it embodies a principle of respect for others, regardless of who they are.

An eye for an eye is hardly the primary theme in the Bible; indeed, the phrase appears only three times. Rather, the primary character of biblical justice can be found in God's own response to wrongdoing.

When confronted with wrongdoing, God is described as exceedingly angry. The terms used connote deep breathing, snorting; they are statements of wrath which sound much like the anger of victims. Anger is a natural response to wrongdoing. Anger is also a stage of recovery.

But the story does not stop there. God is angry at wrongdoing, but nevertheless does not give up! That is the whole story of the people of God: they do terrible things, richly deserving of wrath, but ultimately God does not give up. God is a God of wrath but ultimately of restoration.

The real key to a biblical lens on justice is to be found in the concept of "shalom." Although shalom is often equated with peace, it means much more than that. Rather, it has to do with a sense of "all-rightness," including right relationships. The biblical words translated into English as "justice" have to do with "right-ordering," creating or restoring shalom. Thus the Hebrew word for restitution, paying back, comes from the same root as shalom. Wrongs need to be made right and that often requires something to be restored. Right relationships are the goal. Opportunities for confession, repentance, forgiveness, and reconciliation are essential.

Unlike our justice, biblical justice is not reciprocal, "tit for tat" justice. It is based on need, not merit. The primary focus is not on what people deserve but what they need. Biblical justice is also measured by the outcome—"Have things been made right?"—rather than the process—"Have the rules been followed?" Justice is not a forensic inquiry into guilt but rather a search for solutions which heal people and relationships.

The New Testament's focus on forgiveness is well known, and some see this as a sharp contrast to the retributive tone of the Old Testament. However, as Clarence Jordan has pointed out, there is in fact a kind of logical progression from start to finish.

The Bible opens in Genesis with a recognition of the human tendency to take unlimited revenge. It is called the "Law of Lamech" and is described as "70 times 7," a figure representing infinity. But already in Leviticus there are limits: an eye for an eye—do this much, and only this much. There also is another limit: Love must govern your relationships with your own community. As the Bible progresses, those guidelines are expanded until Jesus urges us to love not just our own kind but also our enemies, and to practice forgiveness. How many times should I forgive? Until 70 times 7, an unlimited number of times. It is probably no accident that he used the same number as that in the Law of Lamech. He stood the law of unlimited retaliation on its head.

In the biblical view, crime is viewed as a violation of people and relationships. Wrongs create obligations to make things right. Shalom, right relationships, are the goal.

So Western history and the Christian tradition point toward a different lens, toward a justice that aims at healing. So too do the traditions of many people throughout the world.

The essence of these traditions suggests a more restorative understanding of justice which might be summarized like this:
Crime
    is a violation or harm to people and relationships.
The aim of justice
    is to identify obligations,
    to meet needs and to promote healing.

The process of justice
    involves victims, offenders, and community
    in an effort to identify obligations and solutions,
    maximizing the exchange of information
    (dialogue, mutual agreement) between them,
    seeking to restore community.

In other words, crime violates people. Violations always create obligations. Justice should involve victims, offenders, and the community in a search to identify needs and obligations so that things can be made right so far as possible.

The three central questions of a restorative approach might look like this: Who has been hurt by this event? What are their needs? What are the obligations, and whose are they?

The restorative approach emphasizes the existential reality of crime: that it represents a violation of people and their relationships. The proper response, then, should seek to heal and restore.

The differences between the two paradigms might be summarized by asking four questions: (1) How is the problem defined? (2) Who are the primary actors or participants? (3) What does a solution or outcome look like? (4) What is the process to get to an outcome?

The prevailing retributive approach defines the problem narrowly, as a legal infraction. A restorative approach defines the problem in relational terms, as a violation of people and relationships, and in its broader context.

In the retributive model, the state is the victim so the state is the primary actor. The offender is placed in a passive or self-defensive mode. The victim is barely in the picture. A restorative or relational approach, in contrast, puts the people involved—victim, offender but also community—center stage. (The state too has an important role but it is less monopolistic, less top-down, than the retributive model assumes.)

Retributive justice defines the "solution" as punishment of the offender. It is predominantly backward-looking. Restorative justice encourages responsibility for past behavior by focusing on the future, on problem-solving, on the needs and obligations resulting from the offense. Reparation and restoration thus take precedence over punishment.

The process of justice in the prevailing paradigm is hierarchical and authoritarian. Having evolved from a battle model, it assumes and heightens conflict and impersonality. Moreover, the process is so technical that in reality, the primary actors are professional stand-ins in the form of prosecutor and defense attorney—as we in the United States saw so dramatically in the O. J. Simpson trial. A restorative approach, however, seeks as far as possible to be participatory, maximizing possibilities for dialogue, for mutual agreement, for an exchange of information, for humanization of the process.

Let me be clear, however, about what I am not saying. I am not arguing that justice can be entirely private, purely a matter between victim and offender. There are both private and public dimensions to crime. Modern society, unfortunately, has emphasized the public and ignored the private dimensions. We must find the proper balance.

Nor am I suggesting that we can develop a wonderful restorative model that can solve everything. Rather, it is a question of what is normative. We have created a system to respond to the most heinous, bizarre cases and imposed that on everything. We need a new (or old) standard, a restorative one.

Perhaps it is most helpful to recognize that these two competing concepts of justice are in reality "ideal types" or poles on a continuum. On the one end is retributive justice; on the other is restorative justice. The legal system as we know it has some very real strengths, but it tends to exacerbate wounds rather than heal them. Our goal, therefore, should be to move our experience of justice as far as we can toward the restorative pole.

At the same time, there are limits to how far we can move toward the restorative pole in specific cases; "true" justice is rarely attainable. Some people do need to be kept from society, at least for a while, and there may be a place for punishment within a larger restorative context. Moreover, there are strengths in the existing system which no one would want to lose.

Throughout the past twenty years, programs throughout the world have demonstrated that justice can indeed be moved toward the restorative ideal. Throughout much of the Western world, victim offender reconciliation or mediation programs work cooperatively with the legal system to provide voluntary mediated encounters between victims and offenders to work out restitution agreements. These allow victims to meet many of their needs while holding offenders directly accountable. Family Group Conferences, which originated in New Zealand but are now being tried in many locations, bring together a larger group. Victims and their supporters, offenders and their families, representatives of the police (who represent the prosecution) and of the legal system all gather to decide—by consensus—what should be done about the offense. Sentencing Circles in Native Canadian communities bring together an even larger circle, including members of the community, to talk about what happened and make recommendations to the court. These approaches have been highly successful in property crimes and "minor" crimes of violence but are increasingly being applied, with appropriate safeguards and modifications, to very serious crimes including murder, with very promising results.

The case of murders demonstrates the meaning of the justice continuum. There is no way, of course, to "make right" the crime of murder. Nor can we assume that we can do without an adversarial truth-finding process to establish facts and culpability when responsibility is denied. People who have murdered may indeed need to be kept from society, sometimes for long periods of time. Within those parameters, however, there is much that can be done that will take seriously survivors' or co-victims' needs while holding offenders accountable for their action.

At one California prison, an inmate group meets regularly to listen to victims, to understand their responsibilities and to carry out fund-raising activities in order to pay symbolic restitution to victim assistance programs.

In another example, a pioneering program at a large maximum-security prison in Pennsylvania has offered an intense program to prisoners who choose to participate. Many of the participants so far are serving life sentences for murder. One of the conditions of entry is that the fact of participation will not be used in legal or parole proceedings; it is intended as a healing journey for offenders and victims who choose to participate. Offenders go through an intense twenty-week seminar designed to help them understand fully the consequences of what they have done. In that process, they begin to meet victims and survivors not related to their own case. Eventually they also work on a letter to their own victims or co-victims. These are deposited with a victim services agency, and victims or survivors have the right to receive them if they wish. Victims who have come into the prison to meet members of the seminar inevitably observe that the experience was extremely helpful for them. Offenders show greatly increased understanding of what they have done and responsibility for it but also have an opportunity to deal directly—usually for the first time—with the sense of guilt and responsibility that has often nagged at them.

Other programs have offered direct encounters, guided by mediators, between survivors and offenders in cases such as homicide with demonstrable benefits for survivors as well as for offenders.

What I am offering here is a vision which is not at all new, but is different from prevailing assumptions. The primary goal of restorative justice is to repair and heal rather than isolate or punish. It is a justice which seeks to give meaning and lay the groundwork for recovery, where justice and healing are not opposites but part of the same cloth. Restorative justice is inherently respectful, putting victim and offender, their relationships, their needs, center stage. It is a justice that aims to heal.

Restorative justice may seem like an impossible goal, especially in a case as tragic as murder. Indeed, we may not be able to fully experience this justice in many cases. Still, it can be the beacon, the ideal, which guides us as we seek to bring some good from the evil that happens. If we seek a justice that restores, at the very least we will work to meet some of the needs of victims and society without reinforcing the cycle of violence. At the very least, we can hope to do some good instead of making things worse.

[4]

The People Want an Alternative
to the Death Penalty

William J. Bowers and Benjamin D. Steiner

SISTER HELEN PREJEAN'S COMPELLING book (and feature film) *Dead Man Walking* exposes the human realities of capital punishment in our society and debunks the myth of its power to relieve the pain and anger of murder victims' survivors.[1] Sister Helen's wrenching experiences with a murderer, his family, and the family members of his two victims reveal the tragedy of the death penalty, especially for the murder victims' families, whose pain is kept alive by recurrent reminders in the protracted judicial process and by repeated exposure to the media's coverage of each new development as the case inches toward the final deadly vengeance of an execution. The victims' families are ravaged, enraged, and desolate. The wounds they have suffered remain unhealed. The offender's family too is unable to escape an endless web of grief and alienation.

A strikingly similar message is delivered by another recent movie, *An Eye for an Eye,* a fictional tale of a privately imposed execution inspired by rage and vengeance for an unpunished murder. The film's protagonist, played by Sally Field, is consumed with avenging her daughter's murder—so much so that it ultimately destroys her family. The execution of the film's deranged serial killer by

SOURCE: Used by permission of the authors.

Field's victimized character, rather than by the state, does not relieve her feelings of loss and grief.

A scene from the film *Dead Man Walking* exposes a profound mistake in the way we think about criminal responsibility and punishment. When Sean Penn's Matthew Poncelet faces his victims' families, as a modern-day antichrist on the "toxic cross" of Louisiana's execution chamber, the unexpected happens. The hollow moment of the death penalty's vengeance is eclipsed by Poncelet's words of sorrow and remorse to the family members of his victims. It is the lost element of responsibility to victims that this scene articulates.

Poncelet's words, which are too little, too late to do much for the victims' survivors, come thanks only to Sister Helen's (Susan Sarandon) arduous intervention in the punishment protocol. The film makes it clear that it is Sister Helen's resolve, despite the execution juggernaut, that awakens Poncelet to his responsibility to the murder victims' families. Our present justice system utterly fails to serve this purpose. Ours is narrowly retributive justice.

The Two Faces of Responsibility

Our law takes a one-sided view of responsibility, dealing only with the defendant's responsibility for the crime and ignoring the defendant's responsibility to the victims and their survivors. In legal parlance, criminal responsibility is exclusively a question of guilt. It is a matter of determining what kind or category of crime the defendant has committed. It is what the prosecution must establish through the presentation of evidence to convict the defendant of the crime.

Virtually forgotten is the other side of responsibility, the offender's responsibility to the victims. The crime has created a debt or obligation; it has caused injury and suffering for which the perpetrator is responsible. Paying for the crime means making amends, providing reparations, doing recompense, seeking atonement with those who have been injured. Isn't the criminal's foremost debt to those who have been victimized rather than to the state? Shouldn't the state's foremost role be to see that the criminal's debt to the victim is repaid? Shouldn't the punishment incorporate this element of responsibility to the victims and impose on the criminal the obligation of repaying the debt the crime has created?

Capital punishment is the ultimate denial of the offender's responsibility to those who have experienced the loss and suffering the crime has caused. It takes the offender's life for the victim's life, but it withholds reparation or restitution to the victim's survivors. *Dead Man Walking* and *An Eye for an Eye* expose the torturous experience of waiting for an execution and the hollow relief the execution provides for victims' families. The death penalty panders to vengeance but forecloses recompense. This reality is not lost on people when they are asked what punishment they would choose for convicted first-degree murderers.

Responsibility and Punishment for First-Degree Murder

If you, like most pundits and politicians, rely only on the standard polling question that asks people whether they "generally favor or oppose the death penalty for convicted murderers," you are apt to conclude that three out of four people want capital punishment for convicted murderers. But you would be wrong. Responses to this polling question are an affirmation of the felt need for severe punishment, but not an endorsement of the death penalty over other punishments for such a crime.[2]

To learn what punishment people want most, when they might favor or accept several options, we must ask them to *choose among alternatives*. We have done just this in surveys of citizens in New York (N = 500), Nebraska (N = 506), Kansas (N = 411), and Massachusetts (N = 603).[3] We posed the death penalty alternatives of a sentence of life without parole (LWOP) and a sentence of life without parole plus restitution to victims' families (LWOP+R) and asked the citizens of those states to choose between the death penalty and each alternative.

LWOP: The first alternative tests the attractiveness of keeping the murderer from ever returning to society without the violence and degradation of executions.[4] The question and citizens' responses were as follows.

If convicted first-degree murderers in this state could be sentenced to life in prison with absolutely no chance of ever being considered for parole, would you prefer this as an alternative to the death penalty?

	New York	Nebraska	Kansas	Massachusetts
Yes	55%	46%	47%	54%
No	36%	43%	49%	38%
Not sure	10%	11%	4%	8%

More people want permanent incapacitation short of execution than want the death penalty. Life without parole is preferred to the death penalty in two of the four states and is a standoff with the death penalty in the other two. Since this alternative categorically eliminates parole, it does away with a major reason for favoring the death penalty—specifically, the worry that convicted first-degree murderers not given the death penalty will be back on the street too soon.[5]

LWOP+R: The second choice we posed tests the attractiveness of making convicted murderers responsible for restitution to murder victims' families, while serving a sentence of life without parole:

If convicted first-degree murderers in this state could be sentenced to life in prison with no chance of parole and also be required to work in prison industries for money that would go to the families of their victims, would you prefer this as an alternative to the death penalty?

	New York	Nebraska	Kansas	Massachusetts
Yes	73%	64%	66%	67%
No	19%	26%	30%	23%
Not sure	8%	10%	4%	10%

Work for restitution to murder victims' families combined with a life sentence and no chance of parole is the overwhelming preference. It wins by a 2-to-1 margin over the death penalty in every state. Only about one in four citizens of these states would stick with the death penalty if they could have restitution to victims' families together with a true life sentence. In a word, the contribution of restitution to people's preference for the death penalty alternative is "decisive." The presence of restitution together with the incapacitative effect of life without parole makes this alternative overwhelmingly preferable to the death penalty. This same preference for a true life sentence plus restitution over the death penalty holds as well in Florida, Georgia, Virginia, Indiana, and California—indeed, wherever surveys have asked this question.[6]

We have also asked this question of jurors from eleven states participating in the Capital Jury Project.[7] These are jurors who have made the life-or-death sentencing decision at the end of a capital trial—435 who imposed a death sentence and 373 who imposed a life sentence.

	Death Jurors	Life Jurors
Yes	53%	60%
No	33%	27%
Not Sure	14%	13%

The results show that life without parole plus restitution is the preference of capital jurors as well as citizens at large. Jurors who imposed a life sentence want this alternative by more than 2 to 1, as do citizens in the four states we surveyed. Even among jurors who have actually imposed a death sentence, more than half prefer this alternative, and only a third would stick with the death penalty. Moreover, the preference for life without parole plus restitution is clear despite the fact that persons who would find it difficult or impossible to vote for a death sentence are excluded from capital juries. Thus the reality of having to decide whether convicted first-degree murderers should live or die does not make people, not even those who decided to impose death, believe the death penalty is preferable.

We also asked the citizens of New York, Nebraska, Kansas, and Massachusetts which punishment for first-degree murder is "harshest," which one "does the greatest good for all concerned," and which one "comes closest to your own personal ideal of justice." The death penalty was unrivaled as harshest. But a life sentence with restitution to murder victims families was seen as the greatest good for all concerned. And critically, people's personal ideals of justice closely mirrored what they saw as the greatest good for all concerned and eschewed harshness.[8] That is to say, people want life without parole plus restitution because they think it "does the greatest good for all concerned" and because it "comes closest to their own personal ideal of justice."

Nor is responsibility to victims a punishment priority in people's minds only when the crime is first-degree murder. Before asking respondents which punishment alternatives they preferred for murder, we presented them with some twenty statements about punishment priorities without any reference to murder. These included statements reflecting the deterrent, incapacitative, and retributive purposes of criminal punishment. Consistently among the most widely endorsed punishment priorities in each of the four states were:

If we really cared about crime victims, we would make offenders work to pay for the injuries and losses their victims have suffered.

A good way to make criminals feel responsibility for their crimes would be to have them work in prison to pay for the harm they have done to others.

The discrepancy between public sentiments and the law on the matter of offenders' responsibility to victims and their families is thus evident for lesser crimes as well as for first-degree murder.[9]

The illusion of deep-seated public support for capital punishment is a self-perpetuating political myth. When legislators in New York, Massachusetts, and Indiana were asked what punishment their constituents would prefer for first-degree murder, they overwhelmingly answered the death penalty over life without parole plus restitution.[10] Pollsters rest their interpretations of death penalty support on a single (flawed) polling question, the media uncritically accepts this interpretation, and politicians say they know their constituents support the death penalty because the polls, as reported in the media, say so. The media's simplistic and sensationalized handling of crime news further tempts politicians to make the death penalty a "get tough" tenet of their election campaigns and legislative strategies.

The Loss of Offender Responsibility to Crime Victims

The lesson of responsibility to victims has ancient roots. Early law that defined an offense of one party against another invariably stated the offender's obligation to the victim to redress the wrong or harm done. German Salic law, for instance, provided compensation for almost every sort of crime including murder. This was known as the *wergild,* in which monetary compensation was made to a family group if a member of that family was injured or killed by another's willful act. Even prior to written law, criminal responsibility in the form of reparation to victims of crime was a societal norm. The African Ossetian people required the offender to make restitution for the crime of murder. Specifically, the murderer's family was required to deliver the murderer to the victim's family, where the murderer's person and labor were at their disposal in perpetuity.

With the transition from feudalism to monarchy in England, the law lost sight of responsibility to crime victims and fixed its gaze instead upon responsibility for criminal actions. The critical ingredient was a transformation of crime from an individual wrong to a societal problem—namely, maintaining the "king's peace." This shift in the conception of crime was buttressed by religious obsession, with the offender as a "sinner," and by political suspicion converted into legal prohibitions against extralegal settlements between offenders and victims that impeded the prosecution of offenders and hence were seen as subverting the king's justice.

These developments, of course, paved the way for the crown to appropriate the offender's person and labor previously due victims. The offender's debt to the victim thus became a debt to society, and with it came an offender-oriented conception of punishment that left victims by the wayside and the offenders' debt to their victims in the hands of the crown.

Consciousness of the law's disregard for crime victims surfaced with the victim's rights movement of the 1970s. The recognition of the victim's right to compensation for the losses and injuries resulting from crime is now manifest, especially in the National Victim Witness and Protection Act of 1982. But recognition of the offender's responsibility to the victims, of the role offenders should play in providing restitution (compensation from the person responsible for the wrong), remains tenuous.

The American Bar Association paid lip service to offender restitution to crime victims in its 1989 guidelines for criminal law reform. Some fifteen states have attached victim-restitution components to their provisions for criminal sentencing. And a few states, notably California and Hawaii, have initiated programs in which offenders work in prison for money that goes to crime victims. Yet offender restitution to victims is treated largely as an administrative afterthought, as an adjunct to offender-oriented punishment, and as a way of diverting the costs of victim compensation otherwise shouldered by taxpayers.

The notion that one should make amends to those who have been harmed is alive, of course, in many homes and families for its value in teaching the message of responsibility for wrongdoing we want our children to learn. It is a factor in the disposition of juvenile cases in some places. And it plays a role in some, usually minor, property offenses where the amount of the loss is easily translated into monetary terms. But it is not being incorporated as fundamental to our conception of punishment for serious crime. Indeed, under the victims' rights banner, victims are being coopted by the state as partners in the quest to strengthen offender-oriented punishments, instead of forcing lawmakers and the justice system to rethink criminal responsibility in terms that make the offender's responsibility to victims an integral part of criminal punishment.

Punishment for What Purpose—Imitation or Redress?

Many things lost or destroyed by crime are irreplaceable. When the loss is a human life, this truth is starkest. But because someone cannot repay a debt fully or in kind, that person is not absolved of responsibility for it. What is owed must be determined and a way to reduce or pay off the debt must be found. Shouldn't we decide what this person owes and provide the place and kind of work in our prisons that will make it possible for the obligation to be met?

The nature of the work to be performed and the distribution of the funds to meet victims' needs and related communitarian purposes will require continuing planning and management. Properly, this is where crime victims should be involved as constituents or stakeholders who play a meaningful role. They must play an integral part in the planning and conduct of the restitution program, not simply as its financial beneficiaries but as representatives of the community's interest in seeing offenders' responsibility to their victims converted into significant contributions to community well-being in the work offenders do, and in the distribution of their earnings to meet victims' needs.

In place of the desperation of victim's families presented in *Dead Man Walking* and the tormented vigilantism depicted in *An Eye for an Eye*, this would give victims a meaningful role in seeing justice done.

Murderers must be punished because they have broken the most fundamental law of society. Their punishment should serve the legitimate ends of retribution, incapacitation, and deterrence in whatever measure and combination is deemed appropriate, as many years or life in prison does. But their debt is also one of restitution to the victim's survivors. To say they owe a debt to society is at best an evasion and at worst a usurpation of what is due the victims.

A New Message of Criminal Responsibility

You might ask, What's so new here? Haven't we already begun to compensate crime victims for their injuries and even their suffering? And haven't we already started putting offenders to work in prisons for money that might go to their victims? The answer is yes on both counts. We are starting to see programs to compensate crime victims, and we are beginning to see work programs for offenders in prisons. But we have not yet appreciated the link of criminal responsibility between the two as an integral part of justice. And, more than this, we have not recognized the importance for our society of such a transformation in our thinking about criminal responsibility.

The new message of criminal responsibility we need is one that places responsibility to victim on a par with, and in partnership with, responsibility for crime. This is a message that can begin the work of healing the wounds of victims and providing redemption for offenders. It means understanding the criminal act in a different way, in a way that sees justice as requiring offenders to take responsibility for what they have done and for those they have victimized, to repair the damage through recompense aimed at regenerating people and relationships instead of degrading and destroying them.

This is a different understanding of punishment, one that extols not the imitation of the crime in the name of justice but the restoration of victims as essential to the meaning of justice. People want something more than to see offenders deprived of liberty or life. They want reparation and recompense to victims. In the case of murder, this means keeping offenders alive and at work to meet their responsibility to the victim's survivors. It is redemptive rather than vindictive. It is harsh but meaningful punishment.

Notes

1. This paper was originally presented as "An Eye for Whom?" at the meetings of the American Society of Criminology, Chicago, November 1996.
2. Citizens express serious misgivings about the way the death penalty is applied in surveys we have conducted in four states (see note 3). For instance, even

greater than the number in each state who say they favor the death penalty is the number who say "the death penalty is too arbitrary because some people are executed while others go to prison for the very same crime" and the number who say "defendants who can afford a good lawyer almost never get the death penalty."

3. Depending on sample size, the margin of sampling error in these surveys is +/- 4 to 6 percentage points. In other words, the results reported here would be within 4 to 6 percentage points of the true statewide populations figures in 95 out of 100 such surveys. The percentages presented below are based on the full samples of respondents; "don't know," and "no answer" responses are included in the "not sure" category.

The New York and Nebraska surveys have been analyzed extensively in William J. Bowers, Margaret Vandiver, and Patricia H. Dugan, "A New Look at Public Opinion on Capital Punishment: What Citizens and Legislators Prefer," *American Journal of Criminal Law* 22 (1994): 77–149. Executive summaries of the Kansas and Massachusetts surveys are available in William J. Bowers and Patricia H. Dugan, "Massachusetts Citizens' Punishment Preferences for First Degree Murder," *Research Program, College of Criminal Justice, Northeastern University* (October 1994), and William J. Bowers and Patricia H. Dugan, "Kansans Want an Alternative to the Death Penalty," *Research Program, College of Criminal Justice, Northeastern University* (April 1994). Similar findings are reported for Indiana in Marla Sandys and Edmund McGarrell, "Attitudes toward Capital Punishment: Preference for the Penalty or Mere Acceptance?" *Journal of Research in Crime and Delinquency* 32 (1995).

4. Robert Johnson calls this option "a civil death penalty." (See Robert Johnson, *Death Work: A Study of the Modern Execution Process,* 1990.)

5. We also know that the sooner capital jurors think a convicted murderer will be paroled if not given the death penalty, the more likely they are to vote for death. (See William J. Bowers and Benjamin D. Steiner, "Death by Default," *Texas University Law Review,* forthcoming. For evidence that citizens in general and capital jurors in particular vastly underestimate how long murderers not given the death penalty will usually spend in prison, see William J. Bowers, "Research Note: Capital Punishment and Contemporary Values: People's Misgivings and the Court's Misperceptions," *Law & Society Review* 27 (1993): 157–75; and William J. Bowers and Benjamin D. Steiner, "Choosing Life or Death: Sentencing Dynamics in Capital Cases," in J. Acker, R. Bohm, and C. S. Lanier, eds., *America's Experiment with Capital Punishment: Reflections on the Past, Present, and Future of the Ultimate Penal Sanction* (Durham, N.C.: Carolina Academic Press, 1997).

6. The results of these other surveys are reported in more detail in Bowers et al., "A New Look at Public Opinion."

7. The principal source of Capital Jury Project research thus far is a symposium issue of the *Indiana Law Journal* 70, no. 4 (fall 1995), that published research

papers (Bowers, Hoffmann, Luginbuhl and Howe, Sandys, Sarat) and commentaries (Baldus, Haney, Hans, Sherman, and Slobogin) presented at a conference on the project held in February 1995 at the Indiana Law School.

8. See Bowers et al., "A New Look at Public Opinion," table 11, p. 123.

9. See Bowers et al., "A New Look at Public Opinion," table 9, pp. 114–15; Bowers and Dugan, "Massachusetts Citizens' Punishment Preferences for First Degree Murder" and "Kansans Want an Alternative to the Death Penalty."

10. See Bowers et al., "A New Look at Public Opinion"; Bowers and Dugan, "Kansans Want an Alternative to the Death Penalty"; and Sandys and McGarrell, "Attitudes toward Capital Punishment."

PART TWO
JUSTICE AS DETERRENCE

[5]

On Deterrence and the Death Penalty

Ernest van den Haag

I

If rehabilitation and the protection of society from unrehabilitated offenders were the only purposes of legal punishment the death penalty could be abolished: It cannot attain the first end, and is not needed for the second. No case for the death penalty can be made unless "doing justice"—or "deterring others"—is among our penal aims. Each of these purposes can justify capital punishment by itself; opponents, therefore, must show that neither actually does, while proponents can rest their case on either.

Although the argument from justice is intellectually more interesting, and, in my view, decisive enough, utilitarian arguments have more appeal: The claim that capital punishment is useless, because it does not deter others, is most persuasive. I shall, therefore, focus on this claim. Lest the argument be thought to be unduly narrow, I shall show, nonetheless, that some claims of injustice rest on premises which the claimants reject when arguments for capital punishment are derived therefrom; while other claims of injustice have no independent standing: Their weight depends on the weight given to deterrence.

SOURCE: Ernest van den Haag, "On Deterrence and the Death Penalty," *Journal of Criminal Law, Criminology, and Police Science,* 1969. Reprinted by permission of the author.

II

Capital punishment is regarded as unjust because it may lead to the execution of innocents, or because the guilty poor (or disadvantaged) are more likely to be executed than the guilty rich.

Regardless of merit, these claims are relevant only if "doing justice" is one purpose of punishment. Unless one regards it as good, or, at least, better, that the guilty be punished rather than the innocent, and that the equally guilty be punished equally, unless, that is, one wants penalties to be just, one cannot object to them because they are not. However, if one does include justice among the purposes of punishment, it becomes possible to justify any one punishment—even death—on grounds of justice. Yet, those who object to the death penalty because of its alleged injustice usually deny not only the merits, or the sufficiency, of specific arguments based on justice, but the propriety of justice as an argument: They exclude "doing justice" as a purpose of legal punishment. If justice is not a purpose of penalties, injustice cannot be an objection to the death penalty, or to any other; if it is, justice cannot be ruled out as an argument for any penalty.

Consider the claim of injustice on its merits now. A convicted man may be found to have been innocent; if he was executed, the penalty cannot be reversed. Except for fines, penalties never can be reversed. Time spent in prison cannot be returned. However, a prison sentence may be remitted once the prisoner serving it is found innocent; and he can be compensated for the time served (although compensation ordinarily cannot repair the harm). Thus, though (nearly) all penalties are irreversible, the death penalty, unlike others, is irrevocable as well.

Despite all precautions, errors will occur in judicial proceedings: The innocent may be found guilty,[1] or the guilty rich may more easily escape conviction, or receive lesser penalties than the guilty poor. However, these injustices do not reside in the penalties inflicted but in their maldistribution. It is not the penalty—whether death or prison—which is unjust when inflicted on the innocent, but its imposition on the innocent. Inequity between poor and rich also involves distribution, not the penalty distributed.[2] Thus injustice is not an objection to the death penalty but to the distributive process—the trial. Trials are more likely to be fair when life is at stake—the death penalty is probably less often unjustly inflicted than others. It requires special consideration not because it is more, or more often, unjust than other penalties, but because it is always irrevocable.

Can any amount of deterrence justify the possibility of irrevocable injustice? Surely injustice is unjustifiable in each actual individual case; it must be objected to whenever it occurs. But we are concerned here with the process that may produce injustice, and with the penalty that would make it irrevocable—not with the actual individual cases produced, but with the general rules which may produce them. To consider objections to a general rule (the provision of any penalties by law) we must compare the likely net result of alternative rules and select the rule (or penalty) likely to produce the least injustice. For however one defines justice, to support it cannot mean less than to favor the least injustice. If the death of innocents because of judicial error is unjust, so is the death of innocents by murder. If some murders could be avoided by a penalty conceivably more deterrent than others—such as the death penalty—then the question becomes: Which penalty will minimize the number of innocents killed (by crime and by punishment)? It follows that the irrevocable injustice sometimes inflicted by the death penalty would not significantly militate against it, if capital punishment deters enough murders to reduce the total number of innocents killed so that fewer are lost than would be lost without it.

In general, the possibility of injustice argues against penalization of any kind only if the expected usefulness of penalization is less important than the probable harm (particularly to innocents) and the probable inequities. The possibility of injustice argues against the death penalty only inasmuch as the added usefulness (deterrence) expected from irrevocability is thought less important than the added harm. (Were my argument specifically concerned with justice, I could compare the injustice inflicted by the courts with the injustice—outside the courts—avoided by the judicial process. I.e., "important" here may be used to include everything to which importance is attached.)

We must briefly examine now the general use and effectiveness of deterrence to decide whether the death penalty could add enough deterrence to be warranted.

III

Does any punishment "deter others" at all? Doubts have been thrown on this effect because it is thought to depend on the incorrect rationalistic psychology of some of its eighteenth- and nineteenth-century proponents. Actually deterrence does not depend on rational calculation, on rationality or even on capacity for it; nor do arguments for it depend on rationalistic psychology. Deterrence depends on the likelihood and on the regularity—not on the rationality—of human responses to danger, and further on the possibility of reinforcing internal controls by vicarious external experiences.

Responsiveness to danger is generally found in human behavior; the danger can, but need not, come from the law or from society; nor need it be explicitly verbalized. Unless intent on suicide, people do not jump from high mountain cliffs, however tempted to fly through the air, and they take precautions against falling. The mere risk of injury often restrains us from doing what is otherwise attractive; we refrain even when we have no direct experience, and usually without explicit computation of probabilities, let alone conscious weighing of expected pleasure against possible pain. One abstains from dangerous acts because of vague, inchoate, habitual and, above all, preconscious fears. Risks and rewards are more often felt than calculated; one abstains without accounting to oneself, because "it isn't done," or because one literally does not conceive of the action one refrains from. Animals as well refrain from painful or injurious experiences presumably without calculation; and the threat of punishment can be used to regulate their conduct.

Unlike natural dangers, legal threats are constructed deliberately by legislators to restrain actions which may impair the social order. Thus legislation transforms social into individual dangers. Most people further transform external into internal danger. They acquire a sense of moral obligation, a conscience, which threatens them should they do what is wrong. Arising originally from the external authority of rulers and rules, conscience is internalized and becomes independent of external forces. However, conscience is constantly reinforced in those whom it controls by the coercive imposition of external authority on recalcitrants and on those who have not acquired it. Most people refrain from offenses because they feel an obligation to behave lawfully. But this obligation would scarcely be felt if those who do not feel or follow it were not to suffer punishment.

Although the legislators may calculate their threats and the responses to be produced, the effectiveness of the threats neither requires nor depends on calculations by those responding. The predictor (or producer) of effects must calculate; those whose responses are predicted (or produced) need not. Hence, although legislation (and legislators) should be rational, subjects, to be deterred as intended, need not be: They need only be responsive.

Punishments deter those who have not violated the law for the same reasons—and in the same degrees (apart from internalization: moral obligation) as do natural dangers. Often natural dangers—all dangers not deliberately created by legislation (e.g., injury of the criminal inflicted by the crime victim)—are insufficient. Thus, the fear of injury (natural danger) does not suffice to control city traffic; it must be reinforced by the legal punishment meted out to those who violate the rules. These punishments keep most people observing the regulations. However, where (in the absence of natural danger) the threatened punishment is so light that the advantage of violating rules tends to exceed the disadvantage of being punished (divided by the risk), the rule is violated (i.e., parking fines are too light). In this case the feeling of obligation tends to vanish as well. Elsewhere punishment deters.

To be sure, not everybody responds to threatened punishment. Nonresponsive persons may be (a) self-destructive or (b) incapable of responding to threats, or even of grasping them. Increases in the size, or certainty, of penalties would not affect these two groups. A third group (c) might respond to more certain or more severe penalties.[3] If the punishment threatened for burglary, robbery, or rape were a $5 fine in North Carolina, and five years in prison in South Carolina, I have no doubt that the North Carolina treasury would become quite opulent until vigilante justice would provide the deterrence not provided by law. Whether to increase penalties (or improve enforcement) depends on the importance of the rule to society, the size and likely reaction of the group that did not respond before, and the acceptance of the added punishment and enforcement required to deter it. Observation would have to locate the points—likely to differ in different times and places—at which diminishing, zero, and negative returns set in. There is no reason to believe that all present and future offenders belong to the a priori nonresponsive groups, or that all penalties have reached the point of diminishing, let alone zero returns.

IV

Even though its effectiveness seems obvious, punishment as a deterrent has fallen into disrepute. Some ideas which help explain this progressive heedlessness were uttered by Lester Pearson, then Prime Minister of Canada, when, in opposing the death penalty, he proposed that instead "the state seek to eradicate the causes of crime: slums, ghettos and personality disorders."[4]

"Slums, ghettos and personality disorders" have not been shown, singly or collectively, to be "the causes" of crime.

(1) The crime rate in the slums is indeed higher than elsewhere; but so is the death rate in hospitals. Slums are no more "causes" of crime than hospitals are of death; they are locations of crime, as hospitals are of death. Slums and hospitals attract people selectively; neither is the "cause" of the condition (disease in hospitals, poverty in slums) that leads to the selective attraction.

As for poverty which draws people into slums, and, sometimes, into crime, any relative disadvantage may lead to ambition, frustration, resentment and, if insufficiently restrained, to crime. Not all relative disadvantages can be eliminated; indeed very few can be, and their elimination increases the resentment generated by the remaining ones; not even relative poverty can be removed altogether. (Absolute poverty—whatever that may be—hardly affects crime.) However, though contributory, relative disadvantages are not a necessary or sufficient cause of crime: Most poor people do not commit crimes, and some rich people do. Hence, "eradication of poverty" would, at most, remove one (doubtful) cause of crime.

In the United States, the decline of poverty has not been associated with a reduction of crime. Poverty measured in dollars of constant purchasing power, according to present government standards and statistics, was the condition of one-half of all our families in 1920; of one-fifth in 1962; and of less than one-sixth in 1966. In 1967, 5.3 million families out of 49.8 million were poor—one-ninth of all families in the United States. If crime has been reduced in a similar manner, it is a well-kept secret.

Those who regard poverty as a cause of crime often draw a wrong inference from a true proposition: The rich will not commit certain crimes—Rockefeller never riots; nor does he steal. (He mugs, but only on T.V.) Yet while wealth may be the cause of not committing (certain) crimes, it does not follow that poverty (absence of wealth) is the cause of committing them. Water extinguishes or prevents fire; but its absence is not the cause of fire. Thus, if poverty could be abolished, if everybody had all "necessities" (I don't pretend to know what this would mean), crime would remain, for, in the words of Aristotle, "the greatest crimes are committed not for the sake of basic necessities but for the sake of superfluities." Superfluities cannot be provided by the government; they would be what the government does not provide.

(2)...Ethnic separation, voluntary or forced, obviously has little to do with crime; I can think of no reason why it should.[5]

(3) I cannot see how the state could "eradicate" personality disorders even if all causes and cures were known and available. (They are not.) Further, the known incidence of personality disorders within the prison population does not exceed the known incidence outside—though our knowledge of both is tenuous. Nor are personality disorders necessary or sufficient cause for criminal offenses, unless these be identified by means of (moral not clinical) definition with personality disorders. In this case, Mr. Pearson would have proposed to "eradicate" crime by eradicating crime—certainly a sound, but not a helpful idea.

Mr. Pearson's views are part as well of the mental furniture of the former U.S. Attorney General Ramsey Clark, who told a congressional committee that "...only the elimination of the causes of crime can make a significant and lasting difference in the incidence of crime." Uncharitably interpreted, Mr. Clark revealed that only the elimination of causes eliminates effects—a sleazy cliché and wrong to boot. Given the benefit of the doubt, Mr. Clark probably meant that the causes of crime are social; and that therefore crime can be reduced "only" by nonpenal (social) measures.

This view suggests a fireman who declines fire-fighting apparatus by pointing out that "in the long run only the elimination of the causes" of fire "can make a significant and lasting difference in the incidence" of fire, and that fire-fighting equipment does not eliminate "the causes"—except that such a fireman would probably not rise to fire chief. Actually, whether fires are checked depends on equipment and on the efforts of the firemen using it no less than on the presence of "the causes": inflammable materials. So with crimes. Laws, courts, and police actions are no less important in restraining them than "the causes" are in impelling them. If firemen (or attorneys general) pass the buck and refuse to use the means available, we may all be burned while waiting for "the long run" and the "elimination of the causes."

Whether any activity—be it lawful or unlawful—takes place depends on whether the desire for it, or for whatever is to be secured by it, is stronger than the desire to avoid the costs involved. Accordingly people work, attend college, commit crimes, go to the movies—or refrain from any of these activities. Attendance at a theater may be high because the show is entertaining and because the price of admission is low. Obviously the attendance depends on both—on the combination of expected gratification and cost. The wish, motive or impulse for doing anything—the experienced, or expected, gratification—is the cause of doing it; the wish to avoid the cost is the cause of not doing it. One is no more and no less "cause" than the other. (Common speech supports this use of "cause" no less than logic: "Why did you go to Jamaica!" "*Because* it is such a beautiful place." "Why didn't you go to Jamaica?" "*Because* it is too expensive." "Why do you buy this?" "*Because* it is so cheap." "Why don't you buy that?" "*Because* it is too expensive.") Penalties (costs) are causes of lawfulness, or (if too low or uncertain) of unlawfulness, of crime. People do commit crimes because, given their conditions, the desire for the satisfaction sought prevails. They refrain if the desire to avoid the cost prevails. Given the desire, low cost (penalty) causes the action, and high cost restraint. Given the cost, desire becomes the causal variable. Neither is intrinsically more causal than the other. The crime rate increases if the cost is reduced or the desire raised. It can be decreased by raising the cost or by reducing the desire.

The cost of crime is more easily and swiftly changed than the conditions producing the inclination to it. Further, the costs are very largely within the power of the government to change, whereas the conditions producing propensity to crime are often only indirectly affected by government action, and some are altogether beyond the control of the government. Our unilateral emphasis on these conditions and our undue neglect of costs may contribute to an unnecessarily high crime rate.

V

The foregoing suggests the question posed by the death penalty: Is the deterrence added (return) sufficiently above zero to warrant irrevocability (or other, less clear, disadvantages)? The question is not only whether the penalty deters, but whether it deters more than alternatives and whether the difference exceeds the cost of irrevocability. (I shall assume that the alternative is actual life imprisonment so as to exclude the complication produced by the release of the unrehabilitated.)

In some fairly infrequent but important circumstances the death penalty is the only possible deterrent. . . . Men who, by virtue of past acts, are already serving, or are threatened, by a life sentence, could be deterred from further offenses only by the threat of the death penalty.

What about criminals who do not fall into any of these (often ignored) classes? Professor Thorsten Sellin has made a careful study of the available statistics: He concluded that they do not yield evidence for the deterring effect of the death penalty.[6] Somewhat surprisingly, Professor Sellin seems to think that this lack of evidence for deterrence is evidence for the lack of deterrence. It is not. It means that deterrence has not been demonstrated statistically—not that nondeterrence has been.

It is entirely possible, indeed likely (as Professor Sellin appears willing to concede), that the statistics used, though the best available, are nonetheless too slender a reed to rest conclusions on. They indicate that the homicide rate does not vary greatly between similar areas with or without the death penalty, and in the same area before and after abolition. However, the similar areas are not similar enough; the periods are not long enough; many social differences and changes, other than the abolition of the death penalty, may account for the variation (or lack of) in homicide rates with and without, before and after abolition; some of these social differences and changes are likely to have affected homicide rates. I am unaware of any statistical analysis which adjusts for such changes and differences. And logically, it is quite consistent with the postulated deterrent effect of capital punishment that there be less homicide after abolition: With retention there might have been still less.

Homicide rates do not depend exclusively on penalties any more than do other crime rates. A number of conditions which influence the propensity to crime, demographic, economic or generally social changes or differences—even such matters as changes of the divorce laws or of the cotton price—may influence the homicide rate. Therefore, variation or constancy cannot be attributed to variations or constancy of the penalties, unless we know that no other factor influencing the homicide rate has changed. Usually we don't. To believe the death penalty deterrent does not require one to believe that the death penalty, or any other, is the only, or the decisive, causal variable; this would be as absurd as the converse mistake that "social causes" are the only, or always, the decisive factor. To favor capital punishment, the efficacy of neither variable need be denied. It is enough to affirm that the severity of the penalty may influence some potential criminals, and that the added severity of the death penalty adds to deterrence, or may do so. It is quite possible that such a deterrent effect may be offset (or intensified) by nonpenal factors which affect propensity; its presence or absence therefore may be hard, and perhaps impossible to demonstrate.

Contrary to what Professor Sellin et al. seem to presume, I doubt that offenders are aware of the absence or presence of the death penalty state by state or period by period. Such unawareness argues against the assumption of a calculating murderer. However, unawareness does not argue against the death penalty if by deterrence we mean a preconscious, general response to a severe, but not necessarily specifically and explicitly apprehended, or calculated threat. A constant homicide rate, despite abolition, may occur because of unawareness and not because of lack of deterrence: People remain deterred for a lengthy interval by the severity of the penalty in the past, or by the severity of penalties used in similar circumstances nearby.

I do not argue for a version of deterrence which would require me to believe that an individual shuns murder while in North Dakota, because of the death penalty, and merrily goes to it in South Dakota since it has been abolished there; or that he will start the murderous career from which he had hitherto refrained, after abolition. I hold that the generalized threat of the death penalty may be a deterrent, and the more so, the more generally applied. Deterrence will not cease in the particular areas of abolition or at the particular times of abolition. Rather, general deterrence will be somewhat weakened, through local (partial) abolition. Even such weakening will be hard to detect owing to changes in many offsetting, or reinforcing, factors.

For all of these reasons, I doubt that the presence or absence of a deterrent effect of the death penalty is likely to be demonstrable by statistical means. The statistics presented by Professor Sellin et al. show only that there is no statistical proof for the deterrent effect of the death penalty. But they do not show that there is no deterrent effect. Not to demonstrate presence of the effect is not the same as to demonstrate its absence; certainly not when there are plausible explanations for the nondemonstrability of the effect.

It is on our uncertainty that the case for deterrence must rest.[7]

VI

If we do not know whether the death penalty will deter others, we are confronted with two uncertainties. If we impose the death penalty, and achieve no deterrent effect thereby, the life of a convicted murderer has been expended in vain (from a deterrent viewpoint). There is a net loss. If we impose the death sentence and thereby deter some future murderers, we spared the lives of some future victims (the prospective murderers gain, too; they are spared punishment because they were deterred). In this case, the death penalty has led to a net gain, unless the life of a convicted murderer is valued more highly than that of the unknown victim, or victims (and the nonimprisonment of the deterred nonmurderer).

The calculation can be turned around, of course. The absence of the death penalty may harm no one and therefore produce a gain—the life of the convicted murderer. Or it may kill future victims of murderers who could have been deterred, and thus produce a loss—their life.

To be sure, we must risk something certain—the death (or life) of the convicted man, for something uncertain—the death (or life) of the victims of murderers who may be deterred. This is in the nature of uncertainty—when we invest, or gamble, we risk the money we have for an uncertain gain. Many human actions, most commitments—including marriage and crime—share this characteristic with the deterrent purpose of any penalization, and with its rehabilitative purpose (and even with the protective).

More proof is demanded for the deterrent effect of the death penalty than is demanded for the deterrent effect of other penalties. This is not justified by the absence of other utilitarian purposes such as protection and rehabilitation; they involve no less uncertainty than deterrence.[8]

Irrevocability may support a demand for some reason to expect more deterrence than revocable penalties might produce, but not a demand for more proof of deterrence, as has been pointed out above. The reason for expecting more deterrence lies in the greater severity, the terrifying effect inherent in finality. Since it seems more important to spare victims than to spare murderers, the burden of proving that the greater severity inherent in irrevocability adds nothing to deterrence lies on those who oppose capital punishment. Proponents of the death penalty need show only that there is no more uncertainty about it than about greater severity in general.

The demand that the death penalty be proved more deterrent than alternatives cannot be satisfied any more than the demand that six years in prison be proved to be more deterrent than three. But the uncertainty which confronts us favors the death penalty as long as by imposing it we might save future victims of murder. This effect is as plausible as the general idea that penalties have deterrent effects which increase with their severity. Though we have no proof of the positive deterrence of the penalty, we also have no proof of zero, or negative, effectiveness. I believe we have no right to risk additional future victims of murder for the sake of sparing convicted murderers; on the contrary, our moral obligation is to risk the possible ineffectiveness of executions. However rationalized, the opposite view appears to be motivated by the simple fact that executions are more subject to social control than murder. However, this applies to all penalties and does not argue for the abolition of any.

Notes

1. I am not concerned with the converse injustice, *which I regard as no less grave.*

2. Such inequity, though likely, has not been demonstrated. Note that, since there are more poor than rich, there are likely to be more guilty poor, and, if poverty contributes to crime, the proportion of the poor who are criminals also should be higher than of the rich.

3. I neglect those motivated by civil disobedience or, generally, moral or political passion. Deterring them depends less on penalties than on the moral support they receive, though penalties play a role. I also neglect those who may belong to all three groups listed, some successively, some even simultaneously, such as drug addicts. Finally, I must altogether omit the far-from-negligible role that problems of apprehension and conviction play in deterrence—beyond saying that, by reducing the government's ability to apprehend and convict, courts are able to reduce the risks of offenders.

4. I quote from the *New York Times,* November 24, 1967, 22. The actual psychological and other factors which bear on the disrepute—as distinguished from the rationalizations—cannot be examined here.

5. Mixed areas, incidentally, have higher crime rates than segregated ones (see, e.g., R. Ross and E. van den Haag, *The Fabric of Society* [New York: Harcourt, Brace & Co., 1957], 102–4). Because slums are bad (morally) and crime is, many people seem to reason that "slums spawn crime"—which confuses some sort of moral with a causal relation.

6. Sellin considered mainly homicide statistics. His work may be found in his *Capital Punishment* (New York: Harper & Row, 1967); or, most conveniently, in H. A. Bedau, *The Death Penalty in America* (Garden City, N.Y.: Doubleday, 1964), which also offers other material, mainly against the death penalty.

7. In view of the strong emotions aroused (itself an indication of effectiveness to me: Might not murderers be as upset over the death penalty as those who wish to spare them?) and because I believe penalties must reflect community feeling to be effective, I oppose mandatory death sentences and favor optional, and perhaps binding, recommendations by juries after their finding of guilt. The

opposite course risks the nonconviction of guilty defendants by juries who do not want to see them executed.

8. Rehabilitation or protection is of minor importance in our actual penal system (though not in our theory). We confine many people who do not need rehabilitation and against whom we do not need protection (e.g., the exasperated husband who killed his wife); we release many unrehabilitated offenders against whom protection is needed. Certainly rehabilitation and protection are not, and deterrence is, the main actual function of legal punishment if we disregard nonutilitarian ones.

[6]

The Deterrent Effect of Capital Punishment: A Cross-State Analysis of the 1960s

Brian E. Forst

DURING THE 1960S, AFTER years of gradual decline, the homicide rate for the United States as a whole increased sharply. Although the homicide rate in most states followed this general pattern, it rose much more sharply in some states than in others, and even declined in a few. This cross-state variation, coupled with the differences from state to state in the rate at which use of the death penalty declined from 1960 to 1970, provides a unique opportunity to estimate the deterrent effect of capital punishment on the commission of homicides. The changes in these and other relevant variables that occurred between 1960 and 1970 in each state for which data are available can be measured and used to estimate the average effect of reductions in the execution rate on the rate at which homicides occur in the population. To the extent that capital punishment deters homicides, the homicide rate should have increased by the largest amounts from 1960 to 1970, *ceteris paribus,* in those states with the greatest reductions in the probability that a person convicted of murder would be executed.

SOURCE: Brian E. Forst, "The Deterrent Effect of Capital Punishment: A Cross-State Analysis of the 1960s," *Minnesota Law Review* 61, no. 5 (May 1977). Reprinted by permission of the *Minnesota Law Review.*

Examining the data in this manner should overcome the potentially serious problems associated with aggregate time-series analysis. Analyzing intertemporal changes in the relevant variables across states should also improve the estimates available from conventional cross-section analysis, partly by reducing biases associated with omitted variables. Moreover, the results of this approach appear less sensitive to alternative assumptions about the mathematical form of the model that describes the relationships among the relevant variables than do those of either the conventional time-series or cross-sectional approaches. By estimating the differential of the homicide rate rather than the parent relationship between the homicide rate and its determinants, one can be sure of describing a function that is additive in the differences of the explanatory variables.

Applying this method of analysis to the 1960s is appealing for other reasons as well. More control variables are available for the most recent census years, and their measurement tends to be more accurate than it was in 1940 or 1950. Moreover, there has been a great deal of controversy about the period from 1960 to 1970 in the reviews of the available time-series evidence. In short, analyzing changes during this decade cross-sectionally would appear to permit one to discover more directly whether the association between the cessation of capital punishment and the upsurge in the homicide rate during the 1960s was primarily causal or coincidental.

The Model

The model that provides the initial structure for this analysis is:

(1) Q/N = f(E/C, C/Q, T, Cr, Age, NW, Male, Urb, Enr, Pop, Div, Y, Pov, Emp, S).

This equation represents the notion that the homicide rate (Q/N) is potentially influenced by the rate at which persons convicted of murder are executed (E/C), the rate at which murders result in conviction (C/Q), the average prison term served by convicted murderers (T), the factors that determine the rate at which crimes other than homicide are committed (Cr), social and demographic characteristics [age (Age), race (NW), sex (Male), urbanization (Urb), school enrollment rate (Enr), resident population (Pop), divorce rate (Div)], economic variables [median family income (Y), proportion of families in poverty (Pov), employment (Emp)], and a binary variable indicating whether the state is southern (S). The sources of data for these variables are given in the Appendix.[1]

Professor Ehrlich has provided theoretical justification for the inclusion of the criminal justice sanction variables and the economic variables.[2] The social and demographic variables have been added to minimize the degree of spuriousness in the estimates of central concern here, those reflecting the effects of the sanction variables on homicides. The rate at which crimes other than homicide are committed and a binary Southern variable are incorporated to capture the effects of additional exogenous factors that the other control variables do not specifically measure. . . .

[Editor's note: Professor Forst's research report includes an initial section showing how his research builds on but corrects errors in a study by Isaac Ehrlich, as well as a lengthy discussion in footnotes of technical matters of statistical methodology, a table, and an appendix on sources of data. I have deleted these in order to stay within economic space limitations. Although I have reproduced his basic equations, I have not reproduced several subsequent equations in his reports on robustness that closely resemble the basic ones. Instead I have simply given his verbal descriptions. I have also omitted equation (2), which is basically identical to equation (1) with coefficients added indicating the change (Δ) in each variable from 1960 to 1970.][3]

Parameter Estimates

These coefficients [measuring the change (Δ) in each variable in equation (1) from 1960 to 1970] can be estimated using ordinary least squares regression analysis, with the full set of independent variables incorporated as regressors. These estimates are based on data from the 32 states for which values of all the variables shown were reported both for 1960 and 1970.

$$
\begin{aligned}
(3)\quad (Q/N) = &\quad -\quad 5.911 \quad + \quad 11.62\Delta(E/C) \quad - \quad 5.714\Delta(C/Q) \\
(R^2=.692) &\qquad\ (2.79) \qquad\quad (12.7) \qquad\qquad\quad (1.92) \\[6pt]
&\quad +\quad .001378\Delta T \quad - \quad 38.68\Delta Pov \quad + \\
.001796\Delta Y &\qquad (.00773) \qquad\qquad (15.8) \qquad\qquad (.0096) \\[6pt]
&\quad +\quad .001430\Delta Cr + 36.97\Delta NW \quad - \quad 189.2\Delta Age \\
&\qquad (.000892) \qquad\quad (17.8) \qquad\qquad (139) \\
&\quad -\quad .9595 S \quad - \quad 29.65\Delta Emp \quad - \quad 9.021\Delta Enr \\
&\qquad (.877) \qquad\qquad (34.2) \qquad\qquad (8.53) \\[6pt]
&\quad +\quad 11.24\Delta Urb \quad + \quad 92.58\Delta Div \quad + \\
.0000002382\Delta Pop &\qquad (15.5) \qquad\qquad (158) \qquad\qquad (.000000411) \\[6pt]
&\quad +\quad 0\Delta Male
\end{aligned}
$$

The numbers in parentheses are standard errors, and R^2 is the coefficient of determination, a measure of the proportion of the variance in the dependent variable that is explained by the independent variables used. Thus, 69 percent of the cross-state variance in the change in the homicide rate from 1960 to 1970 can be attributed to the set of variables in the right-hand side of equation (3).

The first result provides no support for the hypothesis that capital punishment deters homicide. The positive regression coefficient for the execution rate variable is, in fact, consistent with a counterdeterrent effect,[4] but the standard error of this estimate is too large for this finding to be taken seriously. Equation (3) does provide evidence, on the other hand, of a deterrent effect of convictions on homicides. Those states with the largest reductions in the ratio of homicide convictions to homicide offenses tended to have the largest increases in the homicide rate, other factors held constant.

This regression equation, however, has too many shortcomings to allow it to stand alone as an adequate test of the deterrence hypothesis. Foremost among these is the imprecision in parameter estimation caused by the inclusion of 15 independent variables—ten of which are not significant (at the .10 level)—in an equation constructed from only 32 observations. Eliminating these ten variables, except for the variable of primary interest, $\Delta(E/C)$, produces a result that fits the data better:

$$
\begin{aligned}
(4) \quad \Delta(Q/N) = \quad &- \quad 4.222 \quad + \quad 17.64\Delta(E/C) \quad - \quad 5.970\Delta(C/Q) \\
(R^2=.577) \quad & \quad (2.10) \qquad\quad (8.55) \qquad\qquad\quad (1.68) \\[1em]
&- \quad 24.91\Delta Pov \quad + \quad .001515\Delta Cr \quad + \quad 39.60\Delta NW \\
& \quad (7.52) \qquad\qquad\quad (.000507) \qquad\quad (13.3) \\[1em]
&+ \quad .0004679\Delta Y \\
& \quad (.000526)
\end{aligned}
$$

This result is basically similar to (3) for the variables of principal focus, except that elimination of nine weak independent variables increases the adjusted coefficient of determination, a standard measure of goodness-of-fit, from .44 to .48, and increases the statistical significance of five of the six remaining variables.

Equation (4) provides evidence that the sharp increase in the homicide rate during the 1960s was the product of factors other than the abolition of the death penalty. Accounting for what appear to be the most important of these other factors—the murder conviction rate, economic variables, race, and the factors that caused non-capital offenses to escalate during the 1960s—it is apparent that those states in which the actual use of capital punishment ceased during the 1960s experienced no greater increase in the murder rate than did the states that did not use capital punishment in the first place. Under the theory that capital punishment deters murder, one would have predicted the opposite.

Robustness Tests

Before drawing inferences from data that are not produced by controlled experimentation, it is appropriate to test whether the estimates are "robust" to (that is, hold up under) departures from the assumptions on which the estimates are grounded. Equation (4) is based on several assumptions: (1) the murder rate in any given year is influenced by the number of executions in that year; (2) none of the sanction variables is influenced by any of the other variables used in the regression analysis; (3) the variance in the homicide rate is no larger for highly populated states than for the less populated states; and (4) the rate at which non-capital crimes are committed is not affected by, nor does it affect, the other variables in the analysis. Each of these assumptions can be altered to test for robustness, which will indicate the reliability of the estimates obtained in equation (4).

Alternative Constructions of the Execution Rate

Since the execution rate is the independent variable of principal focus in this analysis, it is surely appropriate to vary the methods of measuring it. The construction used in equations (3) and (4) is based on the number of executions and convictions in 1960 and 1970. One alternative is to use executions in 1961 and 1971 instead of executions in 1960 and 1970, respectively, as objective forecasts of the probability that a murder conviction will lead to execution, since executions have been reported to lag behind convictions by about a year. The result . . . is fundamentally no different from equation (4), suggesting that lagging executions does not alter the observed effect of executions on homicides.

To reduce the sampling error associated with the small number of executions that occurred around 1960 and test another lag structure, one can make the numerator of the execution rate the average number of executions over the three-consecutive-year period centered about the year of the convictions in the denominator. Again, this alternative does not produce a result that differs in any important respects from equation (4).

Another execution rate variable can be formed by combining the independent variables (E/C) and (C/Q) into the single variable (E/Q). Although this combination causes an important control variable, the murder conviction rate, to be lost, it allows all 50 states to be included in the analysis. The result is . . . remarkably similar to equation (4) except for the substantial reduction in the proportion of variance in the homicide rate explained by the independent variables, which is produced by the exclusion of the conviction variable and the use of a larger number of observations. This reduction provides further support for the hypothesis that convictions deter homicides, consistent with findings by Ehrlich and Passell and with the results of equations (3) through (6).

A final construction of the execution rate is designed to eliminate whatever bias results from the reverse effect that changes in the homicide rate may have on the execution rate. All of the above regression equations assume that the causality runs strictly from executions to homicides. These results will be biased to the extent that the execution rate is a function of the homicide rate, which would occur, for example, if the demand for capital punishment was stimulated by an increase in the homicide rate. This bias can be reduced by replacing the variable $\Delta(E/C)$ with the estimator $\Delta°(E/C)$, formed separately by regressing $\Delta(E/C)$ on all the predetermined variables in Table 1. This alternative produces [a] result . . . which, again, is basically the same as the other equations. Thus, the major finding—that decreases in the execution rate are not associated with increases in the homicide rate—is robust with respect to alternative methods of constructing the execution rate variable.

Alternative Structures of Simultaneity

Although equation (1) assumes that the causation is unidirectional, some variables in the equation may be both determinants of murder and products of either the homicide rate itself or factors that influence the homicide rate. This phenomenon, known generally as "simultaneity," was assumed in equation (8). One variable other than the execution rate that may be determined simultaneously with the homicide rate is the rate at which homicide offenders are convicted; it may both affect the homicide rate, as is hypothesized in equation (1), and be produced by changes in the homicide rate. The latter would occur if, for example, the ability to convict homicide offenders was hampered by an increase in the load of homicide cases. Failure to account for this reverse effect, or for the effect of changes in the execution rate on the conviction rate, might bias all the regression coefficients estimated. To deal with this problem, the estimator $\Delta°(C/Q)$ is constructed by regressing $\Delta(C/Q)$ on the predetermined variables. . . . Once again, the homicide rate appears unaffected by changes in the execution rate.

Another type of simultaneity may exist with regard to the average term of incarceration served by persons convicted of homicide, T. This would result if, for example, sentences were lengthened in response to an increase in the homicide rate, in an attempt to discourage further homicides. The potential bias produced by this simultaneity can be reduced by forming the variable $\Delta°T$, constructed by regressing ΔT on the predetermined variables. The result produced under this construction is . . . basically similar to the others reported above.

The true system of simultaneity among variables is likely to be considerably more complicated than has been hypothesized. The results obtained by treating the execution rate, the conviction rate, and the average term of incarceration as endogenous variables, however, as was done in equations (8), (9), and (10), respectively, indicate that the biases due to failure to capture these simultaneous effects in equations (3) and (4) are not large.

Use of Weighted Regressions

In cross-section analysis the variance of the dependent variable is often larger for more heavily populated places. This condition, known in a more general form as "heteroscedasticity," produces biased estimates of standard errors of the regression coefficients and biased tests of statistical significance. The presence of heteroscedasticity is commonly identified by visual inspection of a plot of the data, although more rigorous methods are available. To eliminate this bias each observation is generally adjusted by weighting it by the square root of the population. Applying this weighting technique to the observations, under equation (4), the result is [again similar to equation (4), which] suggests that the general findings are robust with respect to conventional weighting.

Exclusion of the Other-Crimes Variable

One of the control variables used in equations (1) through (11) is the rate at which crimes other than homicide are committed. It was included in an attempt to account for the factors that caused crime to increase generally during the 1960s, since the failure of previous analyses to capture these effects may have interfered substantially with their ability to isolate a pure deterrent effect of capital punishment. Certain offenses incorporated in this control variable, however, are likely to differ from homicide only in that the victims did not die. Since it is possible that some nonhomicide offenses may themselves be deterred by capital punishment, having them in the right-hand side of the regression equation may have affected the estimates of the deterrent effect that were reported above.

It is possible to test the effect of this potential bias, whose direction is not obvious, a priori, by estimating a counterpart to equation (4) without other offenses as a control variable. The result is [equation 12]. As before, the deterrent effect of capital punishment is not apparent. While the omission of factors that caused crimes other than homicide to increase during the 1960s produces a result that differs somewhat from equation (4), it does not, in this analysis, materially alter the finding.

Conclusion

The aim of this essay was to investigate empirically the deterrent effect of capital punishment. Building on studies by Ehrlich and Passell, the influence of the execution rate on the homicide rate was estimated by controlling for the effects of other variables and for the reverse effects of the homicide rate on the sanction variables. This analysis differs from previous ones, however, both because it focuses on a unique decade during which the homicide rate increased by over 50 percent and the use of capital punishment ceased and because it examines changes in homicides and executions over time *and* across states.

The findings do not support the hypothesis that capital punishment deters homicides. The 53 percent increase in the homicide rate in the United States from 1960 to 1970 appears to be the product of factors other than the elimination of capital punishment. Foremost among these are a decline in the rate at which homicide offenses resulted in imprisonment (from 41.3 percent in 1960 to 34.6 percent in 1970 for the states that reported in both years) and increasing affluence during the 1960s.

To obtain a sense of how well the estimates, based as they are on individual observations of 32 states, generalize to the United States as a whole, the coefficients of the basic equation, (4), can be combined with changes in the respective independent variables given in the first two columns of Table 1. This produces a predicted increase of 2.68 homicides per 100,000 residents. That the actual increase was 2.7, as shown in Table 1, provides some assurance that the estimates generalize to the aggregate of 18 states not analyzed in equation (4).

The apparent strength of the incarceration rate variable and the apparent weakness of the execution rate and term of imprisonment variables as deterrents to homicide lend some support to Cesare Beccaria's two-hundred-year-old suggestion that certainty of punishment deters more effectively than its severity. There are, however, other explanations for these findings. The appearance of a strong deterrent effect of imprisonments on homicides may be the result of changes in factors omitted from this analysis. And the apparent weakness of the deterrent effect of long imprisonments may be the product of the inaccuracy of our term-of-imprisonment variable since random errors in the measurement of this variable will bias downward estimates of the deterrent effect of the length of imprisonment.

It seems likely, nonetheless, that this finding of a deterrent effect of imprisonments of persons convicted of murder is more real than spurious. Errors in the measure of murder imprisonments are sure to exist, and these are likely to cause estimates of the deterrent effect of incarceration to understate the true effect. Moreover, this particular finding is consistent with empirical results presented by Ehrlich and Passell. And it supports von Hirsch's suggestion that if penalties for homicide were eliminated entirely it is difficult to imagine that the homicide rate would not increase.

The finding that capital punishment, on the other hand, does not deter homicide is remarkably robust with respect to a wide range of alternative constructions of the execution rate, alternative assumptions about simultaneity among the crime and sanction variables, whether or not the observations are weighted, and the inclusion of different subsets of available control variables.

Capital punishment may be a justly deserved and appropriate sanction in some instances. It is certainly an effective way to ensure that a person convicted of murder will not commit further crimes. The results of this analysis suggest, however, that it is erroneous to view capital punishment as a means of reducing the homicide rate.

Notes

1. In the original article in the *Minnesota Law Review.*

2. Isaac Ehrlich, "Participation in Illegitimate Activities: An Economic Analysis," in *Essays in the Economics of Crime and Punishment* 68 (1974), ed. G. Becker and W. Landes, 70–92; and Ehrlich, "The Deterrent Effect of Capital Punishment; A Question of Life or Death," *American Economic Review* 65 (1975): 398–406.

3. Readers who wish to dig deeper into these matters should see the original article in the *Minnesota Law Review* 61, no. 5 (May 1977): 743–67.

4. Ehrlich explained the potential for a counterdeterrent effect as follows: "One may argue that the differential deterrent effect of capital punishment on the incentive to commit murder may be offset by the added incentive it may create for those who actually commit this crime to eliminate policemen and witnesses who can bring about their apprehension and subsequent conviction and execution." Ehrlich, "The Deterrent Effect of Capital Punishment," 398 n. 3. Courts or juries may also be more reluctant "to convict defendants charged with murder when the risk of their subsequent execution is perceived to be undesirably high." Ibid., 405.... Von Weber has suggested as an alternative explanation that capital punishment may induce suicidally inclined persons to commit murder. H. Von Weber, "Selbstmord als Mordmotiv," *Monatsschrift für Kriminalbiologie und Strafrechtsreform* 161 (1937).

[Editor's note: Forst's data show that the homicide rate began to increase sharply in 1963 when the Vietnam War began and continued to rise throughout the Vietnam War. Transnational data show that homicide rates regularly rise during wartime. See Kenneth Haas and James Inciardi, eds., *Challenging Capital Punishment: Legal and Social Science Approaches* (Beverly Hills, Calif.: Sage Publishing, 1988), 49–90; and Ted Gurr, *Why Men Rebel,* passim. Forst's data also show that during World War II, homicide rates had their previous peak; and there was a small rise during the Korean War. Transnational research shows that when government actions and statements in general indicate approval of killing, or less disapproval, killing increases. This may suggest an explanation for the observation that after an execution, homicide rates temporarily increase in the region where the execution took place: the government set an example of justified killing, as it does during wartime. (See W. Bowers and G. Pierce, "Deterrence or Brutalization: What Is the Effect of Executions?" *Crime and Delinquency* 26 (1980): 453–84.) Thus the execution stopped one murderer from ever killing again, but stimulated other murders, as conviction and imprisonment do not stimulate other murders. This hypothesis fits Forst's results well. His results indicate a two-thirds probability that executions cause a net increase in murders, which is suggestive but not high enough to be considered statistically significant.]

PART THREE

JUSTICE AS FAIRNESS AND EQUAL TREATMENT BEFORE THE LAW

[7]

Christian Ethics and Capital Punishment: A Reflection

Alexander Williams Jr.

NEVER WILL THE TIME BE MORE opportune than now for serious reflection and discussion of capital punishment and Christian ethics. The United States of America now holds the dubious distinction of being the world's leader in the area of homicides. General interest in the death penalty has never been greater than it is today as we witness the vicious killings of individuals by fellow human beings in almost every urban community in America. . . .

Arguments in Favor of Capital Punishment

It has been said that "the right of administering punishment is the right of the sovereign as the supreme power to inflict pain upon a subject on account of a crime committed by him."[1] This statement is at the foundation of all arguments favoring capital punishment.

The proponents of capital punishment vigorously support the imposition of death as a punishment for heinous offenses. First, they raise the question as to why law-abiding citizens have to suffer at the hands of law breakers. Inasmuch

SOURCE: From Alexander Williams Jr., "Christian Ethics and Capital Punishment: A Reflection," *Journal of Religious Thought* 49 (summer/fall 1992). Reprinted by permission of the author.

as the public is outraged and disgusted with violence perpetrated against innocent victims and citizens, it is perfectly legitimate for the State to express this anger and vent this outrage by imposing capital punishment. Second, it logically follows that retribution and vengeance should be, and have long been, valid purposes of the criminal justice system. If private acts of vengeance (recent trends in New York suggest that private citizens are now seeking vengeance on their own) and vigilante groups are to be suppressed, citizens must have some assurance that the State will seek retribution on behalf of its citizens.

Third, capital punishment serves as a general deterrent to others who will come to realize what will happen to them if they engage in this kind of violent behavior. The argument here is that although there are no empirical data to verify the role of deterrence, those who claim that it does not deter have the burden to prove their position. It is further insisted that those with that burden cannot themselves prove that it does not deter. Moreover, as the proponents posit, the death penalty serves as a special deterrent. It is beyond dispute that the execution of the offender is the most effective and certain method by which the offender is incapacitated or prevented from perpetrating additional crimes against society.

Fourth, the proponents of the death penalty argue that the majority of people in this country support capital punishment and America has always followed the democratic notion of the majority and consensus as a principle of operation. In support of this argument they point out that approximately thirty-seven state legislatures, representing most of the people in this country, have enacted legislation to impose capital punishment. Candidates for political office campaign on that issue and are elected over those who do not so favor (remember President Bush versus Governor Dukakis in 1988).

Fifth, proponents insist that biblical text supports capital punishment, and, in fact, during the medieval period even the Church recognized the right of the State to execute for the common good. *Lex talionis,* the Law of Retribution, they claim, has long been the basis upon which the State is authorized to protect and defend the common good by using violent means to repel the vicious.

The retributive aspect of the proponents' position has been often repeated by any number of authors. The proponents believe that most of these murderers never express regret for the heinous crimes they commit, nor do they feel the slightest sympathy for the victim or their families. The proponents approve of the Supreme Court's recent attempts to streamline, curtail, and quicken the appeal mechanisms in order that the criminal justice system can become better balanced toward providing more justice to victims rather than always focusing on expanding the rights for criminal defendants.

Arguments against Capital Punishment

Championed by the likes of recently retired Justice William Brennan of the United States Supreme Court, the opponents of capital punishment raise equally forceful arguments. They first argue that the death penalty serves no legitimate utility, and, in fact, they assert, it has demonstrably failed to accomplish its stated objectives. Modern scholars and theologians commencing with the eighteenth century have long rejected retribution as a valid aim of the criminal justice system. They have seriously challenged the right of the State to execute. With respect to deterrence, they claim that with over 20,000 homicides committed each year, and only 300 convicted murders receiving the death penalty, it is clear that the death penalty does not deter. In fact, they suggest that drug dealers are more aware of the death penalty on the streets (for selling bad drugs, or not paying for drugs, or invading another's territory) than the State's imposed capital punishment. Consequently, they posit, when you successfully assail the only two purposes advanced as support for capital punishment (retribution and deterrence), any other purposes can be achieved by other punitive measures. For example, protection of society can be achieved by incarcerating dangerous individuals for the rest of their lives. Moreover, a sentence of life without parole can also serve to deter and can address rehabilitation as a goal, which capital punishment cannot.

Second, they argue that notwithstanding the Supreme Court's opinion in *Gregg v. Georgia*,[2] the evolving standards of decency have not reached a point where society as a whole condones State executions. They reject the notion of the majority on the theory that the majority has frequently been wrong throughout history. (The historical majority favored slavery, favored the separate but equal doctrine until 1954, used to sanction ill treatment for women, and used to cut off a person's hands for being convicted as a thief.) They argue that capital punishment is barbaric and very cruel and unusual in the sense that if we don't abuse a rapist, don't burn down the house of the arsonist, don't beat up the robber or the one who assaults, and don't cut off the hand of the thief, why should we kill the killer?

Third, the opponents argue that capital punishment is arbitrarily and capriciously inflicted as a punishment. It is beyond real debate that the underclass, the poor, and the black in the country disproportionately are the hardest hit and most often the target of capital punishment. Those without money to hire private attorneys and those not the favorite of police, prosecutors, judges, and governors are seen as the victims of discriminatory application of the death penalty. While no effort is being made to cast aspersions on public defender agencies, the reality is that inadequate funding and staffing problems give rise to shortcomings in the quality of representation with respect to the resources of the government.

There has also been statistical evidence established with reference to the discrimination of African Americans. The opponents of capital punishment cite the Baldus study[3] presented by a black defendant who was convicted and sentenced to die in Georgia for the robbery and murder of a white police officer. In the majority opinion by Supreme Court Justice Powell, which held that the Baldus study did not establish that Georgia's capital punishment scheme violated the Equal Protection clause, the Court, nevertheless, referenced the study in detail:

> In support of his claim, McCleskey proffered a statistical study performed by Professors David C. Baldus, George Woolworth, and Charles Pulaski (the Baldus study) that purports to show a disparity in the imposition of the death sentence in Georgia based on the race of the murder victim and, to a lesser extent, the race of the defendant. The Baldus study is actually two sophisticated statistical studies that examine over 2,000 murder cases that occurred in Georgia during the 1970s. The raw numbers collected by Professor Baldus indicate that defendants charged with killing white persons received the death penalty in 11% of the cases, but defendants charged with killing blacks received the death penalty in only 1% of the cases. The raw numbers also indicate a reverse racial disparity according to the race of the defendant: 4% of the black defendants received the death penalty, as opposed to 7% of the white defendants.[4]

Fourth, capital punishment, as a punitive measure, is final and irreversible, which the opponents advance as the strongest reason for rejecting the death penalty. There have been mistakes in convictions throughout history, and the death penalty precludes the opportunity to rectify a miscarriage of justice. Hugo Bedau, in his treatise *The Death Penalty in America,* emphatically asserts that the innocent have been executed and that there is no system of criminal jurisprudence that has on the whole provided safeguards against the conviction and possible execution of an innocent man.[5]

Fifth, similar to assertions by the proponents, there is ample authority in the scripture replete with suggestion for compassion, condonation, and remorse as well as for retribution, which the opponents dismiss as primitive and animalistic.

Sixth, the opponents stress the fiscal impact and argue that the $1,000,000 amount per execution (which includes the entire legal process) is too costly and the sum should be placed elsewhere to meet the State's pressing demands on the treasury from its citizens.

Last, the death penalty, many observers have claimed, has made securing convictions more difficult and has often resulted in the acquittal of obviously guilty defendants. In other words, unpunished criminals are walking the streets because juries won't convict them of capital crimes knowing that they would get mandatory death. In short, many are satisfied that mandatory capital punishment does indeed have a deterrent effect: It deters jurors from convicting probably guilty men.[6] To recap, it is the sacredness of life, the criminal as a victim, and the discriminatory application of the death penalty that undergird the basic position of the opponents to capital punishment.[7]

Developing Christian Paradigms

In developing Christian paradigms with reference to capital punishment, several observations can be made. First, there is clear indication that a significant number of people view the criminal justice system as inequitable and ineffective. Sociologists, penologists, and other professionals admit that many of the theories for punishment such as deterrence and retribution have questionable utility. Many judges and other persons who are part of the criminal justice system are frustrated because of the lack of resources and expertise available to deal with the sociological and psychological issues that must be addressed as part of the overall solution to violent criminal activity. Second, elected and other public officials are also less than candid, with many of them "hustling" in the sense that they must say the right thing in order to get elected and reelected.

The time has come for the religious community to help develop workable rules and paradigms to approach capital punishment and other issues. These new paradigms must "provide uniform justice based on realistic concepts of human and civil rights, morality and acceptable social norms."[8] As we move toward Christian paradigms, it is imperative that we understand that strict adherence to the Old Testament concept of *lex talionis* as justification for supporting capital punishment is as unacceptable as the blind implementation of New Testament principles of love, compassion, and forgiveness.

Guidelines for the development of such paradigms should involve the following factors:

1. The Christian must clearly recognize that dangerous criminals roam our society on a daily basis, a situation that is inimical to our health, safety, and life.
2. Christians must clearly recognize that the society through the mechanism of the state has an absolute right to protect itself from such vicious and dangerous individuals.
3. Christians must face the fact that the criminal justice system has points of unfairness that must be addressed. The disproportionality of blacks

    on death row is of grave concern, as is the possibility of verdicts involving erroneous convictions.

4. There must be some degree of compassion for persons who are the defendants and accused persons in the criminal justice system; however, the nature of this compassion and love deserves clarity in the sense that it should focus on fairness and the elimination of oppressive conditions for the inmate or defendant.

5. Christians must understand that on the dawn of the twenty-first century, the idea of forgiveness as a part and parcel of the criminal justice system is now archaic and of little consequence.

6. We may have visions and anticipations that someday we will live in a utopia that is as close to God's kingdom as possible, but the reality of life is that today no such condition exists. The best thing that we can do as Christians is to anticipate that great day of joy, peace, and the absence of conflict.

A Functional Approach

…A functional approach to the question of capital punishment first requires the elimination of emotion in assessing the issue and then, second, incorporating the six aforesaid paradigms in reaching a clear approach to the issue. A functional approach also requires that after focusing on the various purposes of the Bible, religion, and capital punishment, those purposes then be read harmoniously together in connection with arriving at a reasonable position. In other words, the design of taking a functional approach to deciding the issue is to make every effort to construe the various purposes as complementing and supplementing each other and not as necessarily clashing or conflicting.

    Being uniquely involved in the issue of capital punishment, I take a functional approach to resolving the issue of capital punishment. As the elected State's Attorney for Prince George's County, Maryland,[9] I recognize that the amount of discretion exercised in connection with capital punishment is awesome. In our American system of criminal jurisprudence, the prosecutor has a key role in deciding when to seek the death penalty and against whom. Unless the prosecutor (State's Attorney) in the exercise of his or her discretion notifies the accused that he or she intends to seek the death penalty, neither the judge nor the jury would ever have an opportunity to have an impact on such a case. Accordingly, the prosecutor is obligated to possess clear direction and insight in discharging his or her ethical consideration of this issue.

    The issue of capital punishment is a difficult one for the Christian. Words in the scripture, such as "die," "death," "vengeance," "kill," "murder," "life for a life," and "blood," have meanings and usage that vary according to one's philosophy or interpretation. What does the phrase in John 8:7, "Those who live by the sword will die by the sword," denote? Does the phrase "The wages of sin are death" authorize the death penalty? It appears that both the proponents and opponents of capital punishment may find a phrase or passage to support their position. That is the beauty of the Bible—it is such a flexible and resilient document that it has lasted through many years and is able to be applied today.

There is nothing substantive in the Bible that unequivocally precludes the imposition of capital punishment. If the people of God can accept a self-defense killing or killing in the course of war and defending freedom, then there is nothing so shocking or barbaric about the death penalty as a means of punishment. The Christian must seek to assure fairness in the process. A Christian must subscribe to love ethics, which historically has embodied kindness, forgiveness, forbearance, and redemption. Love ethics must, however, be expanded to include resistance to violence even if it results in the taking of life. Christians may continue to love the vicious criminal, but we need not love violence and oppression, which must at times be forcefully prevented.

The world is not a perfect place. There are some areas of imperfections. Similarly, the criminal justice system has some deficiencies. We must work to cure the shortcomings, such as disproportion in sentencing, and do the best that, as Christians, we can do under very difficult and emotional circumstances. Those in the criminal justice system must seek to promote fairness and compassion wherever they can possibly make a difference. Beyond that, of course, Christians must assume that the majority of citizens struggle to enact just, fair, and well-reasoned rules of law that must be followed in order to maintain the moral order.[10]

As a Christian who happens to be the elected State's Attorney for Prince George's County, Maryland, I support the death penalty and intend to execute it as part of my sworn duty. The Maryland legislature saw fit to impose a penalty of death in appropriate capital cases, and the Council of Appeals of Maryland and United States Supreme Court have determined it to be legal and within the boundaries of the state and federal constitutions.

Traditionally, juries in Prince George's County have expressed a reluctance to impose the death penalty in every capital case. However, it is my view that carefully selected cases setting forth strong, aggravating, and heinous factors warrant being presented as capital cases for consideration and decision by juries. It is my duty, however, as State's Attorney to ensure that a reasonable, fair, and consistent death penalty policy is in place. Accordingly, I have established and implemented a policy pertaining to the procedure to be used in filing notices of intent to seek the death penalty. Each aggravated murder will be reviewed by myself and my executive staff, which consists of two deputies and four division chiefs. Following a full discussion and a recommendation from the executive staff, I shall make the final decisions whether to file a notice of intent to seek the death penalty. Factors to be considered in making this determination include any aggravating or mitigating circumstances, any past criminal history of the accused, the youth of the accused, and the general and specific background of the accused.

In sum, those individuals who have a part in the capital punishment process must make certain that unfairness and unreasonableness are eliminated from the process. Ethical considerations of this nature must be instilled by those who have an opportunity to make such an impact. Only with this kind of ethical reflection and ethical search does the functional approach receive its imprimatur of legitimacy.

Application of the Functional Approach

On October 13, 1989, Damon Bowie and James Edmonds, armed with handguns, entered Stoney's Restaurant located in Prince George's County, Maryland. Once inside the restaurant and after having the money handed over to him, Damon Bowie executed two employees, Kevin Brian Shelby and Arnold James Batson, on his way out of the restaurant. Shelby and Batson died as a result of close-range shootings while they were lying down on the floor in compliance with Bowie's instructions. Two other persons were also shot by Bowie but survived. Damon Bowie and others were indicted on thirty-five counts ranging from murder in the first degree to conspiracy to commit robbery with a deadly weapon.

On July 9, 1990, the Prince George's County State's Attorney, Alexander Williams Jr., pursuant to policies and guidelines established by the State's Attorney,[11] and after extensive debate and reflection by the State's Attorney and his top assistants, filed a notice of the State's intent to seek the sentence of death against Damon Bowie, who at trial was alleged to be the shooter in this matter. The trial commenced on August 27, 1990, and lasted five days. A jury deliberated for about four hours before handing down a guilty verdict on 20 counts, including the murders of Arnold Batson, a black male, and Kevin Shelby, a white male. About two months later, the same jury...reconvened to pronounce sentencing. Under the Maryland Code, a defendant may be given the death penalty if certain aggravating circumstances exist (for example, committing murder while engaging in a crime of violence, to wit, armed robbery).[12] Although the jury found that there were certain mitigating factors, such as the defendant's age and his troubled childhood, they determined that the aggravating circumstances outweighed the mitigating circumstances. Finding that Damon Bowie was, in fact, the shooter in this incident in which two or more persons were killed, and that the murder occurred while he was attempting to commit a robbery, the jury pronounced a sentence of death after deliberating for six hours.[13]

During my first term as the elected State's Attorney, I had fifteen opportunities to file notices of intent to seek the death penalty based on the presence of certain statutory aggravating circumstances. All but one of those fifteen cases involved young black male defendants. In four of those cases, I applied the functional approach and decided to request that the jury return a death sentence. The case of Damon Bowie was one of those cases. My decision to seek the death penalty in that case reflects my overall position as supportive of capital punishment and also illustrates the process upon which that pro–capital punishment point of view is based. Let me be more specific.

First, and from a biblical standpoint, the scripture, in my view, does not preclude capital punishment. God mandates that human beings treat each other in a fair, just, and righteous manner. This means to me that criminal laws and punishment are to be applied evenly, humanely, and fairly to all. Second, I believe that God has directed that my role in this process is to be on the inside of the criminal justice system where certain critical and fair judgments are to be made. Third, I understand and recognize the politics involved in being on the inside as an elected public servant. The political reality of this role is that I am charged with carrying out the letter and spirit of the law while representing all of the citizens, who expect integrity and impartiality on behalf of all. In order to remain on the inside and maintain this key role of administering justice, it is imperative that I enforce capital punishment, which has been declared legally and constitutionally appropriate. My political health and further interest in politics demand that I find some circumstance warranting my requesting capital punishment in a county experiencing record homicide rates for the past four years. Therefore, I candidly admit that politics and public opinion play a part in this decision.

Fourth, I personally believe that retribution is an appropriate criterion for seeking capital punishment. Having spoken to many families of murdered victims, I am thoroughly convinced that a portion of their grief, suffering, and resentment is curtailed and eased once they receive assurance that the State is seeking vengeance by requesting capital punishment. Last, I believe that capital punishment is appropriate where a reasonable procedure is put in place that substantially minimizes the arbitrariness, caprice, and unfairness that has been an inherent part of the history of America where African Americans have been accused of murdering whites.

Under procedures that I have put in place since becoming State's Attorney,[14] every effort is made to obtain consistency of treatment and fair play. In the Damon Bowie case, the decision to seek the death penalty was made without reservation and in compliance with my established policy. The debate and deliberation with my staff prior to deciding to file was thorough and spirited. I determined that Mr. Bowie executed at close range two innocent victims who were lying on the floor as ordered in a completely helpless and defenseless position. One murdered victim was white and the other murdered victim was black. The jury that convicted Bowie and sentenced him to death consisted of six African Americans, one Asian American, and five whites. In view of other aggravating factors, such as a third victim being shot in the face (he is disabled with a severely deformed face) who miraculously lived despite being left for dead, my decision was a correct and ethical one. The community rightfully demanded that I seek the death penalty and a jury of an even number of whites and blacks confirmed my opinion and decision.

In short, then, my ultimate position of pro-capital punishment is based upon a myriad of factors. Some of those factors are religious in the sense that I believe God expects us to participate in delivering justice. Other reasons include my personal feeling that capital punishment has a legitimate utility as a punishment, and also my recognition that politics and public opinion play a significant (though not controlling) role in determining whether a chief law enforcement officer remains in office. This last statement, however, should not be taken out of context. If the majority of citizens through their elected representatives enact a criminal law that is judicially upheld by the courts as legal, then the elected prosecutor ought to reasonably and fairly enforce that law or expect to voluntarily or involuntarily (politically) prepare to leave public service.

Conclusion

As a debatable moral issue, the views relating to the death penalty are varied and stimulating. Despite the deep-seated feelings on both sides, we Christians cannot run from the debate. The bottom line is to approach the issue with reason, respect for both positions, and resolute determination to arrive at a Christian position of fairness and reasonableness.

Notes

1. Michael E. Endres, *The Morality of Capital Punishment: Equal Justice under the Law?* (Mystic, Conn.: Twenty-Third Publications, 1985), 103.

2. *Gregg v. Georgia,* 428 U.S. 153 (1976).

3. Statistical study performed by Professors David C. Baldus, George Woolworth, and Charles Pulaski purporting to show a disparity in the imposition of the death sentence in Georgia based on race.

4. Baldus's 230-variable model divided cases into eight different ranges, according to the estimated aggravation level of the offense. Baldus argued in his testimony to the District Court that the effects of racial bias were most striking in the mid-range cases. "When the cases become tremendously aggravated so that everybody would agree that if we're going to have a death sentence, these are the cases that should get it, the race effects go away. It's only in the mid-range of cases where the decision makers have a real choice as to what to do. If there's room for the exercise of discretion, then the [racial] factors begin to play a role." Under this model, Baldus found that 14.4 percent of the black-victim cases received the death penalty. According to Baldus, the facts of McCleskey's case placed it within the mid-range.

5. Hugo Adam Bedau, *The Death Penalty in America* (Chicago: Aldine Publishing Company, 1964), 189.

6. Hugo Adam Bedau, *Capital Punishment in the United States* (New York: AMS Press, 1975), 49.

7. [Editor's note: Here I have deleted an extensive section quoting many biblical passages that can be used to argue for or against the death penalty, and a section on church teachings that climaxes in quoting the position of the American Baptist churches opposing the death penalty. The biblical passages are discussed more thoroughly in other essays in this book, and here I want to focus on Williams's discussion of justice as fairness.]

8. Lou Torok, *Straight Talk from Prison: A Convict Reflects on Youth, Crime, and Society* (New York: Human Science Press, 1974), 125.

9. Elected in November 1986 as the first African American ever elected as Chief Prosecutor in Prince George's County, Maryland, a suburban jurisdiction in the Washington-Metropolitan area with a population of 700,000 people.

10. Pending before the House recently was the Comprehensive Crime Control Act of 1990 (HR-5269). Under the "Racially discriminatory capital sentencing" chapter of HR-5269 (chapter 177), this congressional bill stated generally that if the percentage of any particular race on death row exceeds that race in the general population, execution of members of that race is prohibited. Exceptions are if the prosecutor can prove by clear and convincing evidence that nonracial factors explain the higher percentage of members on death row or that the sentence being challenged does not fall within a racially discriminatory pattern.

11. Policy and Procedure for Review of Potential Death Penalty Cases (May 1990), Appendix.

12. Prince George's County juries agreed with the State's Attorney in 75 percent of those cases, thereby returning verdicts of death in three of those cases.

13. On appeal the verdict and sentence were reversed and remanded for a new trial due to error attributed to the trial judge.

14. Policy on Death Penalty Cases, Appendix.

[8]

The Case against the Death Penalty

Hugo Adam Bedau

Unfairness

Constitutional due process as well as elementary justice require that the judicial functions of trial and sentencing be conducted with fundamental fairness, especially where the irreversible sanction of the death penalty is involved.[1] In murder cases (since 1930, 99 percent of all executions have been for this crime), there has been substantial evidence to show that courts have been arbitrary, racially biased, and unfair in the way in which they have sentenced some persons to prison but others to death.

Racial discrimination was one of the grounds on which the Supreme Court relied in *Furman* in ruling the death penalty unconstitutional. Half a century ago, Gunnar Myrdal, in his classic *American Dilemma* (1944), reported that "the South makes the widest application of the death penalty, and Negro criminals come in for much more than their share of the executions." Statistics confirm this discrimination, only it is not confined to the South. Between 1930 and 1990, 4,016 persons were executed in the United States. Of these, 2,129 (or 53 percent) were black. For the crime of murder, 3,343 were executed; 1,693 (or 51 percent) were black.[2] During these years African Americans were about 12 percent of the nation's population.

SOURCE: Hugo Adam Bedau, "The Case against the Death Penalty," Capital Punishment Project of the American Civil Liberties Union. Reprinted by permission.

The nation's death rows have always had a disproportionately large population of African Americans, relative to their fraction of the total population. Over the past century, black offenders, as compared with white, were often executed for crimes less often receiving the death penalty, such as rape and burglary. (Between 1930 and 1976, 455 men were executed for rape, of whom 405, or 90 percent, were black.) A higher percentage of the blacks who were executed were juveniles; and blacks were more often executed than were whites without having their conviction reviewed by any higher court.[3]

In recent years, it has been widely believed that such flagrant discrimination is a thing of the past.... In 1990, [however,] the U.S. General Accounting Office reported to the Congress the results of its review of empirical studies on racism and the death penalty. The GAO concluded: "Our synthesis of the 28 studies shows a pattern of evidence indicating racial disparities in the charging, sentencing, and imposition of the death penalty after the Furman decision" and that "race of victim influence was found at all stages of the criminal justice system process...."

These results cannot be explained away by relevant non-racial factors (such as prior criminal record or type of crime), and they lead to a very unsavory conclusion: In the trial courts of this nation, even at the present time, the killing of a white is treated much more severely than the killing of a black. Of the 168 persons executed between January 1977 and April 1992, only twenty-nine had been convicted of the killing of a non-white, and only one of these twenty-nine was himself white.[4] Where the death penalty is involved, our criminal justice system essentially reserves the death penalty for murderers (regardless of their race) who kill white victims.

Both sex and socio-economic class are also factors that enter into determining who receives a death sentence and who is executed. During the 1980s and early 1990s, only about 1 percent of all those on death row were women,[5] even though women commit about 15 percent of all criminal homicides.[6] A third or more of the women under death sentence were guilty of killing men who had victimized them with years of violent abuse.[7] Since 1930, only thirty-three women (twelve of them black) have been executed in the United States.[8]

Discrimination against the poor (and in our society racial minorities are disproportionately poor) is also well established. "Approximately ninety percent of those on death row could not afford to hire a lawyer when they were tried."[9] A defendant's poverty, lack of firm social roots in the community, inadequate legal representation at trial or on appeal—all these have been common factors among death-row populations. As Justice William O. Douglas noted in *Furman,* "One searches our chronicles in vain for the execution of any member of the affluent strata in this society."[10]

The demonstrated inequities in the actual administration of capital punishment should tip the balance against it in the judgment of fair-minded and impartial observers. "Whatever else might be said for the use of death as a punishment, one lesson is clear from experience: this is a power that we cannot exercise fairly and without discrimination."[11]

Justice John Marshall Harlan, writing for the Court, noted: "...the history of capital punishment for homicides...reveals continual efforts, uniformly unsuccessful, to identify before the fact those homicides for which the slayer should die.... Those who have come to grips with the hard task of actually attempting to draft means of channeling capital sentencing discretion have confirmed the lesson taught by history.... To identify before the fact those characteristics of criminal homicides and their perpetrators which call for the death penalty, and to express these characteristics in language which can be fairly understood and applied by the sentencing authority, appear to be tasks which are beyond present human ability."[12]

Yet in the *Gregg* decision, the majority of the Supreme Court abandoned the wisdom of Justice Harlan and ruled as though the new guided-discretion statutes could accomplish the impossible. The truth is that death statutes approved by the Court "do not effectively restrict the discretion of juries by any real standards. They never will. No society is going to kill everybody who meets certain preset verbal requirements, put on the statute books without awareness of coverage of the infinity of special factors the real world can produce."[13]

Even if these statutes were to succeed in guiding the jury's choice of sentence, a vast reservoir of unfettered discretion remains: the prosecutor's decision to prosecute for a capital or lesser crime, the court's willingness to accept or reject a guilty plea, the jury's decision to convict for second-degree murder or manslaughter rather than capital murder, the determination of the defendant's sanity, the final decision by the governor on clemency.

Discretion in the criminal-justice system is unavoidable. The history of capital punishment in American society clearly shows the desire to mitigate the harshness of this penalty by narrowing its scope. Discretion, whether authorized by statutes or by their silence, has been the main vehicle to this end. But when discretion is used, as it always has been, to mark for death the poor, the friendless, the uneducated, the members of racial minorities, and the despised, then discretion becomes injustice.

Thoughtful citizens, who in contemplating capital punishment in the abstract might support it, must condemn it in actual practice.

Inevitability of Error

Unlike all other criminal punishments, the death penalty is uniquely irrevocable.... Although some proponents of capital punishment would argue that its merits are worth the occasional execution of innocent people, most would also insist that there is little likelihood of the innocent being executed. Yet a large body of evidence shows that innocent people are often convicted of crimes, including capital crimes, and that some of them have been executed.

Since 1900, in this country, there have been on the average more than four cases per year in which an entirely innocent person was convicted of murder. Scores of these persons were sentenced to death. In many cases, a reprieve or commutation arrived just hours, or even minutes, before the scheduled execution. These erroneous convictions have occurred in virtually every jurisdiction from one end of the nation to the other. Nor have they declined in recent years, despite the new death penalty statutes approved by the Supreme Court.[14] Consider this handful of representative cases.

In 1975, only a year before the Supreme Court affirmed the constitutionality of capital punishment, two African American men in Florida, Freddie Pitts and Wilbert Lee, were released from prison after twelve years awaiting execution for the murder of two white men. Their convictions were the result of coerced confessions, erroneous testimony of an alleged eyewitness, and incompetent defense counsel. Though a white man eventually admitted his guilt, a nine-year legal battle was required before the governor would grant Pitts and Lee a pardon.[15] Had their execution not been stayed while the constitutional status of the death penalty was argued in the courts, these two innocent men probably would not be alive today.

Just months after Pitts and Lee were released, authorities in New Mexico were forced to admit they had sentenced to death four white men—motorcyclists from Los Angeles—who were innocent. The accused offered a documented alibi at their trial, but the prosecution dismissed it as an elaborate ruse. The jury's verdict was based mainly on what was later revealed to be perjured testimony (encouraged by the police) from an alleged eyewitness. Thanks to persistent investigation by newspaper reporters and the confession of the real killer, the error was exposed and the defendants were released after eighteen months on death row.[16]

In Georgia in 1975, Earl Charles was convicted of murder and sentenced to death. A surviving victim of the crime erroneously identified Charles as the gunman; her testimony was supported by a jail-house informant who claimed he had heard Charles confess. Incontrovertible alibi evidence, showing that Charles was in Florida at the very time of the crime, eventually established his innocence—but not until he had spent more than three years under death sentence. His release was owing largely to his mother's unflagging efforts.[17]

In 1989, Texas authorities decided not to retry Randall Dale Adams after the appellate court reversed his conviction for murder. Adams had spent more than three years on death row for the murder of a Dallas police officer. He was convicted on the perjured testimony of a sixteen-year-old youth who was the real killer. Adams's plight was vividly presented in the 1988 docudrama *The Thin Blue Line,* which convincingly told the true story of the crime and exposed the errors that resulted in his conviction.[18]

Another case in Texas from the 1980s tells an even more sordid story. In 1980 a black high school janitor, Clarence Brandley, and his white co-worker found the body of a missing fifteen-year-old white schoolgirl. Interrogated by the police, they were told, "One of you two is going to hang for this." Looking at Brandley, the officer said, "Since you're the nigger, you're elected." In a classic case of rush to judgment, Brandley was tried, convicted, and sentenced to death. The circumstantial evidence against him was thin, other leads were ignored by the police, and the courtroom atmosphere reeked of racism. In 1986 Centurion Ministries—a volunteer group devoted to freeing wrongly convicted prisoners—came to Brandley's aid. Evidence had meanwhile emerged that another man had committed the murder for which Brandley was awaiting execution. Brandley was not released until 1990.[19]

Each of the five stories told above has a reassuring ending: The innocent prisoner is saved from execution and is released. But when prisoners are executed, no legal forum exists in which unanswered questions about their guilt can be resolved. In May 1992, Roger Keith Coleman was executed in Virginia despite widely publicized doubts surrounding his guilt and evidence that pointed to another person as the murderer—evidence that was never submitted at his trial. Not until late in the appeal process did anyone take seriously the possibility that the state was about to kill an innocent man, and then efforts to delay or nullify his execution failed. Was Coleman really innocent? At the time of his execution, his case was marked with many of the features found in other cases where the defendant was eventually cleared. Were Coleman still in prison, his friends and attorneys would have a strong incentive to resolve these questions. But with Coleman dead, further inquiry into the facts of the crime for which he was convicted is unlikely.

Overzealous prosecution, mistaken or perjured testimony, faulty police work, coerced confessions, the defendant's previous criminal record, inept defense counsel, seemingly conclusive circumstantial evidence, community pressure for a conviction—such factors help explain why the judicial system cannot guarantee that justice will never miscarry.

Notes

1. Editor's note: I have excerpted only that section of Bedau's essay that deals with unfairness, or unequal protection under the law.

2. U.S. Bureau of Justice Statistics, "Capital Punishment," 1977, and NAACP Legal Defense Fund, "Death Row, USA," spring 1992.

3. William J. Bowers, *Legal Homicide: Death as Punishment in America, 1864–1982* (Boston: Northeastern University Press, 1984); Victor T. Streib, *Death Penalty for Juveniles* (Bloomington: Indiana University Press, 1987).

4. "Death Row, USA," spring 1992; and *Sourcebook of Criminal Justice Statistics —1990*.

5. U.S. Bureau of Justice Statistics, "Capital Punishment," 1980–1990.

6. *Uniform Crime Reports*, 1980–1990.

7. Memorandum, National Coalition to Abolish the Death Penalty, January 1991.

8. U.S. Bureau of Justice Statistics, "Capital Punishment," 1979; NAACP Legal Defense Fund, "Death Row, USA," spring 1992.

9. Tabak, in *Loyola of Los Angeles Law Review* (1989).

10. *Furman v. Georgia*, 408 U.S. 238.

11. Samuel R. Gross and Robert Mauro, *Death and Discrimination: Racial Disparities in Capital Sentencing* (Boston: Northeastern University Press, 1989), 224.

12. *McGautha v. California*, 402 U.S. 183 (1971).

13. Charles Black Jr., *Capital Punishment: The Inevitability of Caprice and Mistake,* 2d ed. (New York: Norton, 1982).

14. Michael L. Radelet et al., *In Spite of Innocence: Erroneous Convictions in Capital Cases* (Boston: Northeastern University Press, 1992); Bedau and Radelet, "Miscarriages of Justice in Potentially Capital Cases," *Stanford Law Review* (1987).

15. Gene Miller, *Invitation to a Lynching* (Garden City, N. Y.: Doubleday, 1975); also *The New York Times*, Sept. 10, 1975, 1.

16. "Capital Punishment," Senate Hearings (1981), 713–20.

17. *Atlanta Weekly,* May 30, 1982.

18. Adams, Hoffer, and Hoffer, *Adams v. Texas* (1991).

19. Nick Davies, *White Lies: Rape, Murder, and Justice Texas Style* (New York: Avon, 1993).

[9]

Does It Matter If the Death Penalty Is Arbitrarily Administered?

Stephen Nathanson

I

In this article, I will examine the argument that capital punishment ought to be abolished because it has been and will continue to be imposed in an arbitrary manner.

This argument has been central to discussions of capital punishment since the Supreme Court ruling in the 1972 case *Furman v. Georgia.* In a 5-4 decision, the Court ruled that capital punishment as then administered was unconstitutional. Although the Court issued several opinions, the problem of arbitrariness is widely seen as having played a central role in the Court's thinking. As Charles Black Jr. has put it,

> The decisive ground of the 1972 Furman case anti-capital punishment ruling— the ground persuasive to the marginal justices needed for a majority—was that, out of a large number of persons "eligible" in law for the punishment of death, a few were selected as if at random, by no stated (or perhaps statable) criteria, while all the rest suffered the lesser penalty of imprisonment.[1]

SOURCE: Stephen Nathanson, "Does It Matter If the Death Penalty Is Arbitrarily Administered?" *Philosophy and Public Affairs* 14, no. 2 (spring 1985). Copyright © 1985 by Princeton University Press. Reprinted by permission of Princeton University Press.

Among those justices moved by the arbitrariness issue, some stressed the discriminatory aspects of capital punishment, the tendency of legally irrelevant factors like race and economic status to determine the severity of sentence, while others emphasized the "freakish" nature of the punishment, the fact that it is imposed on a minuscule percentage of murderers who are not obviously more deserving of death than others.

Although the Supreme Court approved new death penalty laws in *Gregg v. Georgia* (1976), the reasoning of *Furman* was not rejected. Rather, a majority of the Court determined that Georgia's new laws would make arbitrary imposition of the death penalty much less likely. By amending procedures and adding criteria which specify aggravating and mitigating circumstances, Georgia had succeeded in creating a system of "guided discretion," which the Court accepted in the belief that it was not likely to yield arbitrary results.

The *Gregg* decision has prompted death penalty opponents to attempt to show that "guided discretion" is an illusion. This charge has been supported in various ways. Charles Black has supported it by analyzing both the legal process of decision-making in capital cases and the legal criteria for determining who is to be executed. He has argued that, appearances to the contrary, there are no meaningful standards operating in the system. Attacking from an empirical angle, William Bowers and Glenn Pierce have tried to show that even after *Furman* and under new laws, factors like race and geographic location of the trial continue to play a large role and that the criteria which are supposed to guide judgment do not separate those sentenced into meaningfully distinct groups. Perhaps the most shocking conclusion of Bowers and Pierce concerns the large role played by the race of the killer and the victims, as the chances of execution are by far the greatest when blacks kill whites and least when whites kill blacks.[2]

The upshot of both these approaches is that "guided discretion" is not working and, perhaps, cannot work. If this is correct and if the argument from arbitrariness is accepted, then it would appear that a return from *Gregg* to *Furman* is required. That is, the Court should once again condemn capital punishment as unconstitutional.

I have posed these issues in terms of the Supreme Court's deliberations. Nonetheless, for opponents of the death penalty, the freakishness of its imposition and the large role played by race and other irrelevant factors are a moral as well as a legal outrage. For them, there is a fundamental moral injustice in the practice of capital punishment and not just a departure from the highest legal and constitutional standards.

II

The argument from arbitrariness has not, however, been universally accepted, either as a moral or a constitutional argument. Ernest van den Haag, an articulate and long-time defender of the death penalty, has claimed that the Supreme Court was wrong to accept this argument in the first place and thus that the evidence of arbitrariness presented by Black, Bowers, and Pierce and others is beside the point. In his words:

> ...the abolitionist argument from capriciousness, or discretion, or discrimination, would be more persuasive if it were alleged that those selectively executed are not guilty. But the argument merely maintains that some other guilty but more favored persons, or groups, escape the death penalty. This is hardly sufficient for letting anyone else found guilty escape the penalty. On the contrary, that some guilty persons or groups elude it argues for extending the death penalty to them.[3]

Having attacked the appeal to arbitrariness, van den Haag goes on to spell out his own conception of the requirements of justice. He writes:

> Justice requires punishing the guilty—as many of the guilty as possible, even if only some can be punished—and sparing the innocent—as many of the innocent as possible, even if not all are spared. It would surely be wrong to treat everybody with equal injustice in preference to meting out justice at least to some. ...
> If the death penalty is morally just, *however discriminatorily applied to only some of the guilty*, it does remain just in each case in which it is applied (emphasis added).[4]

Distinguishing sharply between the demands of justice and the demands of equality, van den Haag claims that the justice of individual punishments depends on individual guilt alone and not on whether punishments are equally distributed among the class of guilty persons.

Van den Haag's distinction between the demands of justice and the demands of equality parallels the distinction drawn by Joel Feinberg between "noncomparative" and "comparative" justice.[5] Using Feinberg's terminology, we can express van den Haag's view by saying that he believes that the justice of a particular punishment is a *noncomparative* matter. It depends solely on what a person deserves and not on how others are treated. For van den Haag, then, evidence of arbitrariness and discrimination is irrelevant, so long as those who are executed are indeed guilty and deserve their punishment.

There is no denying the plausibility of van den Haag's case. In many instances, we believe it is legitimate to punish or reward deserving individuals, even though we know that equally deserving persons are unpunished or unrewarded. Consider two cases:

A. A driver is caught speeding, ticketed, and required to pay a fine. We know that the percentage of speeders who are actually punished is extremely small, yet we would probably regard it as a joke if the driver protested that he was being treated unjustly or if someone argued that no one should be fined for speeding unless all speeders were fined.

B. A person performs a heroic act and receives a substantial reward, in addition to the respect and admiration of his fellow citizens. Because he deserves the reward, we think it just that he receive it, even though many equally heroic persons are not treated similarly. That most heroes are unsung is no reason to avoid rewarding this particular heroic individual.

Both of these instances appear to support van den Haag's claim that we should do justice whenever we can in individual cases and that failure to do justice in all cases is no reason to withhold punishment or reward from individuals.

III

Is the argument from arbitrariness completely unfounded then? Should we accept van den Haag's claim that "unequal justice is justice still"?

In response to these questions, I shall argue that van den Haag's case is not as strong as it looks and that the argument from arbitrariness can be vindicated.

As a first step in achieving this, I would like to point out that there are in fact several different arguments from arbitrariness. While some of these arguments appeal to the random and freakish nature of the death penalty, others highlight the discriminatory effects of legally irrelevant factors. Each of these kinds of arbitrariness raises different sorts of moral and legal issues.

For example, though we may acknowledge the impossibility of ticketing all speeding drivers and still favor ticketing some, we will not find every way of determining which speeders are ticketed equally just. Consider the policy of ticketing only those who travel at extremely high speeds, as opposed to that of ticketing every tenth car. Compare these with the policy of giving tickets only to speeders with beards and long hair or to speeders whose cars bear bumper stickers expressing unpopular political views. While I shall not pursue this point in detail, I take it to be obvious that these different selection policies are not all equally just or acceptable.

A second difference between versions of the argument from arbitrariness depends on whether or not it is granted that we can accurately distinguish those who deserve to die from those who do not. As van den Haag presents the argument, it assumes that we are able to make this distinction. Then, the claim is made that from this class of people who deserve to die, only some are selected for execution. The choice of those specific persons from the general class of persons who deserve to die is held to be arbitrary.

Van den Haag neglects a related argument which has been forcefully defended by Charles Black. Black's argument is that the determination of who deserves to die—the first step—is itself arbitrary. So his claim is not merely that arbitrary factors determine who among the deserving will be executed. His point is that the determination of who deserves to die is arbitrary. His main argument is that

> the official choices—by prosecutors, judges, juries, and governors—that divide those who are to die from those who are to live are on the whole not made, and cannot be made, under standards that are consistently meaningful and clear, but that they are often made, and in the foreseeable future will continue often to be made, under no standards at all or under pseudo-standards without discoverable meaning.[6]

According to Black, even the most conscientious officials could not make principled judgments about desert in these instances, because our laws do not contain clear principles for differentiating those who deserve to die from those who do not. While I shall not try to summarize Black's analysis of the failures of post-*Furman* capital punishment statutes, it is clear that if van den Haag were to meet this argument, he would have to provide his own analysis of these laws in order to show that they do provide clear and meaningful standards. Or, he would have to examine the actual disposition of cases under these laws to show that the results have not been arbitrary. Van den Haag does not attempt to do either of these things. This seems to result from a failure to distinguish (a) the claim that judgments concerning *who deserves to die* are arbitrarily made, from (b) the claim that judgments concerning *who among the deserving shall be executed* are arbitrarily made.

Van den Haag may simply assume that the system does a decent job of distinguishing those who deserve to die from those who do not, and his assumption gains a surface plausibility because of his tendency to oversimplify the nature of the judgments which need to be made. In contrast to Black, who stresses the complexity of the legal process and the complexity of the judgments facing participants in that process, van den Haag is content to say simply that "justice requires punishing the guilty . . . and sparing the innocent." This maxim makes it look as if officials and jurors need only divide people into two neat categories, and if we think of guilt and innocence as factual categories, it makes it look as if the only judgment necessary is whether a person did or did not kill another human being.

In fact, the problems are much more complicated than this. Not every person who kills another human being is guilty of the same crime. Some may have committed no crime at all, if their act is judged to be justifiable homicide. Among others, they may have committed first-degree murder, second-degree murder, or some form of manslaughter. Furthermore, even if we limit our attention to those who are convicted of first-degree murder, juries must consider aggravating and mitigating circumstances in order to judge whether someone is guilty enough to deserve the death penalty. It is clear, then, that simply knowing that someone is factually guilty of killing another person is far from sufficient for determining that he deserves to die, and if prosecutors, juries, and judges do not have criteria which enable them to classify those who are guilty in a just and rational way, then their judgments about who deserves to die will necessarily be arbitrary and unprincipled.

Once we appreciate the difficulty and complexity of the judgments which must be made about guilt and desert, it is easier to see how they might be influenced by racial characteristics and other irrelevant factors. The statistics compiled by Bowers and Pierce show that blacks killing whites have the greatest chance of being executed, while whites killing blacks have the least chance of execution. What these findings strongly suggest is that officials and jurors think that the killing of a white by a black is a more serious crime than the killing of a black by a white. Hence, they judge that blacks killing whites deserve a more serious punishment than whites killing blacks. Given the bluntness of our ordinary judgments about desert and the complexity of the choices facing jurors and officials, it may not be surprising either that people find it difficult to make the fine discriminations required by law or that such judgments are influenced by deep-seated racial or social attitudes.

Both legal analysis and empirical studies should undermine our confidence that the legal system sorts out those who deserve to die from those who do not in a nonarbitrary manner. If we cannot be confident that those who are executed in fact deserve to die, then we ought not to allow executions to take place at all.

Because van den Haag does not distinguish this argument from other versions of the argument from arbitrariness, he simply neglects it. His omission is serious because this argument is an independent, substantial argument against the death penalty. It can stand even if other versions of the argument from arbitrariness fall.

IV

I would like now to turn to the form of the argument which van den Haag explicitly deals with and to consider whether it is vulnerable to his criticisms. Let us assume that there is a class of people whom we know to be deserving of death. Let us further assume that only some of these people are executed and that the executions are arbitrary in the sense that those executed have not committed worse crimes than those not executed. This is the situation which Justice Stewart described in *Furman.* He wrote:

> These death sentences are cruel and unusual in the same way that being struck by lightning is cruel and unusual. For of all the people convicted of rapes and murders in 1967 and 1968, *many just as reprehensible as these,* the petitioners are among *a capriciously selected random handful* upon whom the sentence of death has in fact been imposed (emphasis added).[7]

What is crucial here (and different from the argument previously discussed) is the assumption that we can judge the reprehensibility of both the petitioners and others convicted of similar crimes. Stewart does not deny that the petitioners deserve to die, but because other equally deserving people escape the death penalty for no legally respectable reasons, the executions of the petitioners, Stewart thought, would violate the Eighth and Fourteenth Amendments.

This is precisely the argument van den Haag rejected. We can sum up his reasons in the following rhetorical questions: How can it possibly be unjust to punish someone if he deserves the punishment? Why should it matter whether or not others equally deserving are punished?

I have already acknowledged the plausibility of van den Haag's case and offered the examples of the ticketed speeder and the rewarded hero as instances which seem to confirm his view. Nonetheless, I think that van den Haag is profoundly mistaken in thinking that the justice of a reward or punishment depends solely on whether the recipient deserves it.

Consider the following two cases which are structurally similar to A and B (given above) but which elicit different reactions:

C. I tell my class that anyone who plagiarizes will fail the course. Three students plagiarize papers, but only one receives a failing grade. The other two, in describing their motivation, win my sympathy, and I give them passing grades.

D. At my child's birthday party, I offer a prize to the child who can solve a particular puzzle. Three children, including my own, solve the puzzle. I cannot reward them all, so I give the prize to my own child.

In both cases, as in van den Haag's, only some of those deserving a reward or punishment receive it. Unlike cases A and B, however, C and D do not appear to be just, in spite of the fact that the persons rewarded or punished deserve what they get. In these cases, the justice of giving them what they deserve appears to be affected by the treatment of others.

About these cases I am inclined to say the following. The people involved have not been treated justly. It was unjust to fail the single plagiarizer and unjust to reward my child. It would have been better—because more just—to have failed no one than to have failed the single student. It would have been better to have given a prize to no one than to give the prize to my child alone.

The unfairness in both cases appears to result from the fact that the reasons for picking out those rewarded or punished are irrelevant and hence that the choice is arbitrary. If I have a stated policy of failing students who plagiarize, then it is unjust for me to pass students with whom I sympathize. Whether I am sympathetic or not is irrelevant, and I am treating the student whom I do fail unjustly because I am not acting simply on the basis of desert. Rather, I am acting on the basis of desert plus degree of sympathy. Likewise, in the case of the prize, it appears that I am preferring my own child in giving out the reward, even though I announced that receipt of the award would depend only on success in solving the puzzle.

This may be made clearer by varying the plagiarism example. Suppose that in spite of my stated policy of failing anyone who plagiarizes, I am regularly lenient toward students who seem sufficiently repentant. Suppose further that I am regularly more lenient with attractive female students than with others. Or suppose that it is only redheads or wealthy students whom I fail. If such patterns develop, we can see that whether a student fails or not does not depend simply on being caught plagiarizing. Rather, part of the explanation of a particular student's being punished is that he or she is (or is not) an attractive female, redheaded, or wealthy. In these instances, I think the plagiarizers who are punished have grounds for complaint, even though they were, by the announced standards, clearly guilty and deserving of punishment.

If this conclusion is correct, then doing justice is more complicated than van den Haag realizes. He asserts that it would be "wrong to treat everybody with equal injustice in preference to meting out justice at least to some." If my assessment of cases C and D is correct, however, it is better that everyone in those instances be treated "unjustly" than that only some get what they deserve. Whether one is treated justly or not depends on how others are treated and not solely on what one deserves.[8]

In fact, van den Haag implicitly concedes this point in an interesting footnote to his essay. In considering the question of whether capital punishment is a superior deterrent, van den Haag mentions that one could test the deterrent power of the death penalty by allowing executions for murders committed on Monday, Wednesday, and Friday, while setting life imprisonment as the maximum penalty for murders committed on other days. In noting the obstacles facing such an experiment, he writes, "It is not acceptable to our sense of justice that *people guilty of the same crime would get different punishments* and that the difference would be made to depend deliberately on *a factor irrelevant to the nature of the crime* or of the criminal" (emphasis added).[9] Given his earlier remarks about the argument from arbitrariness, this is a rather extraordinary comment, for van den Haag concedes that the justice of a punishment is not solely determined by what an individual deserves but is also a function of how equally deserving persons are treated in general.

In his case, what he finds offensive is that there is no difference between what the Monday, Wednesday, Friday murderers deserve and what the Tuesday, Thursday, Saturday, and Sunday murderers deserve. Yet the morally irrelevant factor of date is decisive in determining the severity of the punishment. Van den Haag (quite rightly) cannot swallow this.

Yet van den Haag's example is exactly parallel to the situation described by opponents of the death penalty. For, surely, the race of the criminal or victim, the economic or social status of the criminal or victim, the location of the crime or trial and other such factors are as irrelevant to the gravity of the crime and the appropriate severity of the punishment as is the day of the week on which the crime is committed. It would be as outrageous for the severity of the punishment to depend on these factors as it would be for it to depend on the day of the week on which the crime was committed.

In fact, it is more outrageous that death sentences depend on the former factors because a person can control the day of the week on which he murders in a way in which he cannot control his race or status. Moreover, we are committed to banishing the disabling effects of race and economic status from the law. Using the day of the week as a critical factor is at least not invidiously discriminatory, as it neither favors nor disfavors previously identifiable or disadvantaged groups.

In reply, one might contend that I have overlooked an important feature of van den Haag's example. He rejected the deterrence experiment not merely because the severity of punishment depended on irrelevant factors but also because the irrelevant factors were *deliberately* chosen as the basis of punishment. Perhaps it is the fact that irrelevant factors are deliberately chosen which makes van den Haag condemn the proposed experiment.

This is an important point. It certainly makes matters worse to decide deliberately to base life and death choices on irrelevant considerations. However, even if the decision is not deliberate, it remains a serious injustice if irrelevant considerations play this crucial role. Individuals might not even be aware of the influence of these factors. They might genuinely believe that their judgments are based entirely on relevant considerations. It might require painstaking research to discover the patterns underlying sentencing, but once they are known, citizens and policymakers must take them into consideration. Either the influence of irrelevant factors must be eradicated or, if we determine that this is impossible, we may have to alter our practices more radically.

This reasoning, of course, is just the reasoning identified with the *Furman* case. As Justice Douglas wrote:

> A law that stated that anyone making more than $50,000 would be exempt from the death penalty would plainly fall as would a law that in terms said that blacks, those who never went beyond the fifth grade in school, those who make less than $3,000 a year, or those who were unpopular or unstable should be the only people executed. A law which in the overall view reaches the same result in practice has no more sanctity than a law which in terms provides the same.[10]

The problem, in Douglas's view, was that the system left life and death decisions to the "uncontrolled discretion of judges or juries," leading to the unintended but nonetheless real result that death sentences were based on factors which had nothing to do with the nature of the crime.

What I want to stress here is that the arbitrariness and discrimination need not be purposeful or deliberate. We might discover, as critics allege, that racial prejudice is so deeply rooted in our society that prosecutors, juries, and judges cannot free themselves from prejudice when determining how severe a punishment for a crime should be. Furthermore, we might conclude that these tendencies cannot be eradicated, especially when juries are called upon to make subtle and complex assessments of cases in the light of confusing, semi-technical criteria. Hence, although no one *decides* that race will be a factor, we may *predict* that it will be a factor, and this knowledge must be considered in evaluating policies and institutions.

If factors as *irrelevant* as the day of the crime determine whether people shall live or die and if the influence of these factors is ineradicable, then we must conclude that we cannot provide a just system of punishment and even those who are guilty and deserving of the most severe punishments (like the Monday killers in van den Haag's experiment) will have a legitimate complaint that they have been treated unjustly.

I conclude, then, that the treatment of *classes* of people is relevant to determining the justice of punishments for *individuals* and van den Haag is wrong to dismiss the second form of the argument from arbitrariness. That argument succeeds in showing that capital punishment is unjust and thus provides a powerful reason for abolishing it.

V

Supporters of the death penalty might concede that serious questions of justice are raised by the influence of arbitrary factors and still deny that this shows that capital punishment ought to be abolished. They could argue that some degree of arbitrariness is present throughout the system of legal punishment, that it is unreasonable to expect our institutions to be perfect, and that acceptance of the argument from arbitrariness would commit us to abolishing all punishment.

In fact, van den Haag makes just these points in his essay. He writes:

> The Constitution, though it enjoins us to minimize capriciousness, does not enjoin a standard of unattainable perfection or exclude penalties because that standard has not been attained. . . . I see no more merit in the attempt to persuade the courts to let all capital crime defendants go free of capital punishment because some have wrongly escaped it than I see in an attempt to persuade the courts to let all burglars go because some have wrongly escaped imprisonment.[11]

It is an important feature of this objection that it could be made even by one who conceded the injustice of arbitrarily administered death sentences. Rather than agreeing that capital punishment should be abolished, however, this objection moves from the premise that the flaws revealed in capital punishment are shared by *all* punishments to the conclusion that we must either (a) reject all punishments (because of the influence of arbitrary factors on them) or (b) reject the idea that arbitrariness provides a sufficient ground for abolishing the death penalty.

Is there a way out of this dilemma for death penalty opponents?

I believe that there is. Opponents of the death penalty may continue to support other punishments, even though their administration also involves arbitrariness. This is not to suggest, of course, that we should be content with arbitrariness or discrimination in the imposition of any punishment.[12] Rather the point is to emphasize that the argument from arbitrariness counts against the death penalty with special force. There are two reasons for this.

First, death is a much more severe punishment than imprisonment. This is universally acknowledged by advocates and opponents of the death penalty alike. It is recognized in the law by the existence of special procedures for capital cases. Death obliterates the person, depriving him or her of life and thereby, among other things, depriving him or her of any further rights of legal appeal, should new facts be discovered or new understandings of the law be reached. In this connection, it is worth recalling that many people were executed and are now dead because they were tried and sentenced under the pre-*Furman* laws which allowed the "uncontrolled discretion of judges and juries."

Second, though death is the most severe punishment in our legal system, it appears to be unnecessary for protecting citizens, while punishments generally are thought to promote our safety and well-being. The contrast between death and other punishments can be brought out by asking two questions. What would happen if we abolished all punishments? And, what would happen if we abolished the death penalty?

Most of us believe that if all punishments were abolished, there would be social chaos, a Hobbesian war of all against all. To do away with punishment entirely would be to do away with the criminal law and the system of constraints which it supports. Hence, even though the system is not a just one, we believe that we must live with it and strive to make it as fair as possible. On the other hand, if we abolish capital punishment, there is reason to believe that nothing will happen. There is simply no compelling evidence that capital punishment prevents murders better than long-term prison sentences. Indeed, some evidence even suggests that capital punishment increases the number of murders. While I cannot review the various empirical studies of these questions here, I think it can plausibly be asserted that the results of abolishing punishment generally would be disastrous, while the results of abolishing capital punishment are likely to be insignificant.[13]

I conclude then that the argument from arbitrariness has special force against the death penalty because of its extreme severity and its likely uselessness. The arbitrariness of other punishments may be outweighed by their necessity, but the same cannot be said for capital punishment.

Notes

My thanks are due to Hugo Bedau, William Bowers, Richard Daynard, and Ernest van den Haag for reactions to my thinking about the death penalty. I would especially like to thank Ursula Bentel for helpful discussions and access to unpublished research; Nelson Lande for spirited comments (both philosophical and grammatical); and John Troyer, whose keen and persistent criticisms of my views forced me to write this essay.

1. *Capital Punishment: The Inevitability of Caprice and Mistake,* 2d ed. (New York: W. W. Norton, 1981), 20.

2. Ibid., passim. W. Bowers and G. Pierce, "Arbitrariness and Discrimination under Post-*Furman* Capital Statutes," *Crime and Delinquency* 26 (1980): 563–635. Reprinted in *The Death Penalty in America,* 3d ed., ed. Hugo Bedau (New York: Oxford University Press, 1982), 206–24.

3. "The Collapse of the Case against Capital Punishment," *National Review,* March 31, 1978, 397. A briefer version of this paper appeared in the *Criminal*

Law Bulletin 14 (1978): 51–68, and is reprinted in Bedau, *The Death Penalty in America*, 323–33.

4. Ibid.

5. "Noncomparative Justice," in *Rights, Justice, and the Bounds of Liberty: Essays in Social Philosophy* (Princeton, N.J.: Princeton University Press, 1980); originally published in the *Philosophical Review* 83 (1974): 297–338.

6. Black, *Capital Punishment*, 29.

7. Reprinted in Bedau, *The Death Penalty in America*, 263–64.

8. Using Feinberg's terminology, these can be described as cases in which the criteria of comparative and noncomparative justice conflict with one another. I am arguing that in these instances, the criteria of comparative justice take precedence. Although Feinberg does discuss such conflicts, it is unclear to me from his essay whether he would agree with this claim.

9. Van den Haag, "The Collapse of the Case against Capital Punishment," 403 n. 14. (This important footnote does not appear in the shorter version of the paper.)

10. Reprinted in Bedau, *The Death Penalty in America*, 255–56.

11. Van den Haag, "The Collapse of the Case against Capital Punishment," 397.

12. For a discussion of the role of discrimination throughout the criminal justice system and recommendations for reform, see American Friends Service Committee, *Struggle for Justice* (New York: Hill and Wang, 1971).

13. In support of the superior deterrent power of the death penalty, van den Haag cites I. Ehrlich, "The Deterrent Effect of Capital Punishment: A Question of Life and Death," *American Economic Review* 65 (1975): 397–417. Two reviews of the evidence on deterrence, both of which criticize Ehrlich at length, are Hans Zeisel, "The Deterrent Effect of the Death Penalty: Facts v. Faith," and Lawrence Klein et al., "The Deterrent Effect of Capital Punishment: An Assessment of the Evidence." (Both these articles appear in Bedau, *The Death Penalty in America*.) The thesis that executions increase the number of homicides is defended by W. Bowers and G. Pierce in "Deterrence or Brutalization: What Is the Effect of Executions?" *Crime and Delinquency* 26 (1980): 453–84.

[10]

Refuting Nathanson

Ernest van den Haag

Discrimination

... Disagreeing with the Supreme Court, Stephen Nathanson believes that the death penalty still is distributed in an excessively capricious and discriminatory manner.[1] He thinks capital punishment is "unjust" because poor blacks are more likely to be sentenced to death than wealthy whites. Further, blacks who murdered whites are more likely to be executed than those who murdered blacks.[2] This last discrimination has been thrown into relief recently by authors who seem to be under the impression that they have revealed a new form of discrimination against black murderers. They have not. The practice invidiously discriminates against black victims of murder, who are not as fully, or as often, vindicated as white victims are. However, discrimination against a class of victims, although invidious enough, does not amount to discrimination against their victimizers. The discrimination against black victims, the lesser punishment given their murderers, actually favors black murderers, since most black victims are killed by black murderers. ...

Neither the argument from discrimination against black victims, nor the ar-

SOURCE: From Ernest van den Haag, "Refuting Reiman and Nathanson," *Philosophy and Public Affairs* 14, no. 2 (spring 1985). Copyright © 1985 by Princeton University Press. Reprinted by permission of Princeton University Press.

gument from discrimination against black murderers, has any bearing on the guilt of black murderers, or on the punishment they deserve.

Invidious discrimination is never defensible. Yet I do not see wherein it...does make the death penalty "unjust" for those discriminatorily selected to suffer it, as Stephen Nathanson believes.[3] If we grant that some (even all) murderers of blacks, or, some (even all) white and rich murderers, escape the death penalty, how does that reduce the guilt of murderers of whites, or of black and poor murderers, so that they should be spared execution too? Guilt is personal. No murderer becomes less guilty, or less deserving of punishment, because another murderer was punished leniently, or escaped punishment altogether. We should try our best to bring every murderer to justice. But if one got away with murder, wherein is that a reason to let anyone else get away? A group of murderers does not become less deserving of punishment because another equally guilty group is not punished, or punished less. We can punish only a very small proportion of all criminals. Unavoidably they are selected accidentally. We should reduce this accidentality as much as possible, but we cannot eliminate it.[4]

Equal Injustice and Unequal Justice

Nathanson appears to prefer equal injustice—letting all get away with murder if some do—to unequal justice: punishing some guilty offenders according to desert, even if others get away. Equal justice is best, but unattainable. Unequal justice is our lot in this world. It is the only justice we can ever have, for not all murderers can be apprehended or convicted, or sentenced equally in different courts. We should constantly try to bring every offender to justice. But meanwhile, unequal justice is the only justice we have, and certainly better than equal injustice—giving no murderer the punishment his crime deserves.

More Discrimination

Nathanson insists that some arbitrary selections among those equally guilty are not "just." He thinks that selecting only bearded speeders for ticketing, allowing the cleanshaven to escape, is unjust. Yet the punishment of the bearded speeders is not unjust. The escape of the cleanshaven ones is. I never maintained that a discriminatory distribution is just—only that it is irrelevant to the guilt and deserved punishment of those actually guilty.

Nathanson further suggests that it is not just to spare some student plagiarizers punishment for (I suppose) irrelevant reasons, while punishing others.

Again the distribution is discriminatory, i.e., unjust. But the punishment of the plagiarizers selected is not. (The nonpunishment of the others is.) Nathanson thinks that giving a prize only to one of three deserving children (his own) is unjust. Not to the deserving child. Only to the others, just as it was unjust not to punish the others who deserved it, but not unjust to punish the deserving plagiarizers who were irrelevantly selected.[5]

Nathanson taxes me with inconsistency because in a footnote I wrote that irrelevant discriminations are "not acceptable to our sense of justice." They are not. But I did not say that those who deserved the punishment received, or the reward, were unjustly treated, that is, did not deserve it and should not have received it. Rather those equally situated also should have received it, and the distribution was offensive because they did not. Whenever possible this inequality should be corrected, but certainly not by not distributing the punishment, or the reward at issue, or by not giving it to the deserving. Rather by giving it as well to those who because of discrimination did not get it. (I might have done better to write in my footnote that discriminatory distributions offend our sense of *equal* justice. But neither the Constitution nor I favor replacing justice with equality.)

Nathanson quotes the late Justice Douglas suggesting that a law which deliberately prescribes execution only for the guilty poor, or which has that effect, would be unconstitutional. Perhaps. But the vice would be in exempting the guilty rich; the guilty poor would remain guilty, and deserving of prescribed punishment even if the guilty rich escape legally or otherwise.[6]

Further on, Nathanson points out that the inevitable capriciousness in the distribution of punishments (only a very small percentage of offenders are ever punished and the selection unavoidably is morally arbitrary), while no reason to abolish punishment in general, may still be an argument for abolishing capital punishment because of its unique severity, and because we could survive without. We can survive without many things, which is no reason for doing without, if one thinks, as I do, that we survive *better* with. As for the unique severity of the death penalty it is, of course, the reason for imposing it for uniquely heinous crimes. The guilt of those who committed them is not diminished, if they are selected by a lottery from among all those guilty of the crime.

Following Charles Black, Nathanson notes that those executed are not necessarily the worst murderers, since there is no way of selecting these. He is right. It seems quite sufficient, however, that those executed, though not the worst, are bad enough to deserve execution. That others who deserved it even more got away, does not make those executed insufficiently deserving.

Nathanson goes on to insist that "not every person who kills another is guilty of the same crime." True. Wherefore the law makes many distinctions, leaving only a small group of those guilty of homicide eligible for the death penalty. Further, capital punishment is not mandated. The court must decide in each case whether or not to impose it. To impose capital punishment, courts must find that the aggravating circumstances attending the murder outweigh the mitigating ones, both of which must be listed in the law. Nathanson is right in pointing out that the criteria listed in the law are not easy to apply. If they were, we would not need the judgment of the court. That judgment is not easy to make. It may seem too severe, or not severe enough, in some cases, as would mandated penalties. So what else is new?

Notes

1. Stephen Nathanson, "Does It Matter If the Death Penalty Is Arbitrarily Administered?" *Philosophy and Public Affairs* 14, no. 2 [reprinted in this book; see chapter 9]. Unless otherwise noted, all further quotations are taken from Nathanson's essay.

2. Despite some doubts, I am here granting the truth of both hypotheses.

3. Nathanson, "Does It Matter If the Death Penalty Is Arbitrarily Administered?"

4. Discrimination or capriciousness is (when thought to be avoidable and excessive) sometimes allowed by the courts as a defense. Apparently this legal device is meant to reduce discrimination and capriciousness. But those spared because selected discriminatorily for punishment do not become any less deserving of it as Nathanson thinks, although not punishing them is used as a means to foster the desired equality in the distributions of punishments.

5. There will be some difficulty in explaining to the children who did not get the reward, why they did not, but no difficulty in explaining why one deserving child got it—unless the children share Nathanson's difficulty in distinguishing between justice and equality.

6. See note 4.

PART FOUR

SCRIPTURAL GUIDANCE ON CAPITAL PUNISHMENT

[11]

Capital Punishment:
The Classic Jewish Discussion

Gerald J. Blidstein

I

"Kill" and "murder" are words whose integrity is carefully guarded.[1] "Kill" designates any taking of human life, while "murder" is reserved for unauthorized homicide, usually of a malicious nature. This fine distinction has become a vital one, serving in both legal and ethical Jewish thought.

Contemporary Jewish translators of the Bible have unanimously read the Sixth Commandment as a ban upon what we call murder: Old JPS gives, "Thou shalt not murder"; New JPS, "You shall not murder"; Buber-Rosenzweig, "*Morde nicht.*" The Children of Israel were thus commanded at Sinai to desist from unauthorized killing, but they were not commanded regarding homicide of, say, a judicial or military nature. The ideological conclusions to be drawn from this fact would tend to confirm Judaism as a realistic, hard-headed system, committed to a law of justice rather than a chaos of love. An obvious line is being drawn between a faith that reads, "You shall not murder," and one that naively and unrealistically demands, "You shall not kill."

SOURCE: From Gerald Blidstein, "Capital Punishment: The Classic Jewish Discussion." Reprinted with permission from *Judaism* 14, no. 2 (spring 1965). Copyright American Jewish Congress.

This Jewish translation is also insisted upon by the 12th-century exegete, R. Samuel b. Meir (Rashbam), who states in his notes to Exodus 20:13: "*Rezichah* means 'unjustifiable killing' wherever it is used...but *harigah* and *mitah* can be used for both unjustifiable [killing]...and justifiable...." These definitions were denied, however, by Isaac Abarbanel, who finds in the Sixth Commandment a ban on killing per se, and in the word *rezichah* the equivalent of homicide. To illustrate such usage, he cites Numbers 35:27. Actually, Numbers 35:30 makes the point even more dramatically....

Both verses certainly describe legal killings. In one, the blood-avenger takes advantage of the murderer's abandonment of the city of refuge to kill him. In the other, the murderer is killed after his guilt is established by witnesses.

Consider our three translations of these verses:

> But if the manslayer shall at any time go beyond the border of his city of refuge, whither he fleeth; and the avenger of blood find him without the border of his city of refuge, and the avenger of blood slay [*ve-razach*] the manslayer, there shall be no bloodguiltness for him....

* * *

> Whoso killeth any person, the murderer shall be slain [*yirzach et ha-rozeach*] at the mouth of witnesses.
>
> > (Old JPS)

In the first passage, *razach* is consistently rendered "slay." In the second, the *rozeach* is branded a murderer, yet rather than being "murdered" himself (as a consistent translation of *yirzach* would require) he is "slain." Obviously, in English one cannot translate a judicial ("at the mouth of witnesses") killing "murder"—but the Hebrew text does not allow any such latitude.

The New JPS (of which I give the crucial phrases) goes the old version one better:

> ...and the blood-avenger kills the manslayer...

* * *

> If anyone kills a person the manslayer may be executed only on the evidence of witnesses;...

We have three persons in our drama, all described by some form of the root *r-z-h* and all, surprisingly, with different English names: the *manslayer,* the *kill-*

ing blood-avenger, and the *executioner.* Translation, then, reflects contemporary values; slayer, killer, and executioner are named with little regard for their Hebrew root but with much concern for the role (condemned or approved) each plays in our society.

Our third version, Buber-Rosenzweig, has the merit of consistency (of a rather didactic nature, one suspects):

...und der Bluteinloser mordet den Morder ab...

* * *

...nach dem Mund von Zeugen soll man den Morder abmorden...

Both Old and New JPS, by their discriminations, refuse to admit that the Bible makes no verbal distinction between a murderer and the approved surrogate of either family or society. Only Buber-Rosenzweig pursue an offending consistency with the vengeance of *had gadya: r-z-h* is uniformly rendered "murder." But since, on the one hand, "murder" is to be defined by contemporary usage, and, on the other, the killing of the murderer is either commanded or regulated by Divine law, it can only be called killing. The conclusion will then have to be that *r-z-h* must be rendered "kill" in all instances of its use.

One is, therefore, taken aback by the ingenious obscuring of biblical thought in our contemporary translations, by the costuming of biblical statement in diplomatic prose. There are, of course, instances where a translator must interpret an obscure text, but, on the other hand, a translator must always resist the impulse to manipulate the clear yet disconcerting phrase or sentence. This is especially so where preconceived moral judgments threaten to be imposed upon dissenting texts. Otherwise, the original statement becomes at best the victim of oversight; it is subdued by habit.

II

What of rabbinic usage? Does it make a hard and fast verbal distinction similar to that made between murder and kill? How does it deal with *razach?*

Exodus 21:14 states that a murderer is to be brought to justice even from the altar, which implies, if necessary, delaying the sacrificial service. The *Mekhilta* (ed. Horowitz-Rabin, p. 263) wishes to argue from this that executions could take place even on the Sabbath; it uses the term *rezichah.* One might object that the *rezichah* here spoken of is the case of murder committed by the accused, rather than the execution administered by the court. The ensuing discussion in the *Mekhilta* (p. 264, 1:14) specifically includes within the scope of the argument, however, all modes of execution, and hence all to be executed, not merely murderers. Still, the critical reader could justifiably bisect the two passages.

The parallel passage in the Jerusalem Talmud (Sanhedrin 4:6; 92b) places the matter beyond all doubt:

> Resh Lakish says: "Let them try him, convict him, and execute him on the Sabbath. For if the service, which overrides the Sabbath, is overridden by an execution (*rezichath-mitzvah*), . . . certainly the Sabbath, which is overridden by the service, should be overridden by execution (*rezichath-mitzvah*)."

The term *rezichath-mitzvah* could hardly refer to an act of murder; it must, then, denote an execution. *Mitzvah* is perhaps used in its usual sense of "commanded," as opposed to "permitted"; it may even emphasize that the only valid motive for the act is the fulfillment of the Divine command (see the discussion of R. Isaac b. Abdimi, *Yebamot* 39b). Whatever the correct explanation, one thing is clear: the biblical meaning of *razach*—"to kill"—was perpetuated in Talmudic times.

A passage (seemingly from our *Mekhilta*) in the *She'iltot* (*Vayechi*, No. 34) is equally illuminating:

> The burial of a *met mitzvah* (neglected corpse) does not override the Sabbath, as it is stated: [And if a man be put to death] . . . thou shalt surely bury him the same day (Deut. 21:23), on the day on which you execute him (*rozcho*), do you bury him. . . .

—and since no executions (*rezichot*) took place on the Sabbath, neither were such burials permitted. This passage is of the same fabric as the one previously discussed; in both, *rezichah* hardly means "murder."

Rezichah is used similarly in the *Midrash Hagadol:*

> Most severe is the spilling of blood, which finds its atonement only in *rezichah*, as it is stated (Num. 35:33): . . . and no expiation can be made for the land for the blood that is shed therein, but by the blood of him that shed it.

This verse refers, of course, to the execution of the murderer. (A similar use of the term occurs in a medieval *midrash*.) The citation of Numbers 35:33 is indeed relevant in our context. For the Bible pointedly indicates here the reciprocity demanded by the execution of the killer—a reciprocity in harmony with the fact that biblical language does not discriminate between executions and other killings.

The word is similarly understood by the *Zohar*. Noting the dual system of cantillation and pronunciation provided for the Ten Commandments, it comments that without the caesura thus created in v. 13 "...it would be illegal to kill anyone in the world, though he had violated the law of the Torah...." The verbal (as distinguished from the substantial) point implied here is that *razach* is best understood as "killing," rather than as "murder." So too Maimonides: "Anyone who kills a human being violates *lo tirzach* (*Hilchot Rozeach* 1:1)." And in the *Sefer Ha-mizvoth* (negative command 289): "We are commanded not to kill one another, as it is stated, *lo tirzach.*" The dialectic of Halachah can, of course, comprehend both a ban on killing and the duty to execute much as it comprehends a ban on physical violence and a command to administer stripes. Other resolutions of this problem could be suggested. But whatever the final nature of the dialectic, one thing is clear: Maimonides, both in the *Sefer Ha-Mizvoth* and in his Code, applies the Sixth Commandment to killing in general.

We have thus seen that biblical usage does not limit *rezichah* to murder, rather extending it to describe all killing, even to that which is biblically ordained. We have also seen that subsequent Jewish usage never totally abandoned the biblical insight that no word for the spilling of human blood could bear a less prohibitive denotation than any other.

The conclusion to be drawn from this usage is as concerned with the moral vision of the Hebrew language as it is with the proper rendering of the Sixth Commandment. For in the creation of certain words and their meanings and the non-creation of others a basic and irretrievable moral step is taken. Some speak of the genius of the language. This is imprecise, for language itself is but the manifestation of a more significant and responsible entity.

Western thought distinguishes, at a basic and indelible level—at the level of the word—between homicide and murder. Jewish usage does not make this distinction. The verbal integrity of the spilling of human blood is never violated; homicide is not splintered into the justifiable and the criminal. Obviously, I do not speak here of biblical law, which knows of authorized killings of war, self-defense, and execution. I speak of language, of the stuff in which law is articulated, from which it is nourished, and with which it (or any healthy human activity) is ultimately harmonized.

III

Is there a drive within Judaism that reflects the verbal scheme outlined above? Do we have here a linguistic quirk or rather the organic expression of a deeply rooted attitude? Let us examine the debate carried on in the study halls of Talmudic Palestine over the propriety and wisdom of capital punishment.

The famous clash of R. Akiba and R. Tarfon with R. Simeon ben Gamliel is provocative and ambiguous:

> R. Tarfon and R. Akiba say: "Were we in the Sanhedrin [during that period when it possessed capital jurisdiction], no man would ever have been killed." R. Simeon ben Gamliel says: "They, too, would multiply spillers of blood in Israel."

It is clear that R. Tarfon and R. Akiba could not have expected mere sentiment to make the application of capital punishment impossible. They needed a device that would legally bind the Sanhedrin to their point of view; as the Talmud explains, such a device was to be found in an intense and meticulous questioning of witnesses (e.g., "Did the murderer kill a man about to die anyhow?" "Perhaps the murderer's dagger pierced the body at the very spot of the mortal weakness?"), a questioning designed to find the witness wanting. Yet while their strategy is clear enough, the motive of R. Akiba and R. Tarfon is not discussed. Why this radical and total disclaimer of a recognized judicial procedure?

Three possibilities suggest themselves. First, the very device sketched above may embody the germ of their opposition. R. Akiba and R. Tarfon feared human weakness, the inability of man ever to know an event in its accurate facticity. No witness can ever testify with an absolute knowledge, as their examination was designed to show. Execution then becomes no more than a judicial gamble—and the dice are always loaded when a man's life is the stake. The Sanhedrin, they held, must never arrogantly assume a certainty it cannot truly possess.

Yet this approach, though reasonable, is not totally satisfactory. In the Talmud the device of close interrogation answers the question, "What would they have done (to prevent execution)?" It is not adduced to explain the source of R. Akiba's and R. Tarfon's opposition to capital punishment. Furthermore, and most crucially, R. Simeon ben Gamliel's retort ("They, too, would multiply spillers of blood in Israel") is a *non sequitur.* For once the possible innocence of the man in the docket is admitted, one cannot have his head merely to insure public safety.

A second approach would be that R. Akiba and R. Tarfon agreed that human observation of events could be accurate enough to establish the guilt of an individual but that a society that practiced capital punishment was bound to err, that this license would, by the very frailty of human judgment, be abused, leading to the execution of an innocent. Yet, once again, R. Gamliel's reply is not to the point: can society purchase health at the price of innocent lives?

Perhaps, then, the opposition to capital punishment is rooted elsewhere; perhaps its source is not a fear of killing the innocent but a reluctance to kill the guilty. This reluctance to take the life of even a criminal could be translated into an effective legal restraint by the type of questioning outlined above—an interrogation on the unknowable. R. Gamliel's retort is now very much to the point: "You would not kill the guilty," he says, "because of your disdain to take the life of man; but you will in reality cause many more deaths than the one you now seek to avoid."

It were well to emphasize at this point the fact that this approach to capital cases was not a "mere theoretical" one. True, both R. Tarfon and R. Akiba lived at a time when the Sanhedrin did not sit on such cases; hence their teachings had no immediate application. Yet they also lived at a time of intense political and military activity designed to regain for the Jews full autonomy, including, of course, the re-establishment of the Sanhedrin. The precise role played by R. Akiba in this struggle may be a matter of debate; but the existence of this struggle is a fact against which all utterances of the time must be measured. Hence, the teaching of these Tannaim cannot be relegated to the limbo of pure theory. It were also well to emphasize that R. Akiba hardly sanctifies human life beyond all other values. Did he not deliver up his own life for the love of God and His Torah? Naturally, he retained his objectivity in the construction of the Halachic scheme: while many sages understood the "death" decreed for the non-*Kohen* who performed the Temple service (Num. 18:7) as "heavenly (*biy-dei shmayim*)," R. Akiba maintained that capital punishment was intended. Indeed, Jewish law abolished capital punishment in fact not by denying its conceptual moral validity but rather by allowing it only this conceptual validity.

This teaching of R. Akiba would be an accurate reflection of the categories of the Hebrew language. For when a language does not verbally distinguish between authorized and unauthorized killing, it implies one possibility of its people's morality. The point in time at which this morality becomes explicit, the moment at which linguistic insight crystallizes into legal fact, is irrelevant. We must see R. Akiba, then, as the final expositor of a muted tradition. Significantly, R. Akiba is identified as using the term *rezichah* for execution (*Mekhilta Ki Tissah,* p. 304, 1:13). Other teachings of this Tanna and his school fit into this same pattern. Thus, "R. Akiba says: 'Whoever spills blood destroys the image [of God].'" This is the metaphysical fact of the matter, a fact unchanged by the motives behind the slaying. R. Meir (a student of R. Akiba) points out that the sight of an executed criminal hanging from a tree (Deut. 21:22–3) provokes the thought that the King [God, as it were] himself is hung.

IV

It has long been a truism that Jewish law is so weighted as to make execution a virtual impossibility. Again, such an attitude was not "merely theoretical":

the young R. Yochanan ben Zakkai attempted the actual disqualification of murder-witnesses by questioning them concerning the stems of the figs growing on the tree underneath which the crime was committed (*Sanhedrin* 41a). Such questioning (the Talmud [81b] tells us) had as its sole end the possible evasion of the death penalty; it could not prove the innocence of the accused or free him. Similarly, Samuel regards the stringent requirements for proper *ha-tra'ah* (warning) of the murderer as relevant only to his execution but not to his imprisonment. These devices, then, were hurdles placed between the criminal and his execution.

Yet R. Tarfon and R. Akiba go farther—if not in fact, then at least in formulation. Disdaining legal propriety, they bluntly do away with all pretense and announce their goal, a goal which legal ingenuity would then have to achieve. R. Jochanan had attempted the same result (see Rashi, 41a, *s.v. he-hakiroth*) but had not, to our knowledge, publicly acknowledged his aim. (R. Akiba similarly "teaches" a teleological orientation in *Shabbat* 64b.)

As we have seen, R. Tarfon and R. Akiba met with opposition. R. Gamliel was probably not alone in protesting this virtual abolition of the death penalty. His is merely the clearest voice. As we note some other expressions of opposition, we shall also see more fully the basis of the debate.

In *Midrash Tannaim* (p. 115) we find the following comment to Deuteronomy 19:13:

> *Do not pity him*—this is an admonition not mercifully to spare the killer; we should not say, "The one has already been killed—of what use is the killing of the other?" Thus the execution will be neglected. Rather, he must be killed. Abba Hanon says in the name of R. Eliezer: "Wherever the Torah specifies an [apparently] unjust punishment, it is written, *Do not pity.*"

Here we find R. Eliezer (an older contemporary of R. Tarfon) emphasizing the duty to execute; the passage as a whole rebukes those who would eliminate the death penalty as useless.

The corresponding comment in the *Sifre* (Deut. 18:7) is, despite its terseness, most instructive:

> Perhaps you will say, "Since the one has been killed, why should we incur the guilt of spilling the other's blood (*la-hov be-damo*)?" Therefore the Torah says, *Do not pity him.*

Both passages deal with a man whose guilt is established beyond doubt. Nevertheless, there are those who protest his execution. In the *Midrash Tannaim* the uselessness of such execution is cited; the objecting voice in the *Sifre* would take the argument one step further—if such execution is useless, it is *eo ipso* criminal, a "guilty spilling of blood." This is not merely circumstantial opposition to the death penalty; it cuts at the very root of the institution. The guilt of the court, it contends, would be similar to that of the murderer: both would have spilled blood.

Yet the *Sifre* and *Midrash Tannaim* reject the suggestion that the death penalty is useless and immoral. Rather, it is both useful and moral; it functions as a deterrent (as R. Gamliel points out), and its morality is established by the fact that it is an ordinance of the Torah. To paraphrase, "The Judge of all the world has done justly"; is man to be more just than his Lord? In a similar vein, the Talmud tells that God rebukes him who mourns overmuch: "Do you love the departed more than I" (*Mo'ed Katan* 27b)? The correct response to such situations is not to be forged in human freedom. Man must abide not only by the pattern devised by God; he must also accept the evaluation and judgment implied by the set pattern.

This response is a natural one in a religious community; one expects to find it hurled as a general accusation at all departures from the popularly accepted norm. Furthermore, the accusation that man is arrogantly assuming Divine prerogative can, by slurring over man's dynamic responsibility of interpreting and implementing the Divine imperative, simplify the issue to a question of antinomianism.

One senses in the following Aggadah, too, an admonition to man to forgo all reliance upon his own erratic judgment, especially in areas where he claims to be motivated by his moral or ethical sensibility:

> *Be not righteous overmuch* (Eccles. 7:16)—do not be more righteous than your Creator. This refers to Saul . . . who debated with his Creator and said, "God said, 'Go and smite Amalek.' If the men are guilty, the women and children are yet innocent; the oxen and donkeys are innocent too." A voice answered from heaven, "Be not more righteous than your Creator." . . .
>
> Resh Lakish said: "Whoever pities where he should be cruel will ultimately be cruel where he should pity. Whence do we learn that Saul was cruel instead of merciful? As it is stated: *And Nob, the city of the priests, smote he with the sword, both men and women, children and sucklings, and oxen and asses and sheep, with the edge of the sword* (I Sam. 22:19). Is Nob less than the seed of Amalek?"

The problem with which the Aggadah grapples is clearly a crucial one—can man's moral insight, an insight implanted by God and further educated by Him, ever become self-reliant? Can man ever be master in his own house? In fact, any slackening of the rigor of the law is censured; again we hear that the universal terminus of such a course is moral bankruptcy. However generous the motive, the perversion of justice is evil, its motivation misguided. The Rabbis feared that true love of humanity could only be underlined by indiscriminate recourse to "mercy," which, as R. Gamliel pointed out, would deny to an innocent society the concern shown the criminal.

But thus stated, the problem is a simplistic, indeed meaningless, contrast in black and white just as the situation selected by the Aggadist offers only the two opposed options of adherence to the command of God or total revolt against it. The Aggadah illustrates an instance where the answer had to be "No," for an absolutely unconditioned ethos is impossible. And so the Aggadist points out the incontrovertible: man never advances far beyond brutality; he is never educated out of cruelty. The tower, says Pascal, rises on an abyss.

Rabbi Jose b. Bon said: "They do not well who turn of God's *middoth* (attributes) into mercy, and also those who translate: 'My people Israel, just as I am merciful in heaven, so be you merciful on earth—*be it cow or ewe, you shall not kill it and its young both in one day* (Lev. 22:28).'" The ban against killing both mother and young on the same day was apparently a favorite text of those who would sweep away law and enshrine mercy. R. Jose was contending with a spiritual temper that has always had its adherents and which read Leviticus 22:28 as a charge and a program. That the text was so used we see from the following:

> Bar Kappara said: "Doeg is called the Edomite because he forbade Saul to shed the blood (*dam*) of Agag. For Doeg said: 'It is written in the Torah, *Ye shall not kill it and its young both on the same day;* yet you are about to kill young and old, children and women in one day.'"

Doeg (and those he represents) argue that the manifestation of God's mercies in certain rules should become the standard of all conduct. The Rabbis reject this as a superficial understanding of mercy.

V

Yet such statements always remained only one pole of the tension we have been examining; the act of mercy towards those held undeserving of it was practiced and praised, for it was motivated by *imitatio Dei*. Thus we read of R. Joshua b. Levi:

In the neighborhood of R. Joshua b. Levi there lived a Sadducee [*min*] who used to trouble him greatly with [his interpretations of] texts. One day the Rabbi...thought... "I shall curse him." When the moment [propitious for cursing] arrived, R. Joshua was dozing. [On awakening] he said: "I see from this that my intention was improper. For it is written, *And His mercies are over all His works,* and it is further written, *Neither is it good for the righteous to punish.*"

A Scripture-quoting heretic may not be a menace of the first rank. Yet R. Joshua's motive for abandoning the matter remains of interest. He does not withdraw because of the insignificance of the episode, nor because the heretic did not objectively deserve his curse. Rather, he takes his sleep as a sign that justice is to be subdued by mercy. For does not God extend His mercy even where He should visit justice upon the world? The righteous, then, must also stay their hand.

The Aggadah would praise even those reluctant to exact their due from the murderer: "The priests forgave [Saul, for his role in the slaughter at Nob], but the Gibeonites did not forgive him, and therefore God rejected them." We have, then, come full circle: for some, the murder of the priests of Nob limns the irresponsibility and bankruptcy of Saul's earlier desire to save the Amalekite innocents, while for others it proves the opportunity for a merciful act of forgiveness to the guilty. We see, thus, that both legal and Aggadic discussions give witness to two tendencies, one that regards the enforcing of retribution as most just and hence most merciful, and an other, which finds mercy too divinely dynamic a quality to be forever defined and controlled by the demand for retribution.

Both approaches, curiously enough, contend in the Midrashic interpretation of Deuteronomy 13:18: *And there shall cleave nought of the devoted thing to thy hand, that the Lord may turn from the fierceness of His anger, and show thee mercy, and have compassion upon thee, and multiply thee, as He hath sworn unto thy father:*

Show thee [literally, "give" Thee]: to your people is the quality of mercifulness given, and not to others, as we read, *And the Gibeonites were not of the children of Israel.*

Have compassion upon thee: the punishing of the wicked is an act of mercy to the world.

Notes

1. I wish to express my thanks to Dean Isaac Bacon, of Yeshiva College, for discussing certain aspects of this paper with me. [Editor's note: In the original, this essay has extensive technical scholarly discussion in the footnotes, increasing its length by half. Wanting to operate within space limitations, I have deleted these footnotes, and encourage those whose appetite is whetted by this excellent essay to read the extended discussion in the original.]

[12]

Biblical Teaching on Capital Punishment

Glen H. Stassen

THIS BIBLICAL STUDY WAS written at the request of Rev. Joe Doss, then Rector of St. Mark's Episcopal Church in Palo Alto, California, Dr. James Bresnahan, S.J., a member of the Society of Christian Ethics—both of whom are lawyers as well as practicing clergy—and Colleen Rohan, Deputy State Public Defender in California. They requested it because prosecuting attorneys in California and elsewhere were making strong closing arguments that the Bible favors the death penalty and therefore jurors should impose the death penalty in the case at hand. Doss, Bresnahan, and Rohan asked me to write a study of biblical teaching on capital punishment that could be authoritative, and widely supported by leaders of the Society of Christian Ethics—who are trained in careful teaching in Christian ethics.

I wrote briefly so it could be read quickly; simply and concretely so lawyers or juries would find it useful; and fairly basically without developing highly original argument so it might get widespread support from scholars of different denominations and persuasions. All twelve most recent presidents of the Society of Christian Ethics at the time of writing signed the statement, as well as many other members present at the annual meeting in 1992. The Society of Christian Ethics is the professional society of teachers of Christian Ethics in theological schools, colleges, and universities in the United States and Canada.

SOURCE: From Glen H. Stassen, "Biblical Teaching on Capital Punishment," *Review and Expositor* 93 (fall 1996). Reprinted by permission.

The statement was then distributed by the Most Reverend Edmond L. Browning, Presiding Bishop of the Episcopal Church, in 1992, and made available to others for their use.

The Hebrew Scriptures—The Old Testament

It may seem odd that the Torah (the first five books of the Old Testament) prescribes the death penalty even for children who curse their parents, and for adults who have sex during menstruation, but forbids the death penalty for the prototype of all murderers, Cain, who killed his brother, Abel, premeditated and unprovoked.

On the one hand, the Torah authorizes (or perhaps only predicts) the death penalty for murder (Gen. 9:6);[1] for owning an animal that kills people (Exod. 21:14, 29); kidnapping (Exod. 21:16; Deut. 24:7); giving false witness against a defendant in a death penalty trial (Deut. 18:18–21); for a stubborn son's disobedience to his mother or father, or a child's cursing or striking a parent (Exod. 21:15, 17; Lev. 20:9; Deut. 21:18–21); incest, adultery, bestiality, homosexual practice, rape, and having sex during a woman's menstrual period (Exod. 22:19; Deut. 22:21, 24, 25; Lev. 20:10–14; 21:18); for witchcraft and sorcery (Exod. 22:18; Lev. 20:27); Sabbath-breaking (Exod. 31:14; Num. 15:32–36); child sacrifice (Lev. 21:9); false claim to be a prophet (Deut. 13:5, 10); blasphemy (Lev. 24:15–16); and for a non-Levite who enters the sacred place (Num. 1:51, 3:10, 38; 18:7).[2]

On the other hand, Cain is the father of all murderers. He murders his own brother, out of premeditated jealousy. Found out, he cries out, "I shall be a restless wanderer on the earth, and whoever finds me will kill me." But the Lord said to him, "Not so!"...Then the Lord put a mark on Cain, so that no one who found him would kill him" (Gen. 4:14–15). Claus Westermann, the Old Testament scholar who has written what is widely recognized as the most authoritative commentary on Genesis, explains this means "no human being has the right to step in and execute God's prerogative."[3] Similarly, Moses is seen in the act of murder, and instead of receiving the death penalty, is chosen by God to deliver his people from slavery (Exod. 2:11ff.). David not only committed adultery with the beautiful Bathsheba while she was still having her period, but then had Bathsheba's husband killed. Nathan the prophet confronted him, saying, "You have smitten Uriah the Hittite with the sword, and have taken his wife to be your wife." David confessed, saying, "'I have sinned against the Lord.' And Nathan said to David, 'The Lord has put away your sin; you shall not die'" (2 Sam. 11–12). Accused of adultery, Tamar admits she has committed adultery with her father-in-law, an act specifically requiring the death penalty. She is allowed to live, and her adultery produces an ancestor of David and Jesus (Gen. 38; Matt. 1:3; Luke 3:33). The book of Hosea tells how Gomer commits adultery repeatedly, and Hosea, not without great pain, forgives her, welcoming her back into their covenant relationship. In this adultery and forgiveness Hosea sees the picture of God's way of forgiving his people for their whoring with other gods.

The Old Testament rule of retaliation—a life for a life, an eye for an eye, a tooth for a tooth (Exod. 21:24, 25)—is intended not to require vengeance, but to limit it. Otherwise angry family members might take seven or more lives for a life, as Lamech boasted (Gen. 4:23), and as the Hatfields and the McCoys tried to do. The rules of a life for a life and an eye for an eye are supplemented by rules defining acceptable substitutions, which continue to be elaborated down through Jewish history so that by the time of Jesus most of these penalties could be absolved through payments of money. Just as the law of Moses in Deut. 24 does not mean to approve of divorce, but only, as a concession to the hardness of human hearts, to regulate the separations which were already taking place, so the law of retaliation does not command, but rather limits vengeance as a concession.[4]

The Mishnah is the record of authoritative oral interpretation of the written law of the Torah by the Jewish religious leaders from about 200 B.C.E. to about 200 C.E. It makes the death penalty almost impossible. Death penalty trials required 23 judges. The biblical law (Deut. 19:15) requiring at least two eye witnesses to the commission of the crime "prevented many cases from being brought to trial at all, since such crimes are seldom committed with so much publicity." The testimony of near relatives, women, slaves, or people with a bad reputation is not admitted. If the judges find a witness testified falsely with malicious intent, the witness gets the penalty that would have gone to the defendant, as Deut. 19:16 ff. prescribes. "It is clear that with such a procedure conviction in capital cases was next to impossible, and that this was the intention of the framers of the rules is equally plain."[5] The Mishnah brands a court which executes one man in seven years as "ruinous" or "destructive." It summarizes the teaching of authoritative Rabbis: "Rabbi Eliezar ben Azariah says: Or one in even seventy years. Rabbi Tarfon and Rabbi Akiba say: Had we been in the Sanhedrin none would ever have been put to death.[6] . . .

So the death penalty is prescribed for an unworkably long list of crimes and moral, sexual, and religious transgressions, but either unenforced or made almost impossible to enforce even though eyewitnesses were present and the perpetrator admitted the crime.

To understand this seeming contradiction, we have to understand that the

Torah is affirming two moral principles. One is profound moral seriousness about obeying God's will. Disobedience may not be taken lightly. The other is profound seriousness about the sacredness of human life, created in the image of God (Gen. 1:26 f.). Killing people to punish them must be avoided if there is another morally serious way to punish crime. Therefore, in practice, the death penalty becomes increasingly rare. One almost never hears of it in the Prophets and the Writings (the parts of the Old Testament written after the oldest law codes of the first five books were formulated). The Mishnah frowns on it. Modern Israel has never had capital punishment, which shows something of present-day Jewish understanding of the meaning of the tradition. The American Jewish Congress says "capital punishment degrades and brutalizes the society which practices it; and . . . is cruel, unjust, and incompatible with the dignity and self respect of men."[7]

Any effort to interpret biblical teaching on the death penalty without emphasizing the Bible's moral seriousness about disobedience and injustice will fail. Any effort to interpret it without taking seriously its commitment to human life, and to mercy, and its preference for avoiding the death penalty, will likewise fail.

Jesus Rejected the Retaliation of "Life for Life" or "Death for Death"

Once these two principles are fully understood, along with the developing trend to abolish the death penalty in favor of other penalties, the New Testament may be understood as a continuation or further development of the tradition. Jesus was certainly serious about moral obedience. And he especially emphasized the mercy of God and the value of human life: "Be ye merciful, even as your Father is merciful" (Luke 6:36). Not only should we not kill, but even continuing to be angry with one's brother or insulting him leads to judgment (Matt. 5:21 ff.). So Jesus commanded that we take an initiative with someone we are angry with: go talk and seek to make peace (Matt. 5:21 ff.).

Jesus came down firmly on the mercy side of the equation. In Leviticus 19:15 ff., in the Old Testament, the death penalty was justified but limited as "life for life, eye for eye." Jesus named this method explicitly, and changed it to merciful transforming initiatives that avoid vengeance or violence but instead confront the offender and seek repentance:

"You have heard that it was said, 'an eye for an eye and a tooth for a tooth.' But I say to you, do not set yourself in violent or revengeful resistance against an evildoer.[8] But if any one strikes you on the right cheek, turn the other also; and if any one wants to sue you and take your coat, give your cloak as well; and if any one forces you to go one mile, go also the second mile. Give to anyone who begs from you, and do not refuse anyone who wants to borrow from you" (Matt. 5:38 ff.).

If "life for life" is understood as a limiting of revenge by killing only the killer and not also the killer's family, then Jesus is here taking a further leap in the same direction, limiting it all the way down to zero. If "life for life" is understood as justifying or requiring the death penalty, then Jesus directly opposes it. Either way, Jesus opposes taking a life as retribution for a life. The Apostle Paul makes this clear in Romans 12:19, which most New Testament scholars believe quotes or echoes Jesus' teaching against retaliation: "Beloved, never avenge yourselves, but leave it to the wrath of God; for it is written, 'Vengeance is mine, I will repay, says the Lord.'"

Jesus does not only oppose life-for-life retaliation. He points to a "third way," a way of "transforming initiatives," that moves away from vicious cycles of retaliation into creative confrontation and constructive community-building.[9]

Jesus was confronted by the death penalty directly in John 8. The scribes and Pharisees made a woman stand before him to be judged. "Teacher, this woman was caught in the very act of adultery. In the law Moses commanded us to stone such women. Now what do you say? . . . They said this to test him, so that they might have some charge to bring against him." If he replied flatly, "God's mercy forbids the death penalty," they could charge him with the blasphemy of disagreeing with Moses and stone him. Jesus answered, "Let anyone among you who is without sin throw the first stone." When they heard this, they went away one by one, and Jesus was left with the woman standing before him. He said to her, "Woman, where are they? Has no one condemned you?" She said, "No one, sir." Jesus said, "Neither do I condemn you. Go your way, and from now on do not sin again."

Raymond E. Brown, the widely respected scholar who specializes in the Gospel of John, praises the beauty of this story with "its succinct expression of the mercy of Jesus." Brown concludes: "The delicate balance between the justice of Jesus in not condoning the sin and his mercy in forgiving the sinner is one of the great gospel lessons."[10] Here Dr. Brown is pointing to the two principles we saw in the Old Testament: moral seriousness about sin, and mercy toward sinners. Disobedience may not be taken lightly. But mercy and the sacredness of human life require us to avoid killing criminals if there is a morally serious alternative. Jesus releases her from the death penalty. But he admonishes her not to commit adultery again.

Bishop Lowell Erdahl says the accusers "were convicted of their own sins and accepted the fact that there is no justification for the vengeful execution of one sinner by another. If all Christians had followed their example, there would have been no blessing of capital punishment in Christian history."[11] He points out that this fits Jesus' consistent character and teaching. "The woman's accusers knew enough about Jesus to expect that he might oppose her execution. We too are not surprised.... We would be shocked if Jesus had said, '...Go ahead and kill this wretched sinner.'"

Jesus' Crucifixion Was Unjust

Jesus confronted the death penalty one other time. He himself was the victim of capital punishment. Crucifixion was state terrorism. It was given only to slaves and rebels. They were tortured and then killed in full public view to terrorize other slaves and potential rebels, to coerce them into docility in spite of unjust imperialism.[12]

The gospel accounts make clear that Jesus was falsely accused and unjustly condemned (for example, John 18:38). Ironically, Barabbas, who was actually guilty of the crime of insurrection that Jesus was falsely accused of, was freed in Jesus' place. This was clearly unjust. Jesus said from the cross, "Father, forgive them, for they know not what they do" (Luke 23:34). The reason they needed forgiveness is that they were doing terrible wrong. The New Testament witness is that God used their wrong to bring forgiveness and redemption, but this does not alter the fact that it was unjust. Christians who remember their Lord was unjustly and cruelly given the death penalty have a hard time being enthusiastic about imposing the death penalty on others. The cross on Christian churches signifies not that we should advocate more crosses for others, but that we all need mercy. We are not to seek vengeance (Rom. 12:19). We are to love our enemies, and seek to do mercy (Luke 6:35–36).

Here an odd argument is made by William H. Baker.[13] He refers to a conversation in John 19 between Jesus and the Roman colonial government authority, Pilate, as Pilate is about to sentence Jesus to death. Pilate asserts he has authority to crucify Jesus. Jesus answers, "You would have no authority over me, unless it had been given you from above; for this reason he who delivered me up to you has the greater sin."

Jesus is clearly saying that what Pilate is doing is wrong, a sin. Yet Baker argues this shows God approves of capital punishment and governmental authority to order the death penalty. Baker and Pilate both *think* the conversation is about Pilate's secular authority. But read in context, John is clearly showing Pilate misunderstands what the topic is.

The theme of ironic misunderstanding runs throughout the Gospel of John, and this passage is a good example. Jesus is speaking of God's power to bring about the hour of redemption, when he will die so that we will live. Pilate plays a role in *this* death only because God is allowing it. And he misses the point, thinking the topic is his power to command legions and kill people. Jesus is speaking of God's gift of redemption, not engaging in a discussion of whether God approves of capital punishment.[14] As Raymond Brown says, "No one can take Jesus' life from him; he alone has power to lay it down. However, now Jesus has voluntarily entered 'the hour' appointed by his Father (12:37) when he will lay down his life. In the context of 'the hour' therefore, the Father has permitted men to have power over Jesus' life."[15]

The gospels make clear that the governmental authorities acted unjustly in sentencing Jesus to death. By no means do they teach that giving capital punishment to Jesus was justice. Baker himself admits "that Pilate allowed a miscarriage of justice to take place." To use this miscarriage of justice as an argument for the rightness of the death penalty suggests desperation to find a New Testament rationalization for a preconceived interest.

All Death Penalties in the New Testament Are Unjust

Baker makes a similar argument concerning Acts 25:11, although he admits the passage does not have "the express purpose of teaching anything about the subject of capital punishment."[16] The point of the passage is the Apostle Paul's defense against accusers who want to kill him. Paul says: "*if* I . . . have committed anything worthy of death. . . ." He knows he does not deserve the death penalty. The authorities twice explicitly declare they have found that "he had done nothing deserving of death" (Acts 25:25; 26:31).

What Paul says is not that he approves of capital punishment, but that he is not afraid to die. This is a point he makes elsewhere, writing, for example, "For me to live is Christ and to die is gain" (Phil. 1:21). His defense tells how he had once voted for the death penalty for Christians as blasphemers, and how he has now repented for his action (Acts 26:10 ff.).

An individual passage should not be (mis)interpreted as an isolated proof-text. It should be understood in the context of the many instances of capital punishment mentioned in the New Testament. Otherwise it is too easy to read one's own bias into a single passage. The New Testament describes many instances of the death penalty being threatened or imposed. Nowhere do the followers of Jesus advocate the death penalty. Every instance of the death penalty mentioned by the New Testament is clearly presented as an injustice: the beheading of John the Baptist (Matt. 14:9 ff.); the crucifixion of Jesus (John 18:38 and Luke 23:34); the stoning of Stephen (Acts 7); the stoning of other Christians (Matt. 21:35; 23:37; John 10:31 f.; Acts 14:5); the threatened death penalty for Paul (Acts 25:11, 25:25, and 26:31); the persecution of Christians in the Book of Revelation. Furthermore, in the Letter to Philemon, Paul writes persuasively "to save the life of the escaped slave, Onesimus, who under Roman law was liable to execution."[17]

Romans 13 Concerns the Authority to Tax, Not Capital Punishment

Some have argued that the authority of the Roman government to impose capital punishment is specifically endorsed in Romans 13: "Let every person be subject to the governing authorities.... For the authority does not bear the sword in vain.... For the same reason you also pay taxes, for the authorities are God's servants, busy with this very thing. Pay to all what is due them—taxes to whom taxes are due, revenue to whom revenue is due...."

The authoritative study of this passage was written by a team of well-known New Testament scholars in Germany.[18] They point out Paul is urging his readers to pay the Roman taxes and not to participate in a rebellion against Nero's new tax. An insurrection against taxes had recently occurred and had gotten Christians kicked out of Rome. Another one was brewing. The Greek in Romans 13:4 translated "sword" (*machairan*) does not name the instrument used in capital punishment. It names the symbol of authority carried by the police who accompanied tax collectors. Paul was urging Christians to make peace, pay Nero's new tax, and not rebel. He was not arguing for capital punishment. He was arguing *against* violence.

The Central Biblical Themes of Justice and Redemption Define the Context

These discussions of specific scripture passages concerning (or not concerning) the death penalty should be understood in the overall context of fundamental themes that are central to the Bible and that are critically important to the death penalty in its actual practice. One is: "Do not slay the innocent." But errors are made. The death penalty is the one penalty that does not allow reinstatement after it is carried out. Another is the central emphasis on justice for the poor, the powerless, and the oppressed. This is emphasized from the Exodus of the oppressed Jews from Egypt through the redemption of the persecuted followers of the Lamb in the Book of Revelation. "You shall not afflict any widow or orphan. If you do afflict them, and they cry out to me, I will surely hear their cry, and my wrath will burn.... You shall not pervert the justice due to your poor in their suit. Keep far from a false charge, and do not slay the innocent and righteous, for I will not acquit the wicked" (Exod. 22:22 f. and 23:6 f.). Walter Berns, in his book arguing for capital punishment, admits that no affluent person ever has been given the death penalty in U.S. history.[19] It goes primarily to the poor who cannot afford extensive legal help. African American murderers are given the death penalty much more often than Caucasian murderers, and the ratio soars if the victims were white. As in the Roman Empire, where the death penalty was reserved for slaves and rebels, so in the U.S. it is reserved for the poor and the black.

Central to the biblical story is the emphasis on redemption, even of one's enemies.

> "Which of you, having a hundred sheep, and having lost one of them, will not leave the ninety-nine in the wilderness, and go after the one which is lost, until it is found? ... There will be more joy in heaven over one sinner who repents than over ninety-nine righteous persons who need no repentance" (Luke 15:4–7).

The death penalty terminates the chance for repentance. "What hope is there for a dead man's redemption or reformation?"[20]

In sum, the Bible affirms two profound principles. One is profound moral seriousness about obeying God's will. Disobedience may not be taken lightly. The other is profound seriousness about the sacredness of human life. Killing people to punish them must be avoided if there is another morally serious way to punish crime. Therefore, in practice, the death penalty becomes increasingly rare. One almost never hears of it in the Prophets and the Writings, and every mention of it in the New Testament concerns an unjust death penalty. Other penalties develop, and the death penalty is avoided. Mercy becomes central. Vengeance is ruled out: "Beloved, never avenge yourselves, but leave it to the wrath of God; for it is written, 'Vengeance is mine, I will repay,' says the Lord" (Rom. 12:19; Lev. 19:18; Deut. 32:35; Heb. 10:30). And the Bible again and again emphasizes justice for the poor, the powerless, the oppressed, and the innocent. Furthermore, it rejects whatever blocks the possibility of repentance and redemption.

The Way to Deliverance from Homicide's Devastation of Families

But what then of taking the victims seriously? And the devastation to the victims' families? How can we reverse the trend toward ever more murders, a trend which has continued during recent years after the death penalty was reinstated and advocated enthusiastically by national leaders? [Author's note: Since 1991, the U.S. murder rate has decreased each year.]

In the Sermon on the Mount (Matt. 5–7), Jesus did not simply oppose evils such as killing, lying, and hating the enemy; *Jesus consistently emphasized a transforming initiative that could deliver us from the vicious cycle of violence or alienation.*

Simply to oppose the death penalty is unlikely to be effective. Many people feel too much anger about the victims of murder to give up the death penalty if there is not an alternative that takes injustice seriously and does something about the murderous violence in our society. The biblical clue is to look for transforming initiatives that can begin to deliver us from the cycles of violence that we experience.

Otherwise we are back in the days when bloodletting was the known cure for fever and pneumonia. Someone who simply opposed the treatment would encounter great anger: "My father died of pneumonia, and now my brother may too. Why are you telling us not to treat him?" Merely opposing bloodletting because it was ineffective or bad for the patient would be unpersuasive unless you could offer a better alternative. We have to take the injustice of murder with profound moral seriousness.

Scientific studies[21] show capital punishment does not reduce homicide rates and may increase them. They also show what *does* reduce homicides: catching and convicting murderers more promptly and efficiently; governmental example in opposing killing (homicides increase when governments kill, make war, or spread guns); a culture that opposes violence (vs. television violence and ready access to guns); working to achieve equal-opportunity justice for those who are being denied rights and equality; funding drug rehabilitation programs; and developing neighborhood communities rather than depersonalized cities.

Many nations have remarkably fewer murders than the United States does. Some cities and states have fewer than others do. Comparisons are possible. Comparisons across time are also possible. Comparative studies suggest the above actions are in fact effective in decreasing murder rates.[22] That is where our emotions and energies should be directed.

This means as long as people's emotions are diverted into advocating capital punishment as the cure for murder, they are being led to neglect the initiatives that can make a difference. Like the pre-scientific practice of bloodletting, misdirected emotion drives people into vengeful and diversionary destruction and away from constructive and effective action.

The constructive action that is effective in decreasing homicides, as indicated by scientific studies, closely resembles the effective action advocated by biblical ethics: take initiatives to convert the people and change the culture from being pro-violence to anti-violence (Rom. 12:17–21; Isa. 60:17b–20); invest yourselves in remedial justice and equal rights for the poor and the outcasts (Isa. 61:1–4 and 8–11); don't seek a cure by shedding blood, but by compassionate justice for those who need it (Jer. 22:1–5 and 22:13–17); do punish criminals justly (Exod. 23:6 ff.; Isa. 5:22–23; Jer. 12:1); seek the welfare of your city's neighborhoods, not false escapes (Jer. 29:4–9); persuade the government to take steps that make peace rather than war (Jer. 4:19 ff.; 6:13 ff.; 22:3–17; Luke 19:41 ff.). This is the way of deliverance.

Notes

1. Genesis 9:4–6 says we shall not eat meat with any blood still in it; emphasizes that we are made in God's own image and our life is sacred; and says "whoever sheds the blood of man, by man shall his blood be shed." This should probably be interpreted as a realistic prediction that violence causes violence, which is the way Jesus interprets it (Matt. 26:52). Lewis Smedes shows the unworkability and violent extremes we would be led into if we took Genesis 9:6 out of context as a command to execute everyone who kills someone, regardless of motive, circumstance, or accident. It is not a universal moral command for us and all time, but is probably to be understood in its context "as a shrewd observation of what usually happens to killers." Lewis Smedes, *Mere Morality: What God Expects from Ordinary People* (Grand Rapids, Mich.: Eerdmans, 1983), 119–21. Claus Westermann argues that Genesis 9:6 belongs to *sacral* rules of worship which are no longer binding (sacrificing animals on an altar—Gen. 8:20–9:6), and is not intended as a *moral* command, anymore than the command not to eat meat with any blood in it is a moral command for us. See Westermann, *Genesis 1–11: A Commentary* (Minneapolis: Augsburg Publishing House, 1984), 463 ff.

2. I am grateful for the insights and collegiality of my students Gene Gladney, Aubrey Williams, and Michael Westmoreland-White, as well as my colleagues Henlee Barnette and Paul Simmons, each of whom has written papers on capital punishment from which I have learned.

3. Westermann, *Genesis 1–11: A Commentary*, 312.

4. John Howard Yoder, *The Christian and Capital Punishment* (Newton, Kans.: Faith and Life Press, 1961), 6–7.

5. George Foot Moore, *Judaism in the First Centuries of the Christian Era* (New York: Shocken Books, 1971 edition), vol. II, 184–87. See also George Horowitz, *The Spirit of Jewish Law* (New York: Central Book Company, 1963), 165–70 and 176.

6. Herbert Danby, trans., *The Mishnah* (London: Oxford University Press, 1933), 403; Makkoth, 1.10.

7. American Jewish Congress, "Statement on Capital Punishment," adopted at the 66th Annual Meeting, May 6, 1972.

8. The usual English translation of the Greek as "do not resist evil" is inadequate, as is shown by Walter Wink in his book *Violence and Nonviolence: Jesus' Third Way* (Philadelphia and Santa Cruz: n.p., 1987), 13 ff.; and in his well-documented "Beyond Just War and Pacifism: Jesus' Nonviolent Way," *Review*

and Expositor 89:2 (spring 1992): 197–214. The Greek means continuous, violent or vengeful resistance. Paul shows this in Romans 12:19, when he reports the teaching as "Never avenge yourselves." Both Jesus and Paul resisted evildoers, but they never advocated vengeance or violence, never the death penalty.

9. See Pinchas Lapide, *The Sermon on the Mount* (Maryknoll, N.Y.: Orbis, 1986), chapters 10, 13 and 14; and the two pieces by Walter Wink cited above.

10. Raymond E. Brown, S.S., *The Gospel According to John* (Garden City, N.Y.: Doubleday, 1966), vol. I, 336 f.

11. Lowell Erdahl, *Pro-Life/Pro-Peace* (Minneapolis: Augsburg, 1986), 114.

12. Martin Hengel, *Crucifixion in the Ancient World and the Folly of the Message of the Cross* (Philadelphia: Fortress, 1977).

13. William H. Baker, *On Capital Punishment* (Chicago: Moody Press, 1973, 1985), 57 ff.

14. Alan Culpepper, *Anatomy of the Fourth Gospel* (Philadelphia: Fortress Press, 1983), 161 and 172. Cf. Brown, *The Gospel According to John,* 892.

15. Brown, *The Gospel According to John,* 893.

16. Baker, *On Capital Punishment,* 62 ff.

17. Henlee Barnette, *Crucial Problems in Christian Perspective* (Philadelphia: Westminster Press, 1970), 129.

18. Johannes Friedrich, Wolfgang Pöhlmann, and Peter Stuhlmacher, "Zur historischen Situation und Intention von Röm 13, 1–7," *Zeitschrift für Theologie und Kirche* (1976), 131 ff. See also John Howard Yoder, *Politics of Jesus* (Grand Rapids, Mich.: Eerdmans, 1976), 206.

19. Walter Berns, *For Capital Punishment* (New York: Basic Books, 1979), 33 ff.

20. Barnette, *Crucial Problems in Christian Perspective,* 129.

21. A highly sophisticated regression analysis is Brian E. Forst, "The Deterrent Effect of Capital Punishment: A Cross-State Analysis of the 1960's," *Minnesota Law Review* (May 1977), 743 ff. In the two months following an execution the number of homicides and the brutality with which they are executed increases dramatically in the immediate area and increases significantly throughout the area where the execution was publicized. See William Browers's research, in Kenneth Haas and James Inciardi, eds., *Challenging Capital Punishment: Legal and Social Science Approaches* (Beverly Hills, Calif.: Sage Publishing, 1988), 49–90; and Ted Gurr, *Why Do Men Rebel?,* passim.

22. Ibid.; and especially the carefully analyzed transnational and longitudinal statistical research of Dane Archer and Rosemary Gartner, *Violence and Crime in Cross-National Perspective* (New Haven, Conn.: Yale University Press, 1984), 64 ff., 86, 104, 115, 136 f., 159; Ted Gurr, *Why Men Rebel,* which won the annual award of the American Political Science Association. The Archer and Gartner and Gurr research is extremely helpful in pointing toward effective corrective action, and should be widely read and extensively applied.

[13]

Is Capital Punishment Wrong?

Jacob J. Vellenga

THE CHURCH AT LARGE IS giving serious thought to capital punishment. Church councils and denominational assemblies are making strong pronouncements against it. We are hearing such arguments as: "Capital punishment brutalizes society by cheapening life." "Capital punishment is morally indefensible." "Capital punishment is no deterrent to murder." "Capital punishment makes it impossible to rehabilitate the criminal."

But many of us are convinced that the church should not meddle with capital punishment. Church members should be strong in supporting good legislation, militant against wrong laws, opposed to weak and partial law enforcement. But we should be sure that what we endorse or what we oppose is intimately related to the common good, the benefit of society, the establishment of justice, and the upholding of high moral and ethical standards.

There is a good reason for saying that opposition to capital punishment is not for the common good but sides with evil; shows more regard for the criminal than the victim of the crime; weakens justice and encourages murder; is not based on Scripture but on a vague philosophical system that makes a fetish of the idea that the taking of life is wrong, under every circumstance, and fails to

SOURCE: Jacob J. Vellenga, "Is Capital Punishment Wrong?" *Christianity Today,* October 13, 1959. Used by permission, *Christianity Today,* 1959.

distinguish adequately between killing and murder, between punishment and crime.

Capital punishment is a controversial issue upon which good people are divided, both having high motives in their respective convictions. But capital punishment should not be classified with social evils like segregation, racketeering, liquor traffic, and gambling.

Those favoring capital punishment are not to be stigmatized as heartless, vengeful, and lacking in mercy, but are to be respected as advocating that which is the best for society as a whole. When we stand for the common good, we must of necessity be strongly opposed to that behavior which is contrary to the common good.

Old Testament on Capital Punishment

From time immemorial the conviction of good society has been that life is sacred, and he who violates the sacredness of life through murder must pay the supreme penalty. This ancient belief is well expressed in Scripture: "Only you shall not eat flesh with its life, that is, its blood. For your lifeblood I will surely require a reckoning; of every beast I will require it and of man; of every man's brother I will require the life of man. Whoever sheds the blood of man, by man shall his blood be shed; for God made man in his own image" (Gen. 9:4–6, RSV). Life is sacred. He who violates the law must pay the supreme penalty, just because life is sacred. Life is sacred since God made man in His image. There is a distinction here between murder and penalty.

Many who oppose capital punishment make a strong argument out of the Sixth Commandment: "Thou shalt not kill" (Exod. 20:13). But they fail to note the commentary on that Commandment which follows: "Whoever strikes a man so that he dies shall be put to death.... If a man willfully attacks another to kill him treacherously, you shall take him from my altar that he may die" (Exod. 21:12, 14). It is faulty exegesis to take a verse of Scripture out of its context and interpret it without regard to its qualifying words.

The Exodus reference is not the only one referring to capital punishment. In Leviticus 24:17 we read: "He who kills a man shall be put to death." Numbers 35:30–34 goes into more detail on the subject: "If any one kills a person, the murderer shall be put to death on the evidence of witnesses; but no person shall be put to death on the testimony of one witness. Moreover you shall accept no ransom for the life of a murderer who is guilty of death; but he shall be put to death.... You shall not thus pollute the land in which you live; for blood pollutes the land, and no expiation can be made for the land, for the blood that is shed in it, except by the blood of him who shed it. You shall not defile the land in which you live, in the midst of which I dwell; for I the Lord dwell in the midst of the people of Israel." (Compare Deut. 17:6–7 and 19:11–13.)

Deuteronomy 19:4–6, 10 distinguishes between accidental killing and willful murder: "If any one kills his neighbor unintentionally without having been at enmity with him in time past . . . he may flee to one of these cities [cities of refuge] and save his life; lest the avenger of blood in hot anger pursue the manslayer and overtake him, because the way is long, and wound him mortally, though the man did not deserve to die, since he was not at enmity with his neighbor in time past . . . lest innocent blood be shed in your land which the Lord your God gives you for an inheritance, and so the guilt of bloodshed be upon you."

The cry of the prophets against social evils was not only directed against discrimination of the poor, and the oppression of widows and orphans, but primarily against laxness in the administration of justice. They were opposed to the laws being flouted and criminals not being punished. A vivid expression of the prophet's attitude is recorded in Isaiah: "Justice is turned back, and righteousness stands afar off; for truth has fallen in the public squares, and uprightness cannot enter. . . . The Lord saw it and it displeased him that there was no justice. He saw that there was no man, and wondered that there was no one to intervene; then his own arm brought him victory, and his righteousness upheld him. He put on righteousness as a breastplate, and a helmet of salvation upon his head; he put on garments of vengeance for clothing and wrapped himself in a fury as a mantle. According to their deeds, so will he repay, wrath to his adversaries, requital to his enemies" (Isa. 59:14–18).

New Testament on Capital Punishment

The teachings of the New Testament are in harmony with the Old Testament. Christ came to fulfill the law, not to destroy the basic principles of law and order, righteousness and justice. In Matthew 5:17–20 we read: "Think not that I have come to abolish the law and the prophets; I have come not to abolish them but to fulfill them. For truly, I say to you, till heaven and earth pass away, not an iota, not a dot, will pass from the law until all is accomplished. . . . For I tell you, unless your righteousness exceeds that of the scribes and Pharisees, you will never enter the kingdom of heaven."

Then Christ speaks of hate and murder: "You have heard that it was said to the men of old, 'You shall not kill; and whoever kills shall be liable to judgment [capital punishment].' But I say to you that everyone who is angry with his brother shall be liable to judgment [capital punishment]" (Matt. 5:21–23). It is evident that Jesus was not condemning the established law of capital punishment, but was actually saying that hate deserved capital punishment. Jesus was not advocating doing away with capital punishment but urging his followers to live above the law so that law and punishment could not touch them. To live above the law is not the same as abrogating it.

The church, the Body of Christ, has enough to do to evangelize and educate society to live above the law and positively to influence society to high and noble living by maintaining a wide margin between right and wrong. The early Christians did not meddle with laws against wrong doing. Paul expresses this attitude in his letter to the Romans: "Therefore, he who resists the authorities resists what God has appointed, and those who resist will incur judgment. For rulers are not a terror to good conduct, but to bad . . . for he is God's servant for your good. But if you do wrong, be afraid, for he does not bear the sword in vain; he is the servant of God to execute his wrath on the wrongdoer" (13:2–4).

The early Christians suffered many injustices and were victims of inhuman treatment. Many became martyrs because of their faith. Consequently, they were often tempted to take the law in their own hands. But Paul cautioned them: "Beloved, never avenge yourselves, but leave it to the wrath of God; for it is written, 'Vengeance is mine, I will repay, says the Lord.' No, 'if your enemy is hungry, feed him; if he is thirsty, give him drink; for by so doing you will heap burning coals upon his head'" (Rom. 12:19–21).

There is not a hint of indication in the New Testament that laws should be changed to make it lenient for the wrongdoer. Rather the whole trend is that the church leave matters of justice and law enforcement to the government in power. "Let every person be subject to the governing authorities. For there is no authority except from God, and those that exist have been instituted by God" (Rom. 13:1). Note the juxtaposition of love to enemies with a healthy respect for government. The Christian fellowship is not to take law in its own hands, for God has government in his economy in order to take care of matters of justice.

Jesus' words on loving one's enemies, turning the other cheek, and walking the second mile were not propaganda to change jurisprudence, but they were meant to establish a new society not merely made up of law-abiding citizens but those who lived a life higher than the law, so that stealing, adultery, and murder would become inoperative, but not annulled. The law of love, also called the law of liberty, was not presented to do away with the natural laws of society, but to inaugurate a new concept of law written on the heart where the mainsprings of action are born. The church is ever to strive for superior law and order, not to advocate a lower order that makes wrongdoing less culpable.

Love and mercy have no stability without agreement on basic justice and fair play. Mercy always infers a tacit recognition that justice and rightness are to be expected. Lowering the standards of justice is never to be a substitute for the concept of mercy. The Holy God does not show mercy contrary to his righteousness but in harmony with it. This is why the awful Cross was necessary and a righteous Christ had to hang on it. This is why God's redemption is always conditioned by one's heart attitude. There is no forgiveness for anyone who is unforgiving. "Forgive us our debts, as we forgive our debtors" (Matt. 6:12). There is no mercy for anyone who will not be merciful. "Blessed are the merciful for they shall obtain mercy" (Matt. 5:7). There is striking similarity to these verses in Psalm 18:25–26: "With the loyal thou dost show thyself loyal; with the blameless man thou dost show thyself blameless; with the pure thou dost show thyself pure; and with the crooked thou dost show thyself perverse."

Professor C. S. Lewis in his recent book *Reflections on the Psalms* deals with the difficult subject of the spirit of hatred which is in some of the psalms. He points out that these hatreds had a good motivation. "Such hatreds are the kind of thing that cruelty and injustice, by a sort of natural law, produce.... Not to perceive it at all—not even to be tempted to resentment—to accept it as the most ordinary thing in the world—argues a terrifying insensibility. Thus the absence of anger, especially that sort of anger which we call indignation, can, in my opinion, be a most alarming symptom.... If the Jews cursed more bitterly than the Pagans this was, I think, at least in part because they took right and wrong more seriously."

Vindictiveness is a sin, but only because a sense of justice has gotten out of hand. The check on revenge must be in the careful and exact administering of justice by society's government. This is the clear teaching of Scripture in both the Old and New Testaments. The church and individual Christians should be active in their witness to the Gospel of love and forgiveness and ever lead people to the high law of love of God and our neighbors as ourselves; but meanwhile wherever and whenever God's love and mercy are rejected, as in crime, natural law and order must prevail, not as extraneous to redemption but as part of the whole scope of God's dealings with man.

The argument that capital punishment rules out the possibility of repentance for crime is unrealistic. If a wanton killer does not repent when the sentence of death is upon him, he certainly will not repent if he has 20 to 50 years of life imprisonment ahead of him.

We, who are supposed to be Christian, make too much of physical life. Jesus said, "And do not fear those who kill the body but cannot kill the soul; rather fear him who can destroy both soul and body in hell" (Matt. 10:28). Laxness in law tends to send both soul and body to hell. It is more than a pious remark when a judge says to the condemned criminal: "And may God have mercy on your soul." The sentence of death on a killer is more redemptive than the tendency to excuse his crime as no worse than grand larceny.

It is significant that when Jesus voluntarily went the way of the Cross he chose the capital punishment of his day as his instrument to save the world. And when he gave redemption to the repentant thief he did not save him from capital punishment but gave him Paradise instead which was far better. We see again that mercy and forgiveness are something different than being excused from wrongdoing.

No one can deny that the execution of a murderer is a horrible spectacle. But we must not forget that murder is more horrible. The supreme penalty should be exacted only after the guilt is established beyond the shadow of a doubt and only for wanton, willful, premeditated murder. But the law of capital punishment must stand, no matter how often a jury recommends mercy. The law of capital punishment must stand as a silent but powerful witness to the sacredness of God-given life. Words are not enough to show that life is sacred. Active justice must be administered when the sacredness of life is violated.

It is recognized that this article will only impress those who are convinced that the Scriptures of the Old and New Testament are the supreme authority of faith and practice. If one accepts the authority of Scripture, then the issue of capital punishment must be decided on what Scripture actually teaches and not on the popular, naturalistic ideas of sociology and penology that prevail today. One generation's thinking is not enough to comprehend the implications of the age-old problem of murder. We need the best thinking of the ages on how best to deal with crime and punishment. We need the Word of God to guide us.

[14]

The Death Penalty and
Torture in Islamic Thought

Mohammed Arkoun

I AM BOUND TO MAKE it clear from the very beginning that I do not share the current opinion, according to which the traditional religions are ultimate authorities of knowledge and intangible systems for the regulation of individual and collective existence. All that I shall attempt to do in this chapter is to contribute to the renewal of thought about the death penalty and torture, taking as my point of departure the Islamic example.

I shall begin by a brief outline of the sociological and historical conditions that prevailed at the time of Mohammed and the origin of the Quran. I shall then go on to indicate the important positions of religious law or *Sharî'a* with regard to murder (*qatl*) as an offense and a sanction. Finally, I shall provide a (too rapid) survey of the theoretical problems raised by the *Sharî'a* today in the Islamic societies that are confronted by modernization.

SOURCE: Mohammed Arkoun, "The Death Penalty and Torture in Islamic Thought," in *The Death Penalty and Torture*, ed. Franz Bockle and Jacques Pohier, in the Concilium series Religion in the Seventies (New York: Seabury Press, 1978). Reprinted by permission of the Concilium Foundation, Netherlands.

'Urf and Sharî'a

These two Arabic words refer to an anthropological distinction. *'Urf* is the local common law in force in various ethnic and cultural groups not only before, but also after the appearance of the phenomenon known as Islam. *Sharî'a,* on the other hand, is the system of legal and religious norms and categories based on Quranic texts, the authentic prophetic traditions (*Hadîth*), the consensus of the community (*Ijma'*) and reasoning based on an analogy with the explicit rules of the Quran and the *Hadîth.*[1] The Muslim state, which may have had a khalif, a sultan (in the Ottoman period), or a simple emir at its head, has always attempted to introduce the *Sharî'a* in place of the local common laws, but the latter have resisted this change all the more effectively, as their regulations and customs have been transcended by the teaching of the Quran, especially those connected with punishments.

These verses from the Quran may perhaps serve as an illustration:

Those who wage war against God and the one whom he has sent and who do everything to sow disorder on earth will be punished by being put to death, crucified, having opposite hands and feet cut off or being banished far from their own country. They will be held in ignominy in this world and the next and will be cruelly tortured (V. 33).

Produce evidence from four of you against those of your wives who have been guilty of depravity (= illicit sexual act). If they bear witness against them, enclose them inside your dwellings until they are visited by death or God grants them a way of salvation (IV. 15).

We have prescribed for them in the Torah: an eye for an eye, a nose for a nose, an ear for an ear, a tooth for a tooth, life for life. All injuries are subject to the law of talion. A charitable renunciation of the right to retaliate is equal to an expiation of one's sins. Those who do not judge in accordance with what God has revealed are unjust (V. 45).

O believers! The law of talion is prescribed for you in cases of murder: a free man for a free man, a slave for a slave, a woman for a woman. The one who is pardoned by his brother for having murdered will have to pay damages in good grace in conformity with the custom. This is a mitigation and a mercy on the part of your Lord. Anyone who transgresses after that will be cruelly punished (II. 178).

Many more examples could be given of verses in the Quran that go back to practices in Arab society that was subject to what is known in the Quran as the *Jâhiliyya,* in other words, to ideas and forms of behavior that are uncivilized, as opposed to the ideal, humane, and emancipating norms taught by God and his prophet. The emphasis in this primitive teaching is on cases of permanent and bloodthirsty conflicts—rivalries between families, clans, and tribes involving theft, robbery, and murder; women responsible for the honor of the family or the clan (*'irdh*), in other words, the life of men and women who are responsible for the power of the clan to defend itself or attack its enemies (with the consequent insistence on endogamic marriage and inbreeding often restricted to parallel cousins); an endless cycle of revenge (*tha'r*) because every murder calls for another, and so on.

The Quran represents in every case an attempt to mitigate the harsh collective attitudes imposed by a sociological apparatus without any form of political control. The overall direction of its teaching is towards a respect, even an exaltation of the human person (*al-insân*), who is created by God and responsible to him for grave sins (*kabâ'ir*), one of which is murder (*qatl*). One striking example of this mitigating effect is the prohibition of the barbarous Arab custom allowing the father of a family to bury his young daughters alive (*maw'ûda;* VI. 137, 140; LXXXI. 8) for obscure reasons. Another is the general prohibition of murder (IV. 29, 92–93): "The believer has not the right to kill another believer except in error. Anyone who erroneously kills a believer is bound to set a believing slave free and to pay the family of the victim the price of the blood, unless this is charitably renounced. If the victim belongs to an enemy clan and is still a believer, the murderer will have to set a believing slave free. If the victim belongs to a clan with which you are allied by a pact, the murderer will have to pay the price of the blood to the family and set a believing slave free or otherwise fast for two consecutive months as an expression of repentance before God, the all-knowing, wise one. Anyone, however, who intentionally kills a believer will suffer the punishment of eternal hell."

The Quran, then, protects human life, introduces distinctions, and confirms the norms and attitudes that had been in force for a long time in the common law or *'urf*. It is valuable at this point to summarize the position of the Quran with regard to the elaboration of the *Sharî'a* during the first two centuries of the hegira.

1. The death penalty was explicitly prescribed in the case of "those who wage war against God and the one whom he has sent," the wife who was guilty of an illicit sexual act, intentional homicide (the law of talion), and apostasy (*murtadd*).

2. More generally, grave sins (*kabâ'ir*), regarded as direct transgressions of the will of God, would be punished on the Day of Judgment and there was no right of intercession or possibility of remission (II. 48). Torture, torments, eternal fire, cruel punishment, anger, and God's curse were again and again invoked in connection with these sins.

3. All hardened unbelievers (*kuffâr*) and believers who had broken with God because of serious sin were to suffer the death penalty and be tor-

tured. These rules regarding punishment are in fact an expression of a system of protections for the emerging Muslim community that was threatened by the existing tribal society with its clan solidarities. It is worth noting, however, that the new community made use of the same methods for the formation of alliances and oppositions in order to establish itself. To do this, contingent and secular norms and practices were raised in the Quran to a transcendental level (the price of blood, stoning, the emancipation of slaves, and so on). The Islamic doctors and lawyers continued to take the historical and social circumstances surrounding the Quranic interventions (*asbâb al-nuzul*) into account, but they at the same time neglected to study the theological difficulties raised by the legal verses.

The Teaching of the Sharî'a

Attempts to define what is now called the "Islamic" position regarding justice, property, authority, religious freedom, the death penalty, and so on, frequently result in confusion, partly because a search is made at random in the Quran, the *Hadîth* and the *Sharî'a*, all three being regarded as undisputed and indisputable authorities. In this chapter, I shall confine myself to the *Sharî'a*.[2]

It should be borne in mind that the teaching of the *Sharî'a* has two different sources. Until the second half of the eighth century (= the second century of the hegira), the politico-religious leaders (khalifs, governors, and judges) settled cases by considering the data of the local *'urf* and what they knew of the sacred texts. From about 780–800 onwards, however, a body of legal writing was developed. This moved in two directions. On the one hand, a series of theoretical writings about legal decisions (*ahkâm*) emerged and, on the other, a *corpus juris* which was used by the judges was elaborated. This means that the *Sharî'a*, which was raised to a transcendental level by the later theories of the fundamental sources (*Usûl al-fiqh*), is in fact a historical construction with close links with the political and cultural data and the customs and practices of the Arabo-Islamic world during the first two centuries of the hegira.[3] The principles contained in the Quran are incorporated into this construction, but, as I pointed out briefly above, the teachers of the law have given very little attention to the theological difficulties involved in this operation.

The basic difference between the Quran and the *Sharî'a* is that the first makes use of contingent data in order to emphasize the relationship between God and man and to fill men's minds with a consciousness that there is a world beyond this world of events, values, norms, and possessions. All this is clothed in mythical language and structure which opens the way to problems rather than excluding them. The second, on the other hand, systematizes, within the framework of a code of law, the pragmatic solutions that were adopted at an early period. It is understandable, then, why it is wrong to call norms that have been included in this code and perpetuated by an inflexible teaching Islamic.

The penal code and the death penalty in particular are good examples of this. The various categories of men dealt with under different headings in the Quran (ethical, spiritual, eschatological, and so on) are systematized in the Sharî'a from a strictly juridical point of view. The Sharî'a also divides humanity into Muslim believers and non-Muslim unbelievers[4] in the following way: Muslims are either freemen or slaves, non-Muslims include the people of the Book (= Jews and Christians) and unbelievers; among the people of the Book, there are those who agree to pay the tax (*jizya*) and those who refuse to pay and who therefore are likely to be involved in a legal action leading to the death penalty. In lawsuits, the form of the proceedings, the severity of the sentence passed and the type of punishment inflicted differ according to the offense and according to the category of person tried. (For example, he may be crucified, stoned, strangled, or hanged.)

The blood of a Muslim believer can only be shed because he is guilty of the crime of apostasy, deliberate homicide, or an illicit sexual act. Torture and cruel methods of putting to death are excluded. In practice and according to the socio-political context, the usual punishment is a hundred strokes of the whip for fornication, but there is a difference of opinion among authors about the application of this penalty with or without stoning, which should be continued until the person dies. A slave has to suffer only half of this penalty, because he lacks the quality of muḥṣan, which is possessed only by the free Muslim. (The free Muslim is muḥṣan if he is legally married, but has never committed an illicit sexual act and is protected by a penal law against a slanderous charge of fornication or *qadhf.*) In this context, it has also to be pointed out that a distinction is made in the *Sharî'a* between the rights of God and the rights of man. The rights of God (*huqûq Allah*) include apostasy and failure to observe prayer, fasting, or the *zakât* (the prohibition of certain foods). These sanctions are imposed by God and cannot be changed, modified, or remitted. The reduction of the penalty for a slave can be explained by the fact that God has no material interest in mind. The rights of man (*huqûq âdamiyya*) are treated differently and, if they are violated, a material compensation has to be made (talion, the price of blood, and so on). Offences committed against honor are treated as mixed.

The inequality and variety of the penalties awarded to Muslims and non-Muslims can be explained not by political or racial considerations but by the religious criterion on which the hierarchy of legal status is based according to the *Sharî'a*. The highest position in this hierarchy is that of the male Muslim who has reached the age of puberty, is mentally healthy, free, and legally married. He is protected by the penal system as the one who is most responsible in the eyes of the law inaugurated by God (*mukallaf*). If he does not obey the laws of God, he can also be punished by the death penalty. Next in this hierarchy is the free Muslim woman who is muḥsana. If she commits apostasy, she is forced to return to Islam, but she does not suffer the death penalty. She is followed in the hierarchy by the male Muslim slave and then the female Muslim slave, unbelievers who are protected by the Muslim sovereign (*dhimma;* these are mainly Jews and Christians who are tried by their own law-courts except in cases where their offenses concern Muslims), foreign unbelievers who are temporarily protected on Islamic territory, and finally unbelievers who are at war with Muslims.

It is true that some of the distinctions and ideas that were current in early Arab societies are perpetuated, but the *Sharî'a* gives them an explicit legal status by defining them according to the categories of pure and impure, sacred and profane, divine and human, and true and false in the order of revelation and therefore also in the order of knowledge and practical conduct that result from that revelation. The word *Sharî'a* means the clearly defined way followed by believers and *fiqh* means religious knowledge par excellence or an understanding of the deep meaning of religious teaching. These two terms themselves provide a good insight into the values and attitudes discussed here.

Some of the attitudes leading to the application of certain penalties can be understood in this context. For example, the law of talion does not apply to the Muslim who kills a *dhimmî* who is protected by the Muslim sovereign, whereas the *dhimmî* who is the accomplice of a Muslim in a murder is put to death, while the Muslim himself only has to pay the price of the blood (*diya*). The *diya* paid by the *dhimmî* is half that paid by a Muslim. The *dhimmî* who is guilty of blasphemy against God, the prophet, or the angels incurs the death penalty.[5] The life and the possessions of the foreign unbeliever are not protected by any law, although he may be granted a temporary security (*amân*) by a Muslim, who is a responsible man or woman. In such a case, the foreigner is treated as a *dhimmî*.

Space prevents me from saying much about the attitudes towards the struggle that Muslims have to conduct to defend the rights of God, in other words, the so-called holy war or *jihâd*. *Jihâd* is waged against extreme oppressors (*bughât*) who appeal within Islam to a different form of "orthodoxy" (see the Quran XLIX. 9). *Jihâd* is also waged against all unbelievers who refuse to be converted or to pay the *jizya*.[6] In such a case, the blood of all men capable of bearing arms who have not yet been taken prisoner is declared lawful.

Should we include under the heading of torture the penalty against theft—the amputation of the right hand and the plunging of the stump into boiling oil to prevent bleeding? The first time that the offense is repeated, the left foot is cut off, the second time it is repeated, the left hand is cut off, and the third time it is repeated, the right foot is cut off. Only the Hanefites insist on the amputation of the left foot for the second offense and then they apply another punishment, such as imprisonment.

Our modern sensitivity and our concern to respect the physical and moral integrity of the human person lead us to reject such punishments. It should be noted in this context, however, that Pakistan and Libya have followed the example set by Saudi Arabia in reintroducing these classical penalties. This brings us to our final section, in which we consider the present-day tensions between the Sharî'a and modern legislation.

The Sharî'a and Modern Legislation

Generally speaking, legislation is slow to reflect the development of customs, feelings, and ideas. This is so throughout the world. In the particular case of Islam, it is possible to speak not only of conservatism, but also of a recurrence of the traditional form of law in the ideological context of a revival of the "authentic" Arabo-Islamic spirit, as a reaction to the cultural invasion of imperialistic Western ideas into the Arab world. In fact, the leaders have tended to make use everywhere of the only effective psycho-social weapon available to them to control the irresistible rise of popular movements basing their call for autonomy on the 'urf to some extent penetrated with the teaching of the Sharî'a. The present nationalist movement is in favor of a reactivation of the ideological operation brought about by the teachers of the law at the beginning of the Abbasid dynasty. The decisions taken with regard to the law by the judges and administrators between 670 and 730 or thereabouts were transformed into a body of teaching, the Sharî'a in its "Islamized" or "sacralized" form, at a later stage by the theory of the fundamental sources of the law. This Islamized Sharî'a is historically false, but it helped to bring about a socio-cultural integration of the Muslim city. This is why the states are nowadays anxious to preserve the theoretical fiction that has become a myth since the eighth century (second century of the hegira). Every time that a modification is suggested in legislation, the divine nature of the Sharî'a is stressed and its unchangeable aspect is solemnly reaffirmed.

Given these conditions, it is not difficult to understand why it was possible to insist on the death penalty in Egypt in 1977 for the apostasy of a Muslim. The present lawgivers are unable to set aside attitudes that are contrary to the present-day consensus of opinion on the basic rights of the human being. What is more, they can often contribute to a strengthening of traditional beliefs that inevitably slow down the process of renewal. We are bound to admit that public opinion lacks the means to influence the development of ideas and the laws that embody them. The death penalty and torture depend above all on the good will of the leaders if they are to be abolished. If those leaders have the necessary intellectual development, the right religious convictions, and good political aims, they may either reactivate the penal enactments of the *Sharī'a* or encourage such punishments as imprisonment or fines, leaving the passing of sentences to the judges. (This is the *ta'zir* of the classical law.)

It is quite common for rural or Bedouin people to continue to apply the ancient norms of the *'urf* especially in cases of sexual offenses where the honor of the family is involved.[7] The authorities are usually strict when there is a question of eliminating the early law of revenge leading to useless killings. More often, however, the death penalty does not have the same force in modern Muslim societies as it does in Western countries. On the one hand, the violence does not take the same form, nor is it so virulent as in the industrialized societies of the West. On the other hand, the people of the Muslim societies are hard pressed by the ordinary everyday tasks of living and concerned with urgent political, economic, and psychological struggles involved in the radical changes in their traditional family and social relationships. They are therefore less able to take part in humanitarian discussions than intellectuals living in the West.

Space prevents me from analyzing the conditions that may lead to the reapplication or the suppression of the death penalty and torture as an indicator of the movement of the Muslim people towards increased human dignity. To judge from recent experiences in various sociopolitical contexts, it would seem that what has been achieved in certain places is not irreversible, nor is it necessarily well adapted to the biological and socio-historical state of man today. In other words, it is not sufficient simply to abolish the death penalty as a sanction imposed by justice or torture as means of enslaving men's wills. There are also the collective executions, the taking of innocent hostages, the blind acts of terrorism that have been "legalized" each time by the "interests" of a nation, a state, or a group. If violence has biological roots and links with the sacred and if "human beings are historical structures" and the result of "an evolution and an odd job,"[8] then we must no longer approach the problem of the death penalty and torture as a purely ethical or religious phenomenon which disguises its real nature or as a traditionally legal question. It is basically a biological and socio-historical threshold that mankind is very painfully crossing.

Notes

1. See J. Schacht, *An Introduction to Islamic Law* (Oxford: n.p., 1964).
2. As a body of law, it should be distinguished from the Quran, just as the Christian gospel has to be distinguished from canon law.

3. This historical and critical presentation has been rejected by Muslim fundamentalists as a weapon used by "orientalists" against Islam. It is based mainly on the work of I. Goldziher, J. Schacht, C. Chéhata, and others.

4. It is interesting to note that mankind was divided by the Second Vatican Council into non-Christians and non-believers.

5. See A. Fattal, *Le statut légal des non-musulmans en pays d'Islam* (Beirut: n.p., 1958).

6. For this tax, see 'djizya,' in the *Encyclopédie de l'Islam,* 2d ed.

7. See J. Chelhod, *Le droit dans la société bédouine: recherches ethnologiques sur le 'urf ou droit coutumier des bédouins* (Paris: n.p., 1971).

8. F. Jacob, "Evolution et bricolage," *Le Monde,* 6, 7, and 8 September 1977.

PART FIVE

THE CONSISTENT ETHIC OF THE SACREDNESS OF HUMAN LIFE

[15]

A Consistent Ethic of Life and the Death Penalty in Our Time

Joseph Cardinal Bernardin

Address to Criminal Law Committee
Criminal Court of Cook County
May 14, 1985

I WISH TO ACKNOWLEDGE with gratitude your considerable contribution to the quality of life among the people of Cook County as you preserve the value of justice and implement it each day. The court system is an indispensable part of our great American heritage of "justice for all under the law." I am aware that your dedicated work involves considerable frustration as you constantly encounter the seamier side of human behavior.

I am grateful for your invitation to meet with you this afternoon and to share my reflections on an issue of mutual concern: capital punishment. I come before you as a *pastor*—not a legal expert. It is my understanding that the constitutional principle of the separation of Church and State ensures religious organizations the right to engage in debate about public policy, expecting neither favoritism nor discrimination. At the same time, I firmly believe that they must earn the right to be heard by the quality of their arguments.

SOURCE: Joseph Cardinal Bernardin, "A Consistent Ethic of Life and the Death Penalty in Our Time," *Consistent Ethic of Life* (Kansas City, Mo.: Sheed & Ward, 1988). Reprinted with permission of Sheed & Ward.

It has also been my longstanding conviction that civil law and social policy must always be subject to ongoing moral analysis. Simply because a civil law is in place does not mean it should be blindly supported. Encouraging reflective, informed assessment of civil law and policy keeps alive the capacity for moral criticism in society.

I also come before you as a *citizen* who cares deeply about the quality of life in our community.

I will address two dimensions of the topic this afternoon. First, I will situate the issue of capital punishment in the context of a consistent ethic of life and then examine the case for capital punishment in light of this ethic.

I. The Context: A Consistent Ethic of Life

Catholic social teaching is based on two truths about the human person: human life is both sacred and social. Because we esteem human life as sacred, we have a duty to protect and foster it at all stages of development, from conception to death, and in all circumstances. Because we acknowledge that human life is also social, society must protect and foster it.

Precisely because life is sacred, the taking of even one life is a momentous event. Traditional Catholic teaching has allowed the taking of human life in particular situations by way of exception, as, for example, in self-defense and capital punishment. In recent decades, however, the presumptions against taking human life have been strengthened and the exceptions made ever more restrictive.

Fundamental to this shift in emphasis is a more acute perception of the multiple ways in which life is threatened today. Obviously such questions as war, aggression, and capital punishment have been with us for centuries; they are not new. What is new is the *context* in which these ancient questions arise, and the way in which a new context shapes the *content* of our ethic of life.

Within the Catholic Church, the Second Vatican Council acknowledged that "a sense of the dignity of the human person has been impressing itself more and more deeply on the consciousness of contemporary man" (Declaration on Religious Freedom, #1). This growing awareness of human dignity has been a dominant factor within Western culture. Within the United States, the struggle to appreciate human worth more fully is found in the civil rights movement and in the public debate about our foreign policy toward totalitarian regimes of both the right and the left.

This deepening awareness, as I intimated above, has been precipitated in part by a growing recognition of the frailty of human life today. Faced with the threat of nuclear war and escalating technological developments, the human family encounters a qualitatively new range of moral problems. Today, life is threatened on a scale previously unimaginable.

This is why the U.S. Catholic bishops and others have been so visible and vocal in the public debate this past decade or two, asserting belief in the sacredness of human life and the responsibilities we have, personally and as a society, to protect and preserve the sanctity of life.

Nonetheless, it is not enough merely to assert such an ethical principle. If it is to be acknowledged and implemented, it must impact all areas of human life. It must respond to all the moments, places, or conditions which either threaten the sanctity of life or cultivate an attitude of disrespect for it.

A consistent ethic of life is based on the need to ensure that the sacredness of human life, which is the ultimate source of human dignity, will be defended and fostered from womb to tomb, from the genetic laboratory to the cancer ward, from the ghetto to the prison.

II. Capital Punishment in Light of This Ethic

As you undoubtedly know, since the time of St. Augustine, great thinkers in the Roman Catholic tradition—St. Thomas Aquinas, for example—have struggled with such ethical questions as the right of the State to execute criminals. Through the centuries, as I noted above, the Church has acknowledged that the State *does* have the right to take the life of someone guilty of an extremely serious crime.

However, because such punishment involves the deliberate infliction of evil on another, it always needs justification. Usually this has consisted of indicating some good which would derive from the punishment, a good of such consequence that it justifies the taking of life.

As I understand the current discussion about capital punishment, the question is not whether the State still has the *right* to inflict capital punishment, but whether it should *exercise* this right. In present circumstances, are there sufficient reasons to justify the infliction of the evil of death on another human person?

This is the question which the U.S. Catholic Bishops and others have been addressing recently—the United States Catholic Conference in 1980, the Massachusetts Catholic Conference Board of Governors in 1982, the Oklahoma Catholic bishops in 1983, the Tennessee Bishops exactly one year ago today, and Florida church leaders last November. Although there are differences of presentation, basically the reasoning of these positions follows two lines of thought.

First, they review four traditional arguments justifying capital punishment:

retribution, deterrence, reform, and protection of the State. Based on their review, the religious leaders have argued that these reasons no longer apply in our age.

I don't have time this afternoon to present the reasoning in regard to all four areas, but I would like to use the question of retribution as an example. The 1980 U.S. Catholic Conference statement states:

> We grant that the need of retribution does indeed justify punishment. For the practice of punishment both presupposes a previous transgression against the law and involves the involuntary deprivation of certain goods. But we maintain that this good does not require nor does it justify the taking of the life of the criminal, even in cases of murder.... It is morally unsatisfactory and socially destructive for criminals to go unpunished, but the limits of punishment must be determined by moral objectives which go beyond the mere infliction of injury on the guilty. Thus we would argue it is as barbarous and inhumane for a criminal who had tortured or maimed a victim to be tortured or maimed in return. Such punishment might satisfy certain vindictive desires that we or the victim might feel, but the satisfaction of such desires is not and cannot be an objective of a humane and Christian approach to punishment.

Basing their judgment on this and similar lines of reasoning, many religious leaders conclude that, under our present circumstances, the death penalty as punishment for reasons of deterrence, retribution, reform, or protection of society cannot be justified.

Nonetheless, our reflections on this issue do not stop at this level. As religious leaders we argue that there are gospel insights which bespeak the inappropriateness of capital punishment. First, there is the example of Jesus, offering forgiveness at the time of his own unfair death (Luke 23:24).

Another challenging gospel theme is that of "God's boundless love for every person, regardless of human merit or worthiness. This love was especially visible in Jesus' ministry to outcasts, in his acceptance of sinners" (Florida church leaders). Consistent with this theme and flowing from it is the biblical imperative of reconciliation. Wherever there is division between persons, Christ calls them to forgiveness and reconciliation.

While these themes are specifically grounded in the New Testament, I do not believe they are unique to the Christian vision. People of good will recognize that these virtues ennoble human experience and make it more complete. Commitment to these values changes one's perspective on the strengths and weaknesses of the human family.

This change in perspective seems to have been in mind when the ecumenical leaders of Florida stated that Jesus shifted the locus of judgment in this matter to a higher court: a court where there is absolute knowledge of the evidence, of good deeds and of evil, of faith and of works of faith, of things private and things public—a court in which there is both wrath and tenderness, both law and grace.

It is when we stand in this perspective of a "higher court"—that of God's judgment seat—and a more noble view of the human person, that we seriously question the appropriateness of capital punishment. We ask ourselves: Is the human family made more complete—is human personhood made more loving—in a society which demands life for life, eye for eye, tooth for tooth?

Let me acknowledge that your experience is probably quite different from mine. You have had to deal with heinous crimes, with persons so filled with hatred and violence as to chill the heart. You may be wondering whether my colleagues and I are naive or simplistic in our approach.

Perhaps I won't be able to dispel that perception with my response. Nevertheless, I want to affirm that the State *does* have the responsibility to protect its citizens. It deserves and merits the full support of all of us in the exercise of that responsibility. Although we don't have an adequate understanding of the causes of violent crime, society "has the right and the duty to prevent such behavior including, in some cases, the right to impose terms of lifetime imprisonment" (Florida ecumenical leaders).

I am not suggesting that society should be a prisoner of violence or violent crime. On the contrary, the consistent ethic of life requires that society struggle to eradicate poverty, racism, and other systemic forces which nurture and encourage violence. Similarly, the perpetrators of violence should be punished and given the opportunity to experience a change of heart and mind.

But, having said this, I also think that capital punishment is not an appropriate response to the problem of crime in our land. To take any human life, even that of someone who is not innocent, is awesome and tragic. It seems to me and to others that, in our culture today, there are not sufficient reasons to justify the State continuing to exercise its right in this matter. There are other, better ways of protecting the interests of society.

Recently the Gallup organization conducted a poll about capital punishment—something they had done on previous occasions. In 1966, 42 percent of those polled favored capital punishment; in 1981, 66 percent favored it; and this year the percentage was 72 percent.

Why has 24 percent of the population turned to favoring capital punishment in the last nineteen years? This question is even more urgent because that same poll reported that fully 51 percent of the respondents said "they would still support capital punishment even if studies showed conclusively it does not deter crime"! This is striking because people often use deterrence as a main argument to justify capital punishment. If it is not to deter crime, why do people support capital punishment? Thirty percent of those who favored capital punishment indicated their reason was simple: revenge!

One might argue that the cycle of violence has become so intense in our society that it is understandable and appropriate for people to support capital punishment. What alternative is there, some ask, in a violent society other than to meet violence with violence?

As a citizen in a democracy whose founding dream is of human dignity and as a disciple of Jesus, I must reject this alternative. In fact, as a citizen of this city which has recently been alarmed, saddened, and polarized by the senseless killing of a talented high school basketball star and a ten-year-old standing in front of his home, I assert that violence is not the answer—it is not the way to break the cycle of violence.

Pope John Paul II, speaking to Peruvians who were living in the midst of a rebel stronghold, told them: "The pitiless logic of violence leads to nothing. No good is obtained by helping to increase violence."

Capital punishment, to my mind, is an example of meeting violence with violence. What does it say about the quality of our life when people celebrate the death of another human being? What does it say about the human spirit when some suggest a return to public executions which only twenty years ago we would have considered barbaric?

We desperately need an attitude or atmosphere in society which will sustain a consistent defense and promotion of life. Where human life is considered "cheap" and easily "wasted," eventually nothing is held as sacred and all lives are in jeopardy. The purpose of proposing a consistent ethic of life is to argue that success on any one of the issues threatening life requires a concern for the broader attitude in society about respect for life. Attitude is the place to root an ethic of life.

Change of attitude, in turn, can lead to change of policies and practices in our society. We must find ways to break the cycle of violence which threatens to strangle our land. We must find effective means of protecting and enhancing human life.

[16]

Bipartisan Death Rows

Peter L. Berger

THERE USED TO BE AN ideological division of labor in what might be called the terminal issues of American public life. Conservatives were in favor of the death penalty but opposed to abortion. Liberals, conversely, favored abortion but were against the death penalty. This divide is now in process of being bridged. Perhaps this is part of the larger healing process of which much has been written lately, as for instance in connection with the recent lifting of the ban on trade with Vietnam. Perhaps America is finally becoming a more mature nation, its instincts of compassion tempered with realism, its innate toughness fortified by empathy with the victims of injustice. In any case, there is now emerging a new bipartisan consensus in favor of both abortion and the death penalty.

Readers of *First Things* have not had to complain about lack of coverage of the abortion issue, but they may not have been as aware of the progress on the other issue. A number of prominent politicians represent the new consensus. There is Governor William Weld of Massachusetts, whose credentials as a moderate Republican of possibly presidential timber have been enhanced by his firm pro-choice position and his tenacious efforts to reintroduce capital punishment in the state. On the Democratic side there is former Governor Douglas

SOURCE: Peter L. Berger, "Bipartisan Death Rows," *First Things* (May 1994). Reprinted by permission of *First Things*.

Wilder of Virginia, who has been hailed as a living example of the civilizing effect that black elected officials are increasingly having on American government. A few months ago, still on Gov. Wilder's watch, there was a small problem. A prisoner due to be executed was unable to walk. (It should be mentioned that he was also black, so no racial prejudice could be charged.) The state was getting ready to construct a ramp so that this individual could be wheeled right into the death chamber. In the event, this proved to be unnecessary: he felt that being rolled in on a wheelchair was undignified and, somehow, he managed to limp to his execution.

However, without in any way diminishing the achievements of leaders like Weld and Wilder, it is President Clinton himself who embodies the new consensus in the most impressive way. A certain moral high point came in the 1992 electoral champaign when Dan Quayle in one of his speeches questioned Clinton's good faith in claiming to be tough on crime. George Stephanopoulos indignantly pointed out that, during his period as governor of Arkansas, Clinton had allowed four executions to be carried out. So he did. Actually, he signed the orders for about seventy executions, but most of these, through no fault of his, were not carried out. Even in the enlightened state of Arkansas desperate defense lawyers have recourse to various legal maneuvers to stave off executions— just the sort of frivolous delaying tactics that the Supreme Court, in another show of growing ideological consensus, is now determined to stamp out.

The last person executed under Clinton's governorship was Rickie Rector. The details of this case were reported in a long story in, of all places, the *New Yorker.* Rector had participated in a robbery in the course of which he had killed a policeman. He then shot himself in the head in an attempt at suicide, either in an effort to avoid capture or as an act of remorse. He failed to kill himself, but was left severely brain-damaged. He had the mental age of a child of five. As usual, the case made its way through the courts, but in this instance all attempts to avoid the execution of the death sentence failed. Clinton was then out of state on the campaign trail. He returned to Little Rock so as to be in his office while the execution was carried out. Consequently, there is no possibility of denying him due credit for it. According to eyewitness accounts Rector was quite unaware of what was happening to him. When the executioner had difficulty inserting the poison syringe, Rector tried to help him. It had been Rector's habit in prison to save a portion of his dessert cake for an evening snack. When his cell was cleaned out after the execution, the usual piece of cake was found left behind. He had evidently planned to eat it afterward.

The Rector case raises the interesting question of whether a severely retarded individual should be subject to the death penalty. An argument could be made that it is more humane to execute someone who does not know what is happening than someone who is fully conscious of the proceedings. This question cannot be pursued here. Rather, attention should be drawn to the international dimension of this issue. The United States is the only Western democracy that continues to carry out the death penalty. There had, of course, been an interruption while the Supreme Court pondered whether the constitutional prohibition of cruel and unusual punishment applied here. Since the wise (and, incidentally, strict constructionist) decision that it did not, executions have been steadily increasing and in a number of states have become routine. Texas, with the highest number of individuals on death row, has inaugurated a work program just for them—a garment factory. (Assurances have been given that none of its products will be exported to China.) The Clinton crime bill, of course, greatly increases the number of offenses punishable by death under federal jurisdiction. Some foreigners, especially Europeans and Latin Americans, have difficulty understanding this. *The Spectator* of London recently published a cartoon showing an individual being led to an electric chair in front of which a sign said, "Please wait to be seated." This, of course, was intended as a blatantly anti-American comment, such as one has come to expect from the English right. Yet perhaps there was here also an unconscious acknowledgment of a feature of American exceptionalism—the capacity for compassion and courtesy even when robust measures have to be taken.

There is no reason to fear that the United States will abandon its splendidly isolated practice of capital punishment any time in the near future. There is no constituency for abolition either on the right or the left. However, as more and more people move through America's death row, two modest proposals may be in order.

The first (Republicans will note with approval) would require no state intervention. It is high time that the several occupations engaged in life termination be given proper professional training. Increasingly now the death penalty is carried out by lethal injection, a procedure that is not only more humane than the earlier methods but is also inherently a medical procedure. The indicated curriculum would plausibly combine paramedical and paralegal training. It would unite in one program the technical personnel dedicated to abortions, executions, and assisted suicides. In addition to the instructors in practical procedures, the faculty could include morticians, bereavement counselors, and medical ethicists. The course would culminate in a diploma in Individualized Exit Facilitation (IEF). One or another Southern state university could certainly be induced to pioneer in this field.

The second proposal would respond to the aforementioned international aspect of this issue. Yet another growing bipartisan consensus concerns the place of human rights in American foreign policy. The United States Information Agency should make a concerted effort to explain the American position on life termination in all its aspects and its relation to fundamental human rights. The

Agency for International Development should include individuals with IEF diplomas in its programs in the underdeveloped countries. Most important, the State Department should include the status of IEF laws and practices in its annual report on human rights in the world. This last suggestion would also have a domestic benefit. Year by year, Americans can read the State Department report and be proud. They already know how superior they are to China. It is time to feel superior to Switzerland.

[17]

Who Deserves to Live? Who Deserves to Die? Reflections on Capital Punishment

Norman P. Dake

THE CHARGE WAS CAPITAL murder. The accused was a young man whom I had come to know quite well during the several months he was incarcerated while awaiting trial. The inmate's lawyer had asked me if I would be willing to testify in the penalty phase of the capital murder trial.[1] Specifically, he was interested in knowing whether there were any redeeming characteristics that the accused man possessed that might persuade a jury that he deserved to live.

That was an easy question to answer. During the time of our relationship, I had come to know this young man in a way far different from that portrayed by television reporters and the newspapers. It was not a ruthless, cold-hearted killer that I saw, but rather a loving, caring human being. I saw a man who was disturbed by what the publicity of his front-page case was doing to his family. I saw a man who was concerned about the effect a long-term incarceration might have upon his marriage and his relationship with his son. I saw a man who was committed to his Lord Jesus Christ, who had completed a course in the basics of Christian faith, who had been baptized in a jail service, who attended a weekly Bible class, and who genuinely struggled to live out his Christian faith

SOURCE: From Norman P. Dake, "Who Deserves to Live? Who Deserves to Die? Reflections on Capital Punishment," *Currents in Theology and Mission* 10, no. 2 (April 1983). Reprinted by permission.

159

in the hostile environment of his jail cell. I had no trouble coming up with reasons why this man deserved to live.

Yet I had all the trouble in the world answering the attorney's question. It seemed to me to be the wrong question. It assumed that society is justified in deciding that in some circumstances a convicted killer deserves to live and in other circumstances deserves to die. More fundamentally, one is obliged to ask whether anyone—individual or group—has the right, under any circumstances, to take the life of another.

Not Ours to Take

Human life is not ours to take. It belongs to God, who created it. That is a basic affirmation of our Christian faith (Heb. 11:3). Through biology and genetics we understand how life is transmitted from one generation to the next. Through the eyes of faith we see the hand of God at work in the creating and sustaining of life. That divine parenthood makes life precious. What makes human life sacred and uniquely different from any other form of life is that it is life created in God's own image (Gen. 1:27). No matter how dimmed or tainted that image may have become because of sin, it remains an essential part of us (Gen. 9:6), male and female. We were made to be in relationship with our Creator, to be responsive and responsible to God. Our accountability before God requires a recognition that human life is not our private possession to do with as we please.

God has a second claim upon the life that he has created. It is the claim of the cross, by which God has bought back that life [that] has been spawned by sin. Martin Luther, in his explanation of the second article of the Apostles' Creed, dramatically confessed this second form of divine ownership: "I believe that Jesus Christ...has redeemed me, a lost and condemned creature, delivered me and freed me from all sins, from death, and from the power of the devil, not with silver and gold but with his holy and precious blood and with his innocent sufferings and death."[2] Luther has personalized what the Scriptures universalize. Christ's redemptive work was done for the benefit of all (2 Cor. 5:14–15), even convicted criminals (Luke 23:39–43). There is a double mortgage on human life. By virtue of his creating and redeeming activity, God holds title to both.

The giving and the taking of human life is God's domain. Even when overcome by grief, Job was able to affirm this essential truth. "The Lord gave, and the Lord has taken away; blessed be the name of the Lord" (Job 1:21). Whenever a human life is brought to a premature end by forces other than those provided by God in his created order, God's name is not blessed and neither is ours.

This is true whether death occurs on one of our city streets at the hand of a violent killer, or on death row in one of our state penitentiaries at the hand of a public executioner.

The Role of the State

But hasn't God delegated this jurisdiction over life and death to the governmental authorities? Certainly the state has long assumed the authority to carry out the death sentence. John the Baptizer (Mark 6:27), James (Acts 12:2), and Jesus himself are evidence that the Roman government and vassal officials resorted to capital punishment whenever it seemed politically expedient. Yet these very examples should give us pause, lest we concede uncritically the legitimate use of capital punishment to the governing authorities.

In Romans 13:1–7 St. Paul makes one of his strongest statements in support of governmental authority. "If you do what is evil, look out, for the one in authority does not bear the sword in vain" (13:4b). What does St. Paul have in mind when he uses the word "sword"? Does he mean capital punishment? Is he speaking about military force? Or is he using the term in a more general sense to refer to all of the powers possessed by the governing authorities? Based on the context of this statement, the last definition seems to fit best. St. Paul is addressing a community of Christians who had some questions about their obligations to the government. The payment of taxes and customs fees was at issue as was the according of honor and respect to those in authority (13:6–7). While affirming that Christians owe allegiance to God (12:1 ff.) and love to their neighbors (13:8–10), Paul also acknowledges that they have an obligation to conform their behavior to the standards set by the civil authorities (13:1–7).

This conformity, however, is not blind obedience, but rather a declaration on the part of the citizenry that it recognizes in the duly constituted authorities the beneficent hand of the Lord.[3] The authority for any form of government comes from God (13:1). The state has the authority to punish those who do that which is evil rather than the good (13:2–4), because the offenders have subverted the very institution that God has appointed to maintain order and seek the best interests of all citizens. But does this authority to punish include the right to impose the death sentence? That is hardly what Paul had in mind in Romans 13. Paul uses the word "sword" as a "symbol of the penal power of the state"[4] and as a "symbol of the power of the authorities to punish evildoers."[5] Paul is not advocating capital punishment for tax cheaters and flag burners. He is encouraging the Christian community to pay its taxes and to give respect to the governing authorities in response to the government's efforts on behalf of the common good.

The first half of Romans 13:4 is therefore also crucial to our evaluation of the use of capital punishment. "The one in authority is God's servant (*diakonos*) for your good." Two questions arise. The first, which will be discussed later in connection with the purposes of punishment, is whether the execution of criminals is for the good of society. The second is whether the death penalty is in the service of the God who warns us against repaying evil with evil (12:17) and taking vengeance into our own hands (12:19). Such violence is not the stuff of which the Kingdom of God is made.

Jesus himself condemns the use of violence. On the night of Jesus' arrest, Peter (John 18:10) wanted to put up a fight. In the ensuing melee the chief priest's slave lost an ear. Jesus responded to this violent episode by healing the slave's ear (Luke 22:51) and rebuking the offending disciple. "Put your sword back into its place; for all who take the sword will perish by the sword" (Matt. 26:52). This is not Jesus' authorization for the use of capital punishment. It is rather Jesus' affirmation that the Kingdom of God is not going to be established by force of arms. It is a protest against the policy of "eye for an eye, tooth for a tooth" (5:38). Violence breeds violence. Those who engage in violent behavior will suffer at the hand of violence. My friends in jail have another way of saying it. "What goes around, comes around. You reap what you sow." Jesus' words ought to serve as an admonition not only to those individuals who are tempted to use violence, but also to those societies that are bent on institutionalizing violence by legalizing executions.

The Old Testament comes much closer to condoning executions. Following the flood, God made a covenant with Noah and his sons that included this provision: "Whoever sheds the blood of man, by man shall his blood be shed; for God made man in his own image" (Gen. 9:6). Old Testament scholar Otto Eissfeldt suggests that this saying may have been a part of a formal pronouncement made by the elders when a death sentence was imposed or when an execution was carried out.[6] The justification for the death sentence was contained in the solemn saying itself: " . . . for God made man in his own image." The sacredness of human life was an element of the covenant with Noah that God wanted to emphasize.

Yet even the life of a murderer is sacred to God. When Cain killed his brother Abel (Gen. 4:1–16), Cain knew that he deserved to be punished. Yet God did not require Cain's life in return for Abel's. God's verdict against Cain was to make him a fugitive and a homeless wanderer upon the earth. That sentence made Cain fear for his life and he cried out in terror to God, certain that whoever would find him would kill him. But no one killed Cain, because the Lord put a mark on him to protect him from any vengeful hand. Such was the value that God placed on the life of a murderer like Cain.

Why Do We Punish?

Precisely because human life is sacred, the taking of another's life is not to be condoned. From the very inception of civil communities, the human race has sought to condemn in the strongest possible terms those who have usurped God's power over life and death. Murderers have been punished for their offenses against God and society. But what purposes ought punishment to serve? Does capital punishment further those ends?

1. **Retribution.** The offender ought to be "paid back" in some way for the offense that has been committed. There needs to be a distinction, however, between retribution and vengeance. Retributive justice demands, first of all, that punishment be taken out of the hands of an angry mob. In the case of an accidental death—what we would today call manslaughter—Old Testament societies provided cities of refuge where the accused had the right to seek sanctuary until legal proceedings could take place (Num. 35:9–15, 22–28; Deut. 19:1–10). For example, if a person were chopping down trees in the woods and the axe head flew off and struck and killed a neighbor who was standing nearby, the wood chopper could flee to a city of refuge to escape the vengeance of angry friends or neighbors (Deut. 19:5). Punishment is to be meted out after careful evaluation of the circumstances and not on the basis of heated emotions.

Retributive justice demands, secondly, that the punishment fit the crime. This was the intent of the Old Testament Law of Talion:

> *Eye for eye,*
> *tooth for tooth,*
> *hand for hand,*
> *foot for foot,*
> *burn for burn,*
> *wound for wound,*
> *stripe for stripe.*
>
> (EXOD. 21:24–25)

The Law of Talion was to serve as a curb for overzealous law enforcers. Excessive punishment becomes vindictive. The divine admonition "Vengeance is mine" (Deut. 32:35, Rom. 12:19; Heb. 10:30) is a reminder that punishment is not to be a vengeful overreaction to crime, but is to be made commensurate with the offense.

Jesus takes the matter a step further in the Sermon on the Mount. He challenges the Christian community to rise above the "eye for an eye" mentality (Matt. 5:38–42) by responding to hate and evil with love (5:43–48) and mercy

(5:7). Punishment that is not tempered by love and compassion for the offender becomes little more than vindictive retaliation that tempts the offended parties to stoop to the same level as the offenders and to return "evil for evil" (Rom. 12:17).

Although modern society has come a long way from the days of lynching parties and mob rule, much of today's retribution remains vengeful. Angry citizens cry out for capital punishment because they are frustrated by their seeming powerlessness in the face of violent crime; eager prosecutors need little encouragement to launch into emotional tirades in an effort to convince juries that convicted murderers deserve to die. We have succeeded in taking vengeance out of the streets and putting it into our courtrooms, and the second evil is worse than the first. Now our vindictive natures are legitimated under the guise of justice and of law and order. Yet if we are honest with ourselves, we will recognize that most often our motivation for punishing law offenders is nothing less than vengeance, and therefore a usurpation of God's power (Rom. 12:19).

Perhaps one of the reasons our society has not been able to move beyond "an eye for an eye" is that it has only in recent years been able to achieve even this standard of justice. Prior to 1977 rape of an adult that involved no loss of life was punishable by death. However horrified we may be by these violent assaults on human dignity, we should not condemn this violence by condoning capital punishment. The punishment must fit the crime.

Our society has a long history of administering punishments that are vindictive. There is yet room for us to learn new approaches that incorporate the love, mercy, and forgiveness to which our Lord calls us.

To be opposed to capital punishment is not to be soft on crime. The current alternatives to the death sentence—like Missouri's sentence of life in prison with no parole for 50 years—can hardly be regarded as slaps on the wrist. Anyone who has seen the inside of some of our state and federal penitentiaries knows that they are anything but country clubs or college dorms. Prison life is tough and time is hard. Yet there is life, and those who oppose capital punishment value that life and recognize that there are other purposes of punishment besides retribution.

2. **Restitution.** Punishment should not only "pay back" offenders for their crimes, but should provide an opportunity for them to "pay back" their victims. The legal codes of the Old Testament contained provisions for restitution (for example, Exodus 21:18 ff.). They recognized that the guilty parties had a responsibility to those people whom they had wronged.

The victims are often the forgotten people in our criminal justice system. Our legal documents reflect this exclusion of the injured parties when they read, "The State vs. John Doe," as though the state were the only grieved party.

To ignore the needs of the victims is to put the burden of crime disproportionately on their shoulders. Some lose only property; others lose feelings of security and self-worth because of the trauma of their experience; still others lose their lives.

It goes without saying that there can be no adequate compensation for the loss of a life. Murderers cannot bring their victims back to life. A deceased spouse cannot be replaced, even if the survivor should marry again. Another child is no substitute for a child that has been killed. But is there no way for convicted killers to make some amends for their crimes? Is there nothing they can contribute to the society they have wronged? Is there no way for them to be held accountable for the ongoing needs of the victims' families, for support of dependent survivors, or for providing professional assistance to families who must cope with an unexpected loss?

An executed criminal can make no form of restitution. To put convicted killers to death is to deprive them of any opportunity to make amends for their offenses, and to preclude any use of punishment for a compensatory purpose.

3. **Rehabilitation.** Punishment ought to offer some opportunity for the offender to come to repentance and to receive forgiveness. "As I live, says the Lord God, I have no pleasure in the death of the wicked, but that the wicked turn from their ways and live" (Ezek. 33:11). God punished the nations of Judah and Israel for their injustices and unfaithfulness. But it was not punishment for punishment's sake. His overriding purpose was to bring about a change of heart and mind. "Turn again, then, to your God, hold fast to love and justice, and always put your trust in your God" (Hosea 12:6). Even though God felt the hurt and anger of a jilted husband, he could not put away his unfaithful bride. He could not destroy his people (Hosea 11:7–9).

Our society is great at punishing, but it is not so good at forgiving. It has the notion that some crimes, including murder, can not and should not be forgiven. Convicted killers are regarded as being beyond the reaches of reform and rehabilitation. If we cannot put them out of our world through executions, then we would at least like to put them permanently out of our society by locking them up for so long that they will never again see the light of day from outside a prison cell.

Do we not underestimate the power of God? God was able to transform a Saul into a Paul and thereby turn his chief persecutor into his most ambitious witness (Acts 9:1–31). God even used a murderer to bring about a most miraculous deliverance for his people; the man's name was Moses (Exod. 2:11 ff.). Certainly God is able to transform the most despised criminals. As long as we hold sacred the life of even the most notorious killer, God is able to bring about a renewed experience of his love and forgiveness.

4. **Deterrence.** Punishment can sometimes have a beneficial side effect if it

can discourage others from making the same mistake that got a criminal in trouble with the law. Deterrence, however, can never be the primary purpose of punishment, but only a by-product. If deterrence is made the overriding goal of punishment, offenders end up suffering for the criminal inclinations and potential offenses of others rather than solely for their own misdeeds. That is unjust. Except for Christ, God's punishment is directed against those who transgress his law and not against any substitutes. Deterrence, therefore, should never be the only reason for administering punishment.

One of the arguments put forward in support of capital punishment is that it will make an example of a convicted murderer and serve warning that society will not tolerate the taking of human life. The intention is that potential killers will think twice before they strike. Most murders, however, are crimes of passion. They are not planned; there is no premeditation.[7] An argument erupts, a deadly weapon is at hand, and a person is killed. The threat of punishment is not a deterring factor because there is no conscious deliberation.

In cases where intent and premeditation are involved, however, it must be asked whether a deterrent effect can be achieved by the use of capital punishment. Or is there some means less extreme, such as the threat of long-term imprisonment, that would serve the same deterring purpose as the death penalty?

The empirical evidence indicates that capital punishment does not serve as a deterrent.[8] Early research, involving comparison of states with the death penalty to those without it, revealed that the death penalty had "no discernable effect" on homicide rates.[9] In 1967 Canada decided to abolish capital punishment for a five-year trial period, one of the aims being to determine if there was any resulting change in crimes of violence. Results of that experiment indicated no increase in violent crimes attributable to abolition.[10] Consequently, Canada made the abolition of capital punishment permanent. More recent investigations have demonstrated that capital punishment not only has no value as a deterrent, but actually produces the exact opposite results.[11] The death penalty has a "brutalizing effect" upon potential murderers who learn from legally sanctioned executions that killing is the way to deal with people who have given offense. The result is that murder rates *increase* when executions are carried out. All of which suggests that Jesus' words about violence breeding violence (Matt. 26:52) apply to societies as well as to individuals.

The best deterrent to crime is swift and certain punishment. But some crimes go unobserved or unreported. Some offenders are never apprehended. Lack of evidence keeps others from being brought to trial. For those who are prosecuted, conviction is never guaranteed. Consequently, even the deterrent effect of threatened imprisonment becomes watered down. Moreover, because of logjams in the courts and legal maneuverings on both sides. our criminal justice system has rarely been able to provide penalties that are either swift or certain. The deterrent effect of any punishment is therefore somewhat suspect, and the deterrent effect of capital punishment is in any event unproved.

5. **Protection.** Punishment ought to serve two protective functions.

a. *Protection of society.* Protecting its citizens from crime is one of the responsibilities of government. The removal of offenders from society has become the normative pattern for providing this protection. Because the death penalty is such an extreme form of punishment that removes a convicted killer not only from our society but from our world, it can be argued that long-term imprisonment can provide the same degree of protection and is therefore to be preferred as more humane.

There is a danger, however, in any form of punishment that only removes an offender from society. We can delude ourselves into thinking that, once an offender has been sentenced or executed, we have adequately dealt with the crime problem. That is simply not true. It is little wonder that our society has imposed stiffer and stiffer penalties, and its citizens have felt more and more unsafe! Until we as a society have addressed the myriad of factors that contribute to crime—including poverty, inequality, ignorance, underemployment, and drug abuse[12]—the crime rate will continue to grow.

Moreover, a societal attitude that says, "Lock them up and throw away the key" is nothing less than an abdication of our responsibility for those who have broken the law. "Out of sight, out of mind" has become our standard approach to those who are incarcerated, but no one has ever been helped by being forgotten. As Christians we have a word of judgment and a word of forgiveness to bring to law offenders. We would do well not to forget that, but rather to "remember those who are in prison, as though in prison with them" (Heb. 13:3).

b. *Protection of the offender.* Punishment ought to provide in some way for the protection of the convicted. Judicial proceedings that ensure due process, and prison facilities that foster humane treatment, help to protect law offenders from abuse that might be inflicted by others.

Offenders need also to be protected from themselves. When it comes to capital punishment, there is the risk that some offenders may actively seek execution and thereby allow their own evil impulses to do them in. Some may have a death wish, and others may see it as a way of making a name for themselves. But because human life is sacred and is not ours to take, the state should not become the collaborating partner which facilitates the demise of those who seek their own destruction.

When all of the purposes of punishment are taken into account, the death penalty is reduced to questionable value.

Who Decides?

People decide. Police officers decide whom to arrest; prosecuting attorneys decide for whom they will issue warrants; grand juries decide whom to indict; judges and juries decide whom to convict and what the sentence will be. No matter how well intentioned and no matter how well trained, people make mistakes. It is inevitable.[13] In the matter of capital punishment, it is an irreversible mistake. Once an execution has been carried out, the state can no more restore the life of the mistakenly condemned person than convicted killers can bring their victims back to life. This is not just a hypothetical situation. Documented studies have turned up instances of faulty convictions in capital murder cases where the executions had already been carried out before the miscarriages of justice were discovered.[14]

People are also prejudiced. Whether this prejudice is conscious or not, discrimination results. In 1972, the U.S. Supreme Court (in *Furman v. Georgia*) acknowledged that the death penalty is disproportionately imposed and carried out on the poor, black people, and members of unpopular groups.[15] There is also evidence to suggest that if the victim is a white person, a convicted killer is more likely to receive the death sentence than if the victim is black.[16]

Because God has made all people in his image, one human life is as valuable as the next. Punishments that are as discriminatory as the death sentence can have little place in a nation that would pride itself on providing equal protection[17] for all its citizens.

There are now over 1,000 people on death row in the United States.[18] The federal Bureau of Justice Statistics recently suggested that we may soon see executions carried out at the rate of more than three per week.[19] Even if no more people were to be sentenced to die (and it should be noted that in 1981 the number of people on death row increased at a rate of three per week), we could have an execution every other day for the next six years! That is the prospect we face unless, and until, capital punishment is abolished once and for all.

Walter Berns relates the story of a ship that struck a rock in a stormy gale and sank, leaving only one sailor desperately clinging to a piece of wreckage in the dark of night. Eventually he was washed up onto an unknown and deserted beach. When dawn broke and the sailor was able to rub the salt from his eyes, he looked around to learn where he might be. The only human thing he saw was a gallows. "Thank God," he exclaimed, "civilization!"[20]

Is that the kind of civilization we desire? Can that kind of civilization be said to be in the service of God and for the benefit of the human race (Rom. 13:4)? In Jesus Christ we have a Lord who has been to the gallows for us so that we might not receive the sentence we deserve, but might have life instead. That is the message we bring to a world that is struggling with issues of death and life.

Notes

1. In Missouri, capital murder cases have two phases. In the first the jury decides on guilt or innocence. If a guilty verdict is returned, the trial then has a second phase to assess punishment. Either the death penalty or life in prison with no parole for 50 years can be recommended by the jury.

2. Theodore G. Tappert, ed., *The Book of Concord* (Philadelphia: Fortress Press, 1959), 345.

3. See Frederick W. Danker, *Benefactor* (St. Louis: Clayton Publishing House, 1982), 400–401, for a treatment of how rulers are to be channels of the divine benefits to their subjects and, in return, recipients of public respect.

4. Gerhard Kittel, ed., *Theological Dictionary of the New Testament* IV (Grand Rapids, Mich.: Eerdmans, 1967), 525 n. 11.

5. Walter Bauer, *A Greek-English Lexicon of the New Testament,* 2d ed., revised and augmented by F. Wilbur Gingrich.

6. Otto Eissfeldt, *The Old Testament: An Introduction,* trans. Peter R. Ackroyd (New York: Harper & Row, 1965), 68.

7. Robert H. Loeb, Jr. *Crime and Punishment* (New York: Franklin Watts, 1978), 37.

8. One exception is the work of Isaac Ehrlich, "The Deterrent Effect of Capital Punishment: A Question of Life and Death," *American Economic Review* 65 (1975): 397–417, who calculated that one execution saved seven or eight lives. Subsequent researchers, including Peter Passell, "The Deterrent Effect of the Death Penalty: A Statistical Test," *Stanford Law Review* 28 (1975): 61–80, have found fault with Ehrlich's methodology and have been unable to replicate his findings. [Editor's note: See also Brian Forst's study in this book, chapter 6.]

9. Thorsten Sellin, *The Death Penalty* (Philadelphia: American Law Institute, 1959), 34.

10. Ezzat A. Fattah, *A Study of the Deterrent Effect of Capital Punishment with Special Reference to the Canadian Situation* (Canada: Department of the Solicitor General, 1973).

11. Kilman Shin, *Death Penalty and Crime: Empirical Studies* (Fairfax, Va.: Center for Economic Analysis, 1978), 29. See also "Study Links Executions, Homicides," *St. Louis Post-Dispatch,* 9 March 1981.

12. See Shin, *Death Penalty and Crime,* 184; and Loeb, *Crime and Punishment,* 38.

13. See Charles L. Black Jr., *Capital Punishment: The Inevitability of Caprice and Mistake,* 2d ed., aug. (New York: W. W. Norton, 1981), for a discussion of the factors that may produce errors.

14. Hugo A. Bedau, ed., *The Death Penalty in America* (Chicago: Aldine, 1964), 434–52.

15. Although blacks make up only 15 percent of the population of the United States, they represent 41 percent of the inmates of death row. This is not because black people commit 41 percent of the capital murders, but because they tend to be poor, less able to make bond and do the research and interviews that may help their case, and less able to afford quality counsel.

16. "Murder Victims' Race Important," *Sojourners* 7 (February 1978): 7.

17. U.S. Const., amend. XIV, sec. 1.

18. The NAACP put the number at 1,038 as of June 20, 1982.

19. "Nation May See Executions at Rate of Three a Week," *St. Louis Post-Dispatch,* 19 July 1982.

20. Walter Berns, *For Capital Punishment: Crime and the Morality of the Death Penalty* (New York: Basic Books, 1979), 3.

PART SIX

SOCIETY'S VIOLENT SPIRIT AND THE NEED FOR RESTORING JUST ORDER

[18]

Capital Punishment

John Langan

IN MAJOR METROPOLITAN AREAS, it is now customary for the late evening news to begin with a review of the day's murders. This serves as a factual counterpart to the innumerable fictional murders of prime-time entertainment. Crime and the ineffectiveness of our society's response to it have been an important theme in many recent elections. The liberal climate that once led many people to expect that the ten-year moratorium on executions that obtained in the U.S. from 1967 to 1977 might lead to abolition, either by a definitive Supreme Court decision holding that the death penalty was unconstitutional or by public forbearance, now seems irretrievably remote. While the U.S. Catholic Conference's administrative board in its election-year statement on political responsibility reaffirmed its continuing opposition to the death penalty,[1] all three major candidates in the recent election made clear their support for the death penalty. It is only in an atypical jurisdiction such as the District of Columbia that the death penalty fails to find widespread public support. In a November 1992 referendum mandated by Congress, the citizens of the District refused to authorize the imposition of the death penalty. But such victories for opponents of capital punishment are rare.

SOURCE: John Langan, "Capital Punishment," *Theological Studies* 54 (March 1993). Reprinted by permission of *Theological Studies*.

Teaching of the Philippine Bishops

We should notice, however, that the debate over capital punishment is not confined to very violent societies such as the U.S. and South Africa. It has surfaced recently in the Philippines, where President Fidel Ramos has made the reinstatement of capital punishment part of his anti-crime program. This requires a change in the 1986 Constitution, which abolished the death penalty, a change which was opposed by the Catholic Bishops' Conference of the Philippines in a statement issued on 24 July 1992. This statement, which strongly reflects the influence of the 1980 statement of the U.S. Catholic bishops,[2] provides a useful starting point for seeing how this issue is now approached in Catholic teaching. Because of the long history of church acceptance of the death penalty and because of the explicit scriptural authorization of the death penalty, it is not possible for the Philippine bishops to argue that the death penalty is inherently and necessarily a violation of the biblical commandment against killing or that it is an intolerable violation of human rights. Rather, they have to offer a more complex argument which is more prudential than demonstrative but which illuminates connections between capital punishment and other contemporary concerns of the church. Their line of argument falls into three parts: (1) a critical assessment of arguments for the death penalty, (2) a setting forth of objections to the death penalty, and (3) the recommendation of alternative ways to bring crime under control.

Criticism of Death Penalty Arguments

The Philippine bishops begin by affirming that "the abolition of the death penalty by the 1986 Constitution was a very big step towards a practical recognition of the dignity of every human being created to the image and likeness of God and of the value of human life from its conception to its natural end."[3] Three aspects of this preliminary judgment are noteworthy. First, it is about means, not ends ("a very big step"). Second, it is about practice and what makes values effective. Third, it is about values that the Catholic community regards as morally urgent and supremely important (human dignity and the value of human life). The first two points remind us that the bishops are dealing here in the realm of policy and prudential judgments. In fact, one of the Philippine politicians who opposes the bishops' stand, Senator Ernesto Herrera, observes that both sides agree that life is sacred and must be protected and that "we differ only in our approaches."[4] But it is the third point that accounts for the insistence with which those who call for the abolition of capital punishment pursue their cause.

The bishops, along with most observers, believe that the actual deterrent effect of capital punishment as a practice has not been established. Their response to the essentially retributivist claim that capital punishment contributes intrinsically to the restoration of the order of justice is to insist that what society needs is "a humane and Christian approach to punishment."[5] The last point may well be true; but here it amounts to begging the question. The bishops do better in rejecting the standard analogy comparing the criminal to a diseased organ, an analogy which goes back at least to Thomas Aquinas. Against such a comparison they object that the "human being has a value in himself/herself and is the goal or purpose of the human body."[6] One can discuss capital punishment as a means to protect certain values, but one ought not to make the life of the individual person a means.

Objections to the Death Penalty

Two of the objections that the bishops make to the death penalty are familiar and obvious, namely, the possibility of error in applying it and the congruence between abolition and the teaching of Jesus on God's mercy. But two of the other objections are more theologically provocative. The bishops maintain that "the imposition of the death penalty will have a bias against the poor" and that therefore it is not compatible with the church's preferential option for the poor.[7] Given the great differences in access to quality legal advocacy in most societies, including both the Philippines and the U.S., one can normally expect that the recipient of punishment will be a poor person who does not have the financial resources or the educational background or the social sophistication to mount an effective defense against capital charges. There are also, we should note, a certain number of highly publicized cases where prominent or affluent people are on trial where prosecutors and other officials make strenuous efforts to ensure that there is no appearance of favoritism or softness in the way they are treated. Proponents of the death penalty would be correct in observing that most of the victims of violent crimes are themselves poor, and they would also be correct in arguing that, if capital punishment is right, then the way to correct inequitable application of the penalty is to apply greater severity to the affluent or well connected. This reply may have some merit in the abstract, but in most societies we are more likely to get equivalent treatment of rich and poor defendants if criminal penalties do not include capital punishment. It is also important for the legitimacy of the criminal justice system that justice be seen to be done; patterns which support the inference that one class or ethnic group fares better under the system undermine its legitimacy.

The other theologically significant consideration that the Philippine bishops offer is their claim that supporting the abolition of capital punishment is a better way of defending their stand for life. Their language here suggests that the connection between their views on capital punishment and on such life issues as abortion and euthanasia is not one of logical inference and is more a matter of affinity, of public perception, and of tactics. The proposal to connect Catholic positions on capital punishment, disarmament, war, aid to the poor, abortion, and euthanasia is the substance of the "seamless garment" approach to life issues championed by Cardinal Bernardin of Chicago and by many U.S. bishops.[8] This approach has recognized that the church finds allies and supporters in different parts of the political spectrum for different parts of its program for the defense of life; and it has attempted to make a pedagogical and persuasive effort to urge people to develop a broader understanding of what kinds of social and legal measures are needed to protect human life in our time.

But such an approach which attempts to group a range of seemingly disparate issues under one rubric suffers from two inherent limitations. The first is that the connection between norm and practice varies across the range of issues so that church teaching endorses no abortions, lower levels of nuclear and conventional weapons, no executions, some possible uses of military force, and some withholding of life-sustaining measures. This variability does not show that the church's positions on the defense of life are mutually inconsistent; rather, it shows that other values are being taken seriously and that they require a more complex set of prescriptions than if one focused on life to the exclusion of other values. The other limitation is that since the separate issues are connected by the common thread of their reference to life and not by the chains of inference and deduction, they remain distinguishable and separable. The person who affirms the absolute prohibition of abortion and refuses to accept the recent rejection of capital punishment by most conferences of bishops and by the most recent popes is not guilty of logical inconsistency.

Alternative Recommendation

On the most positive side, the Philippine bishops make a set of recommendations for alternatives to the death penalty that are to a large extent, I believe, applicable to U.S. society as well. These include: a comprehensive attack on poverty; reform of the criminal-justice system; reform of the penal system; dealing with such causes of crime as gangs, drugs, and gambling; cleansing of the police and the military; a lessening of the atmosphere of violence; and enforcement of the ban on wearing guns in public places.[9] Since every execution comes at the final stage of a history of personal conflict, destructive behavior, police and judicial processes, society needs to review on a continuing basis how it can alter the various stages in this history so that it does not end with yet another person being violently expelled from the human community and from life in this world. The murders and capital crimes which occur in a society are both the work of the individuals who commit them and who must be pre-vented from repeating them and an expression of the values and conflicts that are prevalent in society at large.

In sum, then, what the Philippine bishops give us in their recent statement is a compact statement of a tripartite case against the death penalty: objecting to reasons for it, stating reasons for abolition, and proposing alternatives that do not involve the taking of yet another human life. This is similar in structure to the 1980 statement of the U.S. bishops on the same topic; and it is in fact what is needed when a social practice is to be assessed which affects a number of dis-tinct values and whose moral acceptability or unacceptability is not to be set-tled simply by the invocation of a single value. What this sort of argument yields is a reflective assessment of a practice and its connections with a range of values. It is less clear and less decisive as an assessment of particular actions. As I will argue later, it may even be true that a particular criminal (e.g., Ted Bundy) is justly executed but that capital punishment itself is a generally bad practice which ought to be terminated.

Societal Considerations

The connection between capital punishment and the values of society at large is central to the argument of a provocative essay by Mark Tushnet, a professor of law at Georgetown University, who observes that "society's position on the ex-istence and use of the death penalty both expresses and constitutes the kind of society it is."[10] Tushnet draws a contrast between a remark made by Jürgen Habermas on the inappropriateness of the death penalty in Germany after the Nazi period and his own reading of the current moral condition of American society. He says: "Abolition of capital punishment, I suggest, would amount to a similar denial of the actual condition of society in the United States. That is, it falsifies the experience of that society to claim that it has gotten beyond the retributive urges that most easily justify the practice of capital punishment."[11] Abolition of capital punishment in Tushnet's view would be like eliminating a symptom rather than a disease; it would encourage a "misplaced self-satisfaction" and might have distorting effects on other social institutions. This last claim is not easy to specify or to substantiate. Tushnet's view also has the disturbing implication that on this matter the U.S. lags behind Germany. This may well be a crudely progressivist simplification of Tushnet's view, which is probably closer to a claim that Germany has by painful historical experience learned the indispensability of extreme caution in the taking of human life.

Where Tushnet's view seems to me to be particularly illuminating is on the rise and subsidence of the movement to abolish capital punishment. He observes: "Law is an effort to move from the world as it is—committed to social violence—to a different world. Abolition could then be seen as a bridge that, by prefiguring a world that had abandoned its commitment to social violence, might lead us there."[12] The distance from where we are as a society to what kind of society we would be without capital punishment and without the attitudes toward capital punishment that legitimate it would on this understanding simply have been too great to sustain. The moratorium that began in 1967 and the expectations aroused by the Supreme Court's 1972 decision requiring the revision of the existing death-penalty statutes confronted the separate states and the country as a whole with a choice of either reaffirming the death penalty or of moving to a new attitude toward violence. Most of the states (36 out of 50) decided to keep the death penalty in a modified and constitutionally acceptable form. The bridge to a new order of society, in this area at least, collapsed. The conclusion that Tushnet draws from this episode is that we ought not to press for the abolition of the death penalty, but that we can criticize the method by which it is applied so that arbitrariness is diminished. He writes: "One can reject abolitionism as a denial of the society's commitment to social violence and simultaneously object to the manner in which the death penalty is administered."[13]

In Tushnet's view there is no real social base for abolition. As he puts the matter, "Support for abolition does not emerge from a social group with an alternative vision of the world."[14] This is a formulation that needs some clarification or amplification; for it seems to me that abolitionists do have some vision of a nonviolent, nonvindictive form of society; but it also seems to me doubtful that they are effectively identified with one or more coherent interest groups (such as religious or ethnic groups, professional or trade associations, regional groups) that are constituted independently of the capital-punishment issue. The constituency for abolition, with the exception of African Americans and some church groups, is simply an ad hoc coalition of moral conviction.

One way of reading Tushnet's position is to take it as an announcement that abolition is not a politically appealing cause and does not generate sufficient public support. This is true, but it does not seem to require more than the ability to read opinion polls or the election returns. But it can also be taken as making a more controversial and interesting point, namely, that abolition is a case whose time has not yet come, a cause that has not yet "ripened." Abolition is the right thing to do, but society is not yet ready to accept this, and so it is best not to press the matter now; indeed, it may even be wrong to do so. This is a complex judgment that combines a moral position with a reading of social and political history. It may seem to belong to the realm of politics rather than jurisprudence or ethics. But we should notice that it expresses an attitude that we should only adopt toward a practice which has both positive and negative aspects and whose continuation for an interim we can contemplate with some equanimity. To grasp the point here, it may be helpful to reflect how we would react to a parallel treatment of slavery. Tushnet's piece does not resolve the underlying ethical issues about capital punishment, but it does direct our attention to important and difficult questions about the legitimacy of violence in our culture and about the anomalous position of the U.S. as the main practitioner of capital punishment among advanced industrial societies even while it is a country which tolerates notably higher murder rates, especially in its cities, than any nation of even remotely comparable economic and educational levels.[15]

A Deterrent to Violent Crime

The public is rightly concerned about the rise in crime, especially violent crime. The FBI Uniform Crime Reports for 1990 recorded over 1.8 million crimes of violence, of which 23,440 were cases of murder and non-negligent manslaughter. This is up from 1.25 million crimes of violence in 1983, of which 19,310 were murders.[16] This rise, it should be observed, occurred precisely during a time when capital punishment was being more widely used. Against these figures we should set the fact that there have been only 18,880 official executions recorded in the entire history of the U.S., of which 180 have occurred since the reinstitution of the death penalty in 1977. Capital punishment resolves only a minute fraction of the crime problem that so troubles our society. Secondly, defense of capital punishment rests to a large extent on confusing two issues: whether a given individual has been justly executed, and whether capital punishment is a justifiable practice. In a case such as the trial and execution of Ted Bundy, the defender of capital punishment can point to many considerations that justify the execution of such a heinous killer, who is at the same time an intelligent and persuasive individual. This seems to establish the rightness of capital punishment in at least some cases. But it mistakes the actual problem of administering capital punishment when most of the condemned are neither so chillingly psychopathic nor so photogenic as Mr. Bundy, when in fact the great majority of them are black, poor, and emotionally disturbed, and when many of them are mentally retarded and ill equipped to understand their situation.

A case that illustrates the unsatisfactoriness of the way the death penalty is currently understood and applied in the U.S. is the Penry case. Johnny Paul Penry was convicted of rape and murder committed in 1979. Rebecca Dick-Hurwitz summarizes his capabilities thus:

> Johnny Paul Penry was twenty-two years old at the time of his crime and had an IQ measured through the years as between 50 and 63. His social maturity has

been assessed as equivalent to that of a nine or ten year old child. He had always exhibited erratic behavior, had never finished first grade and had labored for a year trying to learn how to print his name.[17]

The U.S. Supreme Court held that the execution of the mentally retarded did not in itself violate the Eighth Amendment's prohibition of cruel and unusual punishment, though they did decide that in the Penry case insufficient attention had been [given] to mental retardation as a mitigating circumstance. As Dick-Hurwitz pointedly observes:

> It is beyond dispute that the mentally retarded face profound difficulties when dealing with the criminal justice system. Many of these problems have the potential for catastrophic consequences. *Penry* is a case in point. This unreliability should be a matter of grave concern to the Supreme Court, particularly with regard to the imposition of the death sentence. In light of past decisions, the Court should make every effort to see that this "extreme sanction, suitable to the most extreme of crimes" is reserved only for the most culpable of criminals. Mentally retarded defendants such as Johnny Paul Penry simply do not fit this description.[18]

The abiding difficulty here is that even if a future Supreme Court decision were to rule out capital punishment of the gravely retarded, the death penalty will still be imposed on a certain number of people who have only a marginal capacity for deliberation and for moral agency. It is neither likely nor desirable that capital punishment will ever rise to the level of frequency where it becomes American society's standard response to murder or where it becomes a reasonably reliable deterrent. Rather, it serves as an intermittent and ominous response by a society that tolerates the careless and extensive distribution of guns and the deterioration of basic living conditions for the poor, while it declines to invest in improving educational and correctional institutions and makes the unrealistic depiction of extensive and brutal violence a central part of its entertainment and its imaginative life. It is simply not credible for such a society to present its reliance on capital punishment as a sign of its deep and passionate commitment to justice.

The conclusion reached in an ecumenical statement by the Christian religious leaders of Arizona, including Bishop O'Brien of Phoenix, seems both right and reasonable: "The death penalty cannot be justified as a legitimate tool of society's justice system."[19]

Notes

1. U.S. Catholic Conference Administrative Board, "Political Responsibility: Revitalizing American Democracy," *Origins* 21 (1991): 313–23, at 319.

2. U.S. Catholic Conference, "Statement on Capital Punishment," *Origins* 19 (1980): 373–77.

3. Catholic Bishops' Conference of the Philippines, "Restoring the Death Penalty: 'A Backward Step,'" *Catholic International* 3 (1992): 886–55, at 886.

4. Ibid., 887.

5. Ibid., 886.

6. Ibid. The analogy can be found in *Summa theologiae* 2–2, q. 64, a. 2.

7. Ibid., 887.

8. The most prominent presentation of the "seamless garment" approach was the Gannon Lecture given by Cardinal Joseph Bernardin at Fordham University in December 1983 and published in *Origins* 13 (1983): 491–95. A perceptive account of the political uses and limitations of this approach can be found in Timothy A. Brynes, "How 'Seamless' a Garment? The Catholic Bishops and the Politics of Abortion," *Journal of Church and State* 33 (1991): 17–35.

9. "Restoring the Death Penalty," 887–88.

10. Mark Tushnet, "Reflections on Capital Punishment: One Side of an Uncompleted Discussion," *Journal of Law and Religion* 7 (1989): 21–31, at 24.

11. Ibid.

12. Ibid., 26.

13. Ibid., 27.

14. Ibid., 30.

15. Here I have deleted a lengthy section of the essay on "Special Problems for the Medical Profession." It discusses whether patients who are found to be mentally disturbed, and therefore incompetent to be executed, can rightly be treated by psychiatrists so that they can be restored to competence and then executed; and whether it is right for health care professionals to participate in conducting an execution [editor].

16. Federal Bureau of Investigation, Uniform Crime Reports, 1990, cited in *World Almanac 1992* (New York: Pharos, 1991), 954.

17. Rebecca Dick-Hurwitz, "*Penry v. Lynaugh:* The Supreme Court Deals a Fatal Blow to Mentally Retarded Capital Defendants," *University of Pittsburgh Law Review* 51 (1990): 699–725, at 700.

18. Ibid., 725. The quotation is from the Supreme Court's decision in *Gregg v. Georgia,* 428 U.S. 153, 187 (1976).

19. Arizona Ecumenical Leaders, "The Retaliatory Violence of Capital Punishment," *Origins* 21 (1992): 517–18, at 517.

[19]

Capital Punishment as the Unconstitutional Establishment of Religion: A Girardian Reading of the Death Penalty

James McBride

When the switch is thrown, the prisoner "cringes," "leaps," and "fights the straps with amazing strength." "The hands turn red, then white, and the cords of the neck stand out like steel bands." The prisoner's limbs, fingers, toes, and face are severely contorted. The force of the electrical current is so powerful that the prisoner's eyeballs sometimes pop out and "rest on [his] cheeks." The prisoner often defecates, urinates, and vomits blood and drool.

"The body turns bright red as its temperature rises," and the prisoner's "flesh swells and his skin stretches to the point of breaking. Sometimes the prisoner catches on fire, particularly if [he] perspires excessively." Witnesses hear a loud and sustained sound "like bacon frying," and "the sickly sweet smell of burning flesh" permeates the chamber. This "smell of frying human flesh in the immediate neighborhood of the chair is sometimes bad enough to nauseate even the Press representatives who are present." In the meantime, the prisoner almost literally boils: "the temperature in the brain itself approaches the boiling point of

SOURCE: From James McBride, "Capital Punishment as the Unconstitutional Establishment of Religion: A Girardian Reading of the Death Penalty," *Journal of Church and State* 37 (spring 1995). Reprinted by permission.

water, and when the post-electrocution autopsy is performed "the liver is so hot that doctors have said that it cannot be touched by the human hand." The body frequently is badly burned and disfigured.[1]

So argued Justice William Brennan in his 1985 dissent to the denial of a writ of certiorari in *Glass v. Louisiana* in which he compared electrocution to "disemboweling while alive, drawing and quartering, public dissection, burning alive at the stake, crucifixion, and breaking at the wheel."[2] Although capital punishment was temporarily struck down by the High Court in 1972 in the *Furman v. Georgia* decision on the grounds that its arbitrary and discriminatory application was "cruel and unusual punishment,"...that case was overturned in 1976 by the *Gregg v. Georgia* decision which held that statutory adoption of sentencing guidelines would eschew constitutional impediments to the death penalty.... Today thirty-eight states retain capital punishment and use such methods of execution as electrocution (13), the gas chamber (7), lethal injection (24), hanging (3), and the firing squad (2). Those executed since *Gregg* number 270, including thirty-eight in 1993, the largest annual figure since capital punishment was resumed in 1977 with the execution of Gary Gilmore before a Utah all-volunteer firing squad.[3] Although executions numbered thirty-one in 1994, the death penalty has been carried out fifteen times so far in 1995 (April)—a record-setting pace. Michael Radelet, a sociologist and one of the country's leading opponents of the death penalty, has documented among those 270 cases at least fifteen botched executions, including eight electrocutions, ranging from instances where the prisoner's head and/or leg caught on fire and eyeballs literally exploded to taking up to one hour and four minutes to kill the victim.[4]

The Irrelevance of Factual Innocence

As horrendous as these figures and the methods of execution are to critics of the death penalty, many observers have been even further appalled by the High Court's *Herrera v. Collins* decision in 1993 which, by a 6–3 margin, rejected the appeal of Lionel Torres Herrera to overturn his murder conviction on the grounds that new evidence demonstrated his factual innocence. Although the Court has made an exception for habeas relief in cases of a fundamental miscarriage of justice,[5] such relief is forthcoming "'only where the prisoner *supplements* his constitutional claim with a colorable showing of factual innocence' *Kuhlmann v. Wilson*, 477 U.S. 436, 454 (1986) [emphasis added]. We have never held that it extends to free-standing claims of actual innocence. Therefore, the exception is inapplicable here."[6] Since appeals are based on issues of law rather than those of fact, claims of actual innocence alone are deemed irrelevant. In his dissent to Chief Justice William Rehnquist's majority opinion, Justice Harry Blackmun lamented that "the execution of a person who can show that he is innocent comes perilously close to simple murder."[7] In his most recent book, *In Spite of Innocence: Erroneous Convictions in Capital Cases,* Michael Radelet has argued that at least 139 innocent persons in the United States have been condemned to death since 1900, twenty-three of whom have been executed,[8] and his colleague Hugo Adam Bedau, a philosophy professor at Tufts University, has suggested that in the United States perhaps as many as four innocent persons per year have been convicted of murder since 1900.[9] The Rehnquist opinion admits that, although unlikely, there exists the possibility of convicting and executing the innocent, legitimated in the eyes of the Chief Justice by the admission of human fallibility, something on the order of a judicial "law of double effect" that the state is blameless when the execution of a factually innocent person is foreseen but not intended.

Although the Chief Justice opined in *Herrera* that "the central purpose of any system of criminal justice is to convict the guilty and free the innocent,"[10] such is not the case in the appeals process. For according to the logic of the majority opinion in *Herrera,* prisoners are not condemned because they are guilty; they are guilty because they are condemned. In other words, whether or not they committed the crime is irrelevant; insofar as they stand condemned, they are legally guilty, regardless of the question of their factual innocence. Accordingly, the execution of a factually innocent person, if condemned, would violate neither the Eighth Amendment's prohibition of "cruel and unusual punishment" nor the Fourteenth Amendment's protection of an individual's right to "due process." This conclusion suggests that something is sorely amiss: the standards of justice, fairness, and human decency are being perverted, but to what end? What purpose does it serve to execute the condemned, regardless of the question of their factual innocence?

The Interests of the State: Deterrence and Retributive Justice

What seemed manifestly unfair to the three justices who dissented—Blackmun, David Souter, and John Paul Stevens—is legitimated on the grounds that, particularly in capital cases, more than the fate of the individual is at stake. Citing the *Patterson* case (1977), Rehnquist noted that "due process does not require that every conceivable step be taken, at whatever cost. . . . To conclude otherwise would all but paralyze our system for the enforcement of the criminal law."[11] Hence, the claim of actual innocence is not sufficient to overcome either the permissible legal grounds for appeal (a primarily constitutional rather than factual claim) or the utilitarian arguments of economic costs.[12] The Rehnquist opinion suggests that something else is at stake which outweighs the fate of the individual: the fate of society itself as represented by the state. In other words, the criminal justice system must operate efficiently in order to preserve the interests of society which clearly, in his view, come first.

Those interests are allegedly served by the death penalty itself, for its purpose is not merely to punish the individual but to protect the social order at large. For example, Donald Hook and Lothar Kahn have argued that (based on the average of 1985–86) some 196 persons on death row each year have had previous homicide convictions before the conviction for which they stand condemned. "This means that, out of the group of offenders alone, 196 innocent lives were lost as a result of the release of murderers. Extrapolating from these figures and taking into rough account the increase in the U.S. population since 1900, we may estimate that between 1900 and 1986, at least 1,380 *additional* and unnecessary murders occurred as a result of our having released convicted murderers."[13] According to this utilitarian calculus, the loss of twenty-three innocents to the death penalty (as calculated by Michael Radelet) is a small price to pay compared to the 1,380 innocent victims murdered.

Hence, capital punishment has been frequently justified as a form of deterrence. It is a tautology that dead murderers do not rise from their graves to kill again. However, the argument for deterrence means more than incapacitation. It suggests that persons who would otherwise kill are deterred from murder by the threat of capital punishment for their contemplated crime. But as the majority opinion admitted in *Gregg,* "there is no convincing evidence either supporting or refuting"[14] the deterrent effect of the death penalty. However, Justices Potter Stewart, Powell, and Stevens speculated that common sense says that there must be others for whom capital punishment serves as a significant deterrent, e.g., cases of premeditated murder. Yet as Justice Brennan pointed out in *Furman,* that presumes "a particular type of potential criminal"—one who would be deterred by the death penalty but would not be by life imprisonment. "On the face of it," wrote Brennan, "the assumption that such persons exist is implausible."[15] "No one can know how many people have refrained from murder,"[16] insisted the late Justice Marshall, since, as one sociologist has adroitly pointed out, deterrence is an *"inherently unobservable* phenomenon. . . . We never *observe* someone omitting an act."[17] Yet, despite the fact that there is neither empirical nor logical proof for the supposed deterrent effect of the death penalty, the Chief Justice at the time of the *Furman* decision, Warren Burger, suggested that it is up to opponents of the death penalty to conclusively prove that capital punishment is not a deterrent! "To shift the burden of proof to the States is to provide an illusory solution to an enormously complex problem,"[18] wrote Burger. Inverting the established rules of debate, Burger's argument echoes the claim to magisterial authority exercised by religious institutions which substantiate truth claims by fiat. Yet, this crypto-theological justification of the death penalty reflects the belief adapted by his successor, Chief Justice William Rehnquist (and implicitly affirmed in *Herrera*), that the presumption is granted the interests of the state and society-at-large over that of the individual. As Ernest van den Haag, one of the most vocal academic defenders of the death penalty, has concluded, "wherefore I prefer over- to under-protection."[19] In light of the *Herrera* decision, this endorsement of the deterrence position (despite the lack of either empirical or logical proof) indicates that the support of the majority for the constitutionality of the death penalty is derived from a deep-seated *irrational* belief in the need to execute the condemned, even though they might be factually innocent, in order to defend the well-being of the social order as a whole.

The Court's overriding interest in the protection of society as a legitimation of capital punishment also appears in another guise: that of retributive justice. In the stead of friends and family members who might feel obligated by a desire for vengeance, the state *in principle* acts to enforce the *lex talionis*—"an eye for an eye," a life for a life—by putting to death those it deems responsible for murder. Admittedly, wrote Justice Stewart in *Gregg*, "Retribution is no longer the dominant objective in criminal law (*Williams v. New York*, 337 U.S. 241, 248 (1949)), but neither is it a forbidden objective nor one inconsistent with our respect for the dignity of men."[20] Citing his own opinion in *Furman*, Stewart claimed that capital punishment safeguards "the stability of a society governed by law. When people begin to believe that organized society is unwilling or unable to impose upon criminal offenders the punishment they 'deserve,' then there are sown the seeds of anarchy—of self-help, vigilante justice, and lynch laws."[21] Stewart's claim concerning retributive justice puts the deterrence argument in a new light, for *it is not that the death penalty deters criminals from acts of violence* (there is no proof for that assertion), *but that capital punishment deters law-abiding citizens from vigilantism.* Putting the condemned to death—even if they be factually innocent—is therefore a surrogate for the bloodletting that would otherwise ensue if the state did not substitute its own ritual of government-sponsored executions for the extra-legal spiral of citizen violence.

Yet here there is a significant shift in the argument from legal justifications, based upon the guilt and innocence of the individual, to manipulating the psychic economy of the body politic. The death penalty is justified not as a legal recourse to punish the individual but rather as a social mechanism to vent the violence which would otherwise destroy the social order. It is in this context that a Girardian reading of the death penalty might be offered, that is, that capital punishment is essentially a religious ritual of the state.

René Girard's Theory of Religion

Although most mainstream religious organizations in the United States today oppose the death penalty,[22] the late Justice Thurgood Marshall noted in *Furman* that capital punishment had its origins in colonial America in religious prohibitions mandated by the Old Testament. Capital offenses in the Massachusetts Bay Colony included "idolatry, witchcraft, blasphemy, murder, assault in sudden anger, sodomy, buggery, adultery, statutory rape, rape, manstealing, perjury in a capital trial, and rebellion."[23] The incremental secularization of the state in the nineteenth century reduced the number of capital crimes and loosened them from their religious moorings. Yet even today, as Justice Brennan has observed, there seems to be a barbaric similarity between electrocution and former religiously identified methods of capital punishment. How, he asked in a 1986 speech at Harvard Law School, can "'frying in a chair' be distinguished from burning at the stake?"[24] While, on its face, this relationship seems limited to a physiological similarity, René Girard's theory demonstrates that this similarity is not merely incidental, but rather substantive.

Girard argues that violence is a product of mimetic rivalries that are endemic to all human societies. In that human beings model themselves on each other, they imitate the attributes of their respected elders and peers and seek to acquire their emblematic signs of social status. Desire (variously described as "natural" or "instinctive") is in fact derivative of this primary social dynamic. Hence, when violence erupts among individuals over social status or possessions, it has a potential which far exceeds the instinctual aggression of the animal kingdom. Because of the clan structure of human societies, violence is intimately tied to retributive justice, begetting a spiral of morally based vengeance.[25] Invoking the language of the medical model, Girard suggests that such violence infects the body politic, and, like the physical body, can only be overcome through an inoculation of what infects the body. Violence is therefore both the disease and the cure. "Only violence can put an end to violence," he argues. "The aim is to achieve a radically new kind of violence, truly decisive and self-contained, a form of violence that will put an end once and for all to violence itself."[26] Girard has noted in numerous works that this new kind of violence could be found in the sacrifice of a scapegoat which appeared in Western culture not only as a religious fixture among the Hebrews and the Greeks but also as the very foundation of Christendom: the Christ as the scapegoat of humanity.[27] Through the suffering and death of the scapegoat, the violence which convulses the social order and threatens its very foundation is cathartically exhausted.

Although a substitute for the original transgressor, the scapegoat as surrogate victim is more than a proxy for the perpetrator of an isolated incident. On the contrary, the scapegoat embodies the very meaning of transgression and bears the weight of collective hatred expressed by members of the community toward all those who violate the norms and persons of the social order. Girard notes that in ancient Hellenic society, the scapegoat or *pharmakos* was selected from a separate class of surrogate victims, drawn largely from foreigners, slaves, women, and children.[28] The surrogate was most often dragged through the streets to absorb, as it were, the hostilities which beguiled the community—at large. Likewise, in the Christian tradition, Jesus—the "lamb of God" who dies for us, *pro nobis*—suffers the indignities of the stations of the cross by which he is made to bear the transgressions of all humanity. Like all scapegoats, he is the screen on which are projected all instances of mimetic rivalry, which are interchangeable and therefore ultimately abstract and impersonal. As a social mechanism designed to vent the violence which would otherwise destroy the social order, the execution of the scapegoat becomes the *sine qua non* for the restoration of a healthy community.

In order to be an effective inoculation, the surrogate victim must be both similar and different from those perceived as transgressors in the body politic: without similarity the transfer of affect from transgressors to surrogate is impossible; without sufficient difference, the violence done to the scapegoat threatens to spill over back into the body politic. That similarity is underwritten by choosing a scapegoat who is recognized for sharing the attributes of all those who are capable of obeying social norms, i.e., a "sane" human being who lives in the midst of the community. But insofar as the scapegoat is a member of a class of transgressors (e.g., foreigners, slaves, etc.), s/he is sufficiently different from members of the community to guarantee that the spasm of violence directed toward the scapegoat will not overflow its channels and flood the society-at-large. Although indicted for a particular crime, it is irrelevant whether the scapegoat is personally innocent or guilty. The scapegoat is categorically guilty. "The persecutors," contends Girard, "do not realize that they chose their victim for inadequate reasons, or perhaps for no reason at all, more or less at random."[29] Since the scapegoat is *tautologically* guilty, s/he is *in fact* guilty in the eyes of members of the society, whether or not s/he committed the crime of which s/he has been accused.

This social mechanism is, however, fraught with certain dangers. If the substitution is too obvious, then the vilification of the surrogate victim is dispelled. The transfer of affect is interrupted and, while the execution of the condemned may take place, the expression of public violence continues to mount precipitously. If the substitution is too obscure, the scapegoat is desymbolized and again the transfer of affect fails to take place. Both of these possibilities, however, may be avoided, especially if the scapegoat is seen as coming from a category of lawbreakers, i.e., a class of potential "criminals," who live amidst the walks of everyday life.

Hence, this social dynamic is precarious. The irrational substitution of the scapegoat for transgressors-at-large is carried out on an unconscious level, for to consciously recognize this displacement of hostility is to risk its success. The effectiveness of the religious expiation of violence from society is therefore predicated on misunderstanding. That is to say, only insofar as this religiously based social mechanism is misunderstood can it save the social order from anarchy. The members of the community must believe the scapegoat to be guilty even though s/he may be factually innocent.

The Death Penalty Revisited

In light of the *Herrera* decision, capital punishment may be read as a religious ritual, practiced by the state in order to vent the hostility directed toward all those who transgress social norms, as was specifically suggested by Justice Stewart in the *Furman* and *Gregg* decisions. As one witness testified before the U.S. Congress, the condemned serves as a "sacrificial lamb"[30] who dies for us and thereby saves us from the spiral of violence which otherwise would surely ensue. Although the overtly religious language which once surrounded this ritual, e.g., in the Massachusetts Bay Colony, has all but disappeared, the religious character of this ritual of the state remains. Indeed, *the very denial of its religious nature,* i.e., its substitutionary dynamic, *is necessary in order for it to effectively exorcise violence from the social order.* In other words, public denial of its religious character supports the proposition that the death penalty is, in fact, a religious ritual. It could not be otherwise, for to acknowledge the substitutionary atonement of the surrogate victim for transgressors-at-large would negate the cathartic release of affect which infects the body politic. The effectiveness of this social mechanism is predicated on the socio-legal destination of the condemned who, according to *Herrera,* is categorically guilty, whether or not s/he is factually innocent.

The surrogate victim comes from a specific class set aside for ritual execution. Whereas in ancient social orders that class included foreigners, slaves, women, and children, the members of this class in modern America are prisoners on death row, today numbering some 2,800. Since the ratio of homicide arrests to death sentences in the United States runs roughly 100 to 1 (1976–80)[31] and the ratio of murder convictions to executions stands currently at about 115 to 1 (1993),[32] it is evident that, consistent with Girard's analysis, those who are executed are chosen arbitrarily and at random. As Justice Brennan argued in *Furman,* "When the punishment of death is inflicted in a trivial number of the cases in which it is legally available, the conclusion is virtually inescapable that it is being inflicted arbitrarily. Indeed, it smacks of little more than a lottery system."[33] Many prisoners have been languishing on death row for up to fifteen years. Even if the death penalty was asserted to be a deterrent to crime (lack of evidence notwithstanding), there are simply far too few executions per year to be effective.[34] Instead, this class of prisoner—or surrogate victim—serves the interest of the state by appealing to a religious reflex that is deeply ingrained in Western culture, that is, to arbitrarily execute a scapegoat in order to transfer and expel the hostilities which characterize everyday life.

This reflex has been most evident in the public reaction to the prosecution and condemnation of "cop-killers." Whereas scapegoating remains largely unconscious in most other cases, "cop-killings" make plain this substitutionary dynamic by consciously recognizing the representative character of both the deceased and the transgressor. According to the legislative intent mandating capital punishment for "cop-killing," the death penalty is imposed not simply because an individual has been killed but because the social order itself has been violated. Unpunished "cop-killing," it is said, would lead to social anarchy, but that is no different from the spiral of violence which is feared would result from morally based retribution in cases involving civilian deaths. To execute a "cop-killer," then, is not only to avenge the death of the individual police officer; it also purges the fear and anger which the populace-at-large feels for being subjected to the lawlessness of everyday life. Those accused of murdering police officers are therefore particularly vulnerable to bearing the full weight of all transgressions since, in the public mind, scapegoating the accused is consciously intended. Yet the desire to execute "cop-killers" is just the tip of the iceberg. That same dynamic is present in all cases of capital punishment since the condemned as a class serve as a means to vent the build-up of violence in society-at-large. The hysteria which drives the bloodlust for capital punishment has more recently been evident in the suggestion from some quarters that HIV-positive persons and PWAs (people with AIDS) who engage in nonconsensual sexual activity be subject to the death penalty as well.[35]

While ideologically speaking the execution of the condemned is couched in terms of the humane termination of life, the prisoner is not permitted to exercise the option of suicide. Condemned prisoners do not have the right to decide for themselves the method or time of execution. There is no room for privacy and individuality here. The condemned is to play a role in the psychic economy of the state which extends far beyond his/her own personal story. As a scapegoat who bears the transgressions of the social order, the body no longer belongs to the inmate, but to the state itself. And as the virtual materialization of Jeremy Bentham's panopticon, death row serves as a prison within a prison, "a cruel, ingenious cage"[36] where the inmates are watched continually, lest the prisoner attempt to take his/her own life. . . .

There is no escape from the eyes of the state, no matter which guard is on duty or whether s/he is in fact conducting surveillance at any given moment. Death row is a state of being—a state of being watched abstractly by the ever-present eye of the state which eliminates the privacy necessary for a sense of human subjectivity. It is not just a waiting for death; it is a process of dying in which the prisoner is eventually reified into a body—a thing indispensable for the social mechanism of expiation. Intervention by prison chaplains to the contrary, the nature of death row produces an anomaly in human society: the living dead. In her book *Dead Man Walking*, Helen Prejean, a member of the Sisters of St. Joseph of Medaille, recalls one visit to the condemned in a Louisiana prison and her revulsion for this process, despite its alleged rationality:

> The reality of this waiting place for death is difficult to grasp. It's not a ward in a hospital where sick people wait to die. People here wait to be taken out of their cells and killed. This is the United States of America and these are government officials in charge and there's a law sanctioning and upholding what is going on here, so it all must be legitimate and just, or so one compartment of my brain tells me, the part that studied civics in high school, the part that wants to trust that my country would never violate the human rights of its citizens. The red block letters say "Death Row." My stomach can read the letters better than my brain.[37]

But however much clergy and other persons religious—even the odd sympathetic guard—may attempt to bring a kind word to the condemned, they cannot unwrite the dehumanizing inscription of power in the very structure of death row.

For those who are insane or have been driven to insanity by their lives on death row, prison authorities have subjected the condemned to psychiatric therapy and in some cases even drug treatment in order to render the prisoner sane enough for execution.[38] Strangely enough, the condemned must be assisted in his/her efforts to resist the inevitable dehumanizing effects of death row so that the process might someday bear fruit in the form of the prisoner's own death. In this ironic double-bind, psychiatric professionals—dedicated to "doing no harm"—have provided both drugs and therapy to make their inmate patients sane enough to submit to a prospect which any sane person would resist. Criminally insane patients are thereby forced to live a ghostly existence in the twilight between insanity and death. Although the courts have sometimes been ambivalent, prison authorities in the past have even encouraged the condemned to undergo life-saving operations in order to preserve the body for execution....

Although the religious dynamic of capital punishment preempts the vigilantism of extra-legal moral retribution, there is always the risk that public inoculation of violence may unleash what it is trying to cure. Hence, the state must ensure that the degree to which the public may witness expiatory violence does not spill over into mimetic behavior. Indeed, it is the very danger of infectious violence that led state authorities in this country to change the manner of execution from publicly staged to privately staged acts.... In his book on the history of public executions, Louis P. Masur cites numerous documents which evince real concern that publicly staged executions threaten the social order itself. "Legislators, editors, ministers, and merchants all decried public hangings as festivals of disorder that subverted morals, increased crimes, excited sympathy with the criminal, and wasted time..." producing, as one politician feared, a "deleterious effect on the public morals."[39] ... Insulated from direct exposure to executions, the public nonetheless was informed of the executions by the medium of mass culture during the nineteenth and early twentieth centuries— the newspapers—lest the citizenry not experience the cleansing effect of the sacrificial killing.

In contemporary America where electronic media has displaced print media as the primary vehicle of mass communication, it should not be surprising that there has been a surge of interest in televising executions of the condemned.... Although it is a matter of some speculation, it is worth noting that the demand for televised executions coincides with the epidemic of murders throughout the country and the concomitant proliferation of guns in the hands of its citizenry. It is as if the alarming spiral of violence begets a public interest in televised executions as a means to alleviate the fears and hostilities which infect the populace.

Although this class of surrogate victims includes both men and women, adults and juveniles, as well as whites and nonwhites, it is evident that some categories of persons in society-at-large are statistically more likely to be assigned to the class of the condemned. In other words, the state, through the criminal justice system, is predisposed toward classing some groups of people as scapegoats. Blacks,[40] the poor,[41] and the illiterate are all disproportionately represented on death row.[42] Although these figures may reflect racial and class bias in the nation as a whole, the presence of the marginalized on the list of the condemned helps to emphasize the difference rather than the similarity of the surrogate victim and to prevent the spillover of violence into mainstream white, predominantly middle-class communities. Perhaps this injustice is most blatantly evident in the case of African Americans. Whereas blacks number some 12 percent of the general population, they constitute 39 percent of those executed since the reinstitution of the death penalty in 1976[43] and nearly 40 percent of those presently on death row.[44] This statistical imbalance was heavily influenced by the race of the murder victim. In perhaps the best-known study on this topic, David Baldus found that, in the state of Georgia, a defendant was 4.3 times more likely to receive the death sentence if the victim was white than if the victim was black.[45] And as the *New York Times* reported in 1991, "although whites represent only 35 percent of murder victims, 85 percent of capital cases brought by local prosecutors involve white victims. Prosecutors have sought the death penalty in one of three murders involving whites; with black victims the ratio drops to 1 in 17."[46] In a culture still infected by the scourge of racism, capital punishment therefore serves as a means to vent the hostility of a predominantly white society by scapegoating blacks as members of a subclass of the condemned rather than executing them as individuals. As the 1990 GAO report to the Congressional Judiciary Committees on "Death Penalty Sentencing" concluded, "the black defendant/white victim combination was the most likely to receive the death penalty."[47]

Cruel and Unusual Punishment and the Establishment of Religion

The Supreme Court ruled over one hundred years ago that the death penalty in itself is not cruel and unusual punishment.[48] In *In re Kemmler*, the justices interpreted the Eighth Amendment to refer to the method of execution and concluded that methods which would ensure a swift and relatively painless death were constitutional, including electrocution, even though the latter may take as much as fifteen to twenty minutes. Supposedly compared to drawing and quartering while alive or burning at the stake, state execution by "modern" methods is far preferable. Despite the lack of evidence, it is presumed that victims of such modern methods suffer far less than they would otherwise, even if it is frankly admitted that such procedures are rarely swift and painless. The courts have seen fit to dismiss claims that the intentional infliction of the death penalty implies any state responsibility for the concomitant death agonies which accompany various methods of execution, including electrocution, lethal injection, hanging, or shooting. Again, the moral law of double effect seems to be invoked whereby the pain inflicted may be foreseen but not intended. Instead it is viewed as an unfortunate side effect: the collateral damage of the state's legitimate purpose.

Yet the *Oxford English Dictionary* defines "cruel" as "causing or characterized by great suffering; extremely painful or distressing."[49] The fact that the death agony may not be as painful as could be imagined by the most monstrous and bestial minds does not make the death agonies of the condemned less "painful or distressing." Ironically, conservative jurists (who insist on a "plain reading" of the text) frequently seem too quick to wash their hands of such responsibilities. In the *Furman* decision, however, Justice Thurgood Marshall argued (following Justice Field's dissent in *O'Neil*)[50] that punishment is "cruel and unusual" wherever it is "excessive."[51] He concluded that, since capital punishment cannot be shown to have a greater deterrent effect than life imprisonment, it is, on its face, excessive.

A Girardian reading would agree with Marshall's conclusion that it is excessive but *not* that it is needlessly excessive. On the contrary, the death penalty is, in fact, *necessarily* excessive because the scapegoat must bear the weight of all transgressors. The scapegoat dies *pro nobis,* for the redemption of the social order, and not merely to pay his own due. On its face, capital punishment is unusual, not just empirically (due to the rarity with which those convicted of capital crimes are executed), but structurally, since paying the blood debt owed by all transgressors guarantees that it will be unusual. *The very purpose of the death penalty is therefore "cruel and unusual punishment"; else it would make no sense at all.*

Yet, it is not only that the death penalty violates the Eighth Amendment's prohibition against "cruel and unusual punishment"; it is also manifestly an establishment of religion—a ritual which is intended to sanctify and reinscribe the law-making and law-preserving violence of the state[52] and to counter the spiral of violence which plagues contemporary America. Although, as Justice Brennan argued in *Furman,* "there is no evidence whatever that utilization of imprisonment rather than death encourages private blood feuds and other disorders,"[53] religion does not need a rational foundation for its beliefs. The existence of capital punishment in thirty-six states and the strong support of the citizenry for the death penalty evidences an irrational belief that public executions spare the public from physical harm. In the religious psychic economy, it is irrelevant whether it does in fact exorcise violence from the body politic....

The precedent of the conscientious objector cases holds forth an interesting perspective on the nature of the death penalty, for it is not only that capital punishment fits the scapegoat model of Girard's theory of religion, it is that, according to legal precedent, a belief or practice may be religious if it holds a parallel position in the lives of the practitioners to that of traditional believers even though they may deny its religious character. It is clear that capital punishment, as practiced by the state, parallels the role of the scapegoat in traditional Western religious belief. Although the religious character of the death penalty may be disavowed by representatives of an allegedly secular state, such a denial in itself is *not* dispositive in determining its religious status. On the contrary, both analysis and evidence show that, despite such a denial, public execution is in fact a form of ritual sacrifice, intended to magically redeem the body politic from the infection of violence....

Whereas it is open to question whether humanist values are religious or nonreligious in particular contexts, there can be little doubt as to what structural function capital punishment plays in the broader social context according to recent Supreme Court precedent: it is the arbitrary execution of a member of the condemned class for the purpose of purging the community of violence, a function which is the essential characteristic of the Western religious tradition. The *Herrera* decision—sanctioning the legal execution of the "factually innocent"—unveils the religious imperative which motivates death penalty advocacy in all capital cases—an unconscious but barely hidden desire for blood sacrifice rooted in the Western paradigm of the sacred social order.

Although a critic of the High Court's interpretation of the religion clauses, Michael McConnell has aptly summarized the Court's separationist tendencies developed over the past twenty years: "what the free exercise clause requires the establishment clause forbids. . . ."[54] Whereas the advocacy of blood sacrifice for the redemption of the social order is permitted under the Free Exercise Clause, it is proscribed to the government under the Establishment Clause. That certainly is the premise which underlies the classic *Lemon* test which has survived despite criticism from numerous legal scholars and Supreme Court justices themselves. Under the *Lemon* test, legislation must show a secular purpose, must neither advance nor inhibit religion, nor involve the state in excessive entanglement with religion.[55] As the above analysis shows, advocates of capital punishment may claim to show a secular purpose for the death penalty, but such claims are disproven by the underlying psychic economy of substitutionary atonement. As a reinscription of state authority, executions enhance the civil religious claims of the state and therefore excessively entangle government with religious soteriology as public policy. Hence, according to the separationist standards which have dominated Supreme Court jurisprudence on the religion clauses, capital punishment appears to be unconstitutional.

However, many constitutional scholars would prefer a more accommodationist viewpoint, one influenced by what was once articulated by former Chief Justice Warren Burger as a "benevolent neutrality" between religion and nonreligion.[56] Under this paradigm, the state should not vigorously assume an antireligious stance and attempt to push religious beliefs and practices into the private sphere, far from the public forum. Instead, government should acknowledge the role which religious beliefs and practices play in the public lives of its citizens and should accommodate those beliefs and practices as long as they do not effectively endorse one religion over another or prefer religion over nonreligion. Yet the accommodationist viewpoint should be no more tolerant of religious practices *by the state* than that of separationists, particularly in light of the fact that accommodationists come from traditional Western religious backgrounds. Religious practices *by the state*—particularly that of blood sacrifice—which mime traditional Western sacred rituals are deeply offensive to both Christian and Jewish faiths, for such practices are, on their face, idolatrous. From the Christian perspective, the secular state uses the death row prisoner in place of the *agnus Dei*. Guilt for such a theological transgression does not lie with the prisoner but with the cultic structure that imposes this religious role on the condemned. By this act the state ascribes to itself a place which Christians reserve for God alone. "The principal crime of the human race, the highest guilt charged upon the world, the whole procuring cause of judgment," wrote the church father Tertullian, "is idolatry.... The essence of *fraud,* I take it, is, that any should seize what is another's, or refuse to another this due; and, of course, fraud done toward man is a name of greatest crime. Well, but idolatry does fraud to God, by refusing to Him, and conferring on others, His honours; so that to fraud it also conjoins *contumely*."[57]

The aura of sanctification which surrounds and embellishes state authority is therefore not merely a matter of invoking God's blessing, as Robert Bellah and other scholars of civil religion have noted,[58] but rather is embedded in the very structure of state power. Historically, Jews and Christians have refused to bow before such idolatrous power, most notably in their persecution by the Roman state for their refusal to acknowledge the divinity of the state in the person of the emperor. Such demands violated the first and primary stipulation of the Mosaic covenant in Exodus 20:3, "You shall have no other Gods before me"— a prohibition reiterated in Isaiah 44:6, "I am the first and the last: there is no other God beside me." Likewise, idolatry violates the spirit of the Christian new covenant, founded on the blood of Christ who died *pro nobis* and undermines the Christocentric exclusivity which animates Christian *koinonia* itself. "This is the reason, my dear brothers, why you must keep clear of idolatry. I say to you as sensible people: judge for yourselves what I am saying. The blessing cup that we bless is a communion with the blood of Christ, and the bread that we break is a communion with the body of Christ. *The fact that there is only one loaf means that, though there are many of us, we form a single body because we all have a share in this one loaf*" (1 Corinthians 10:14–17, emphasis added). It is therefore logical that many religious organizations have opposed the death penalty.[59] These religious traditions are not necessarily pacifist, yet it is evident that capital punishment is more than just violence. It is a particular form of violence—an idolatrous claim by the state over life and death in the community. The death penalty is therefore not just an establishment of religion; it is an endorsement of a particular theological position which prefers its own version of substitutionary atonement over that of Jewish and Christian soteriologies. As Chief Justice Burger himself noted in his description of "benevolent neutrality," "The general principle deducible from the First Amendment and all that has been said by the Court is this: that we will not tolerate either governmentally established religion or governmental interference with religion."[60] The death penalty does both. Hence, it is not only the separationists who should oppose the death penalty on constitutional grounds; it is also believing accommodationists who should condemn capital punishment for *both* legal *and* theological reasons.

Conclusion

The arguments presented above against the death penalty may be regarded by some as eccentric, novel, or extreme, but in actuality they only reflect what has been long recognized in that antecedent of American jurisprudence, English law. In his recently published historical study of public execution in Britain, Harry Potter concluded that "whether imposed in the name of the king, the representative of God on earth, or by priests, or in the name of a society considered as a sacred body, the infliction of the death penalty was seen not just as a punishment for a crime, but as a repudiation by society of the evil in its midst, ridding the land of its blood-guilt."[61] Indeed, Potter notes that the attempt to abolish the death penalty in Britain's post-war era was opposed in the House of Lords by the leading bishops of the Anglican Church on the grounds that it served "a *religious* function."[62] Dr. Mervyn Haigh, the Bishop of Winchester, argued that

> The execution of a murderer is a solemn ritual act and its object is not only to demonstrate that murder does not pay but that it is shameful. The penalty is not only death but death with ignominy. The death penalty fulfills this rule in an unequalled way because of this quasi-religious sense of awe which attaches to it. In wantonly taking a life, the murderer is felt somehow to have invaded the sphere of the sacred and to be guilty of profanity. His impious act can only be countered by imposing on him a penalty which also has a numinous character. This is a deeply rooted belief which cannot be wholly rationalized but should not be summarily dismissed.[63]

Inasmuch as the English common law tradition has left an indelible mark on American jurisprudence, it should not be surprising that a Girardian reading of the American death penalty bears out what remains at heart—objections to the contrary—a religious practice. As two anthropologists noted in their comparative analysis of Aztec ritual sacrifice and American capital punishment, "Just as Aztec ripping out of human hearts was couched in mystical terms of maintaining universal order and well-being of the state...capital punishment in the United States serves to assure many that society is not out of control after all, that the majesty of the Law reigns, and that God is indeed in his heaven."[64] Although English law has no such impediment to the endorsement and adoption of religious practices by Her Majesty's government, the United States Constitution proscribes the state from either the endorsement of religion or the preference of one religious interpretation over another, even if the religious character of the practice is disavowed by the legislature which established it. While the death penalty is opposed by those religious groups who find it to be a violation of the reverence for life, these moral claims against capital punishment as cruel and unusual punishment have fallen short of the constitutional threshold needed for its abolition. A Girardian reading of the death penalty, however, presents an alternative strategy which demonstrates the numinous character of public execution, embraced by the state for the expiation of violence in the American body politic. As such, the death penalty is an establishment of religion which violates the First Amendment. In the name of humanity, in the name of the Constitution, it ought to be abolished.

Notes

1. *Glass v. Louisiana,* 471 U.S. 1080 (1985) at 1086–88.

2. Ibid. at 1084.

3. Some scholars argue that Idaho and Utah's adoption of execution by firing squad, like the now abolished practice of beheading, is based on the Mormon religious principles of "blood atonement." This principle holds that some sins, such as murder, are so heinous that they are not covered by Christ's substitutionary atonement. Instead, such sinners are required literally to spill their own blood in order to receive forgiveness. "The strongest link between blood atonement and mainstream Mormondom exists in the simple fact that to this day the states of Utah and Idaho, unlike the other forty-eight, provide a condemned prisoner the option of dying by firing squad rather than by lethal injection in order that his or her blood might mix with the soil and become that 'smoking incense' that will 'atone for their sins.'" James Coates, *In Mormon Circles: Gentiles, Jack Mormons, and Latter-Day Saints* (Reading, Mass.: Addison-Wesley, 1991), 66.

4. "Post-*Furman* Botched Executions." Documents accompanying affidavit of Michael L. Radelet, 15 April 1992, in appeal of Steven Douglas Hill, State of Arkansas.

5. *Sawyer v. Whitley,* No. 91–6382, 4–6 (1992).

6. *Herrera v. Collins,* No. 91–7328 (1993), Chief Justice William Rehnquist (majority opinion), 13 (emphasis added). Also ibid., at 8: "Claims of actual innocence based on newly discovered evidence have never been held to state a ground for federal habeas relief absent an independent constitutional violation occurring in the underlying state criminal proceeding."

7. Ibid., Justice Harry Blackmun, joined by Justice Souter and Justice Stevens (dissenting opinion), at 18.

8. Michael L. Radelet, Hugo Adam Bedau, and Constance E. Putnam, *In Spite of Innocence: Erroneous Convictions in Capital Cases* (Boston: Northeastern University Press, 1992).

9. Hugo Adam Bedau, *The Case against the Death Penalty* (Washington, D.C.: Capital Punishment Project [ACLU] 1992), 12.

10. *Herrera* at 6.

11. *Patterson v. New York,* 432 U.S. 197 (1977) at 208, cited in *Herrera* at 7–8.

12. Legal theorist Ronald Dworkin heavily criticizes the latter, which favor a single value instrumentalism over the principle of innocence, i.e., the "right" not to be convicted, if innocent. He recommends a normative calculus based upon "multi-value instrumentalism." Although taking the risk of convicting the innocent may reduce economic costs, it also entails a moral cost—the violation of the principle of innocence—not sustained if the guilt elude conviction; see Ronald Dworkin, *A Matter of Principle* (Cambridge: Harvard University Press, 1985).

13. Donald D. Hook and Lothar Kahn, *Death in the Balance: The Debate over Capital Punishment* (Lexington, Mass.: D. C. Heath, 1989), 97.

14. *Gregg* at 185.

15. *Furman* at 301. Justice Brennan further contended that a deterrent effect, even if it were accepted in principle , would be undermined by the present administration of the death penalty which makes it "remote and improbable; in contrast, the risk of long-term imprisonment is near and great." Ibid. at 302.

16. *Furman* at 347.

17. Jack P. Gibbs, *Punishment and Deterrence* (New York: Elsevier, 1975), 3. See Justice Marshall's comment in *Furman* at 347: "This is the nub of the problem and it is exacerbated by the paucity of useful information."

18. *Furman* at 396.

19. Ernest van den Haag, "Refuting Reiman and Nathanson," in *Philosophy of Punishment,* ed. Robert M. Baird and Stuart E. Rosenbaum (Buffalo: Prometheus, 1988), 145.

20. *Gregg* at 183.

21. *Furman* at 308. See Brennan, ibid., at 303. "Moreover, we are told, not only does the punishment of death exert this widespread moralizing influence upon community values, it also satisfies the popular demand for grievous condemnation of abhorrent crimes and thus prevents disorder, lynching, and attempts by private citizens to take the law into their own hands."

22. These organizations include the American Baptist Churches in the USA, American Ethical Union, American Friends Service Committee, The American Jewish Committee, Christ Church (Disciples of Christ), Christian Reformed Church in North America, Church of the Brethren, Church Women United, The Episcopal Church, Fellowship of Reconciliation, Friends Committee on National Legislation, Friends United Meeting, The General Association of Regular Baptists, General Conference Mennonite Church, Lutheran Church in America, Mennonite Central Committee US, The Mennonite Church, The Moravian Church, National Board YWCA of the USA, National Council of the Churches of Christ in the USA, The Orthodox Church in America, Presbyterian Church (USA), Reformed Church in America, Unitarian Universalist Association, United Church of Christ, United Methodist

Church, and United States Catholic Conference; see *The Death Penalty: The Religious Community Calls for Abolition* (Washington, D.C.: National Coalition to Abolish the Death Penalty, National Interreligious Task Force on Criminal Justice, 1988).

23. *Furman* at 335.

24. Associate Justice William Brennan, speech before the Harvard Law School, 5 September 1986.

25. Cf. Justice Marshall's remarks in *Furman* at 333: "[Capital punishment's] precise origins are difficult to perceive, but there is some evidence that its roots lie in violent retaliation by members of a tribe or group itself, against persons committing hostile acts toward group members. Thus, infliction of death as a penalty for objectionable conduct appears to have its beginnings in private vengeance."

26. René Girard, *Violence and the Sacred,* trans. Patrick Gregory (Baltimore, Md.: Johns Hopkins University Press, 1972), 26–27.

27. See René Girard. *Des choses cachée depuis la fondation du monde* (Paris: Bernard Grasset, 1978); and René Girard, *Le bouc émissaire* (Paris: Bernard Grasset, 1982).

28. Girard, *Violence and the Sacred,* 93 ff.

29. Ibid., 81.

30. Hearings on S. 1760 before the Subcommittee on Criminal Laws and Procedures of the Senate Committee on the Judiciary, 90th Cong., 2d sess. (1968), cited in *Furman* at 364.

31. Samuel R. Gross and Robert Mauro, *Death and Discrimination: Racial Disparities in Capital Sentencing* (Boston: Northeastern University Press, 1989), 3.

32. *The Death Penalty: Cruel and Unusual Punishment* (New York: Amnesty International, 1993), and "Execution Update" (New York: Amnesty International, 6 October 1993), 1.

33. Brennan, *Furman* at 293.

34. Executions rose from one in 1977 to thirty-eight in 1993.

35. S. S. Werner, "The Death Penalty: A Solution to the Problem of Intentional AIDS Transmission through Rape," *John Marshall Law Review* 26 (summer 1993): 941–76.

36. Michel Foucault, *Discipline and Punish: The Birth of the Prison,* trans. Alan Sheridan (New York: Pantheon, 1977), 205.

37. Helen Prejean, C.S.J., *Dead Man Walking: An Eyewitness Account of the Death Penalty in the United States* (New York: Random House, 1993), 27–28.

38. While the Supreme Court has ruled that executing the insane is unconstitutional (*Ford v. Wainwright,* 407 U.S. 399 (1986)), such a prisoner may be executed if successfully treated through the use of drugs or therapy. The ruling fits the Girardian theory insofar as insanity makes the surrogate victim too dissimilar from original transgressors to effect the transference of affect through

his or her execution. The pharmacological method of alleviating psychosis in order to carry out the death sentence was used in the state of Louisiana prior to *State v. Perry*, 608 So. 2d 594 (La. 1992), which held that a death row inmate could not be forcibly administered antipsychotic drugs in order "to make him sane enough to be executed." Again, from the Girardian perspective, rendering the person "sane," i.e., similar, through artificial means, however, is too obvious a simulation to be genuine. It risks producing pity rather than the expiation of hostility. Only an "authentic cure" through psychotherapy returns the prisoner to the requisite state of similarity necessary for execution.

39. Louis P. Masur, *Rites of Execution: Capital Punishment and the Transformation of American Culture, 1776–1975* (New York: Oxford University Press, 1989), 95, 97.

40. See, e.g., "Death Penalty Sentencing: Research Indicated Pattern of Racial Disparities," GAO/GGD 90–57, Report to Senate and House Committees on the Judiciary, United States General Accounting Office, February 1990.

41. Helen Prejean, in *Dead Man Walking*, 47, reported that one Louisiana attorney, Millard Farmer, who specialized in death penalty appeals estimated that "99% of death-row inmates are poor."

42. Fifty-four percent of death row prisoners did not complete high school, including 8 percent who have the benefit of only an elementary school education; see Bureau of Justice Statistics, Sourcebook of Criminal Justice Studies—1992, ed. Kathleen Maguire, Ann L. Pastore, Timothy J. Flanagan (Washington, D.C.: GPO, 1993), Table 6.127, 670. In his dissent in *Murray v. Giarratano*, Justice John Paul Stevens noted the "typically low educational attainment of prisoners. In 1982 more than half of Florida's general inmate population was found to be functionally illiterate, while in 1979 the state's death row inmates possessed a ninth-grade mean educational level." 492 U.S. 1 at 28, n. 23.

43. "Execution Update," 1.

44. Sourcebook—1992.

45. *McCleskey v. Kemp*, 481 U.S. 279 at 286–87. The February 1990 GAO report to the Senate and House Committees on the Judiciary, "Death Penalty Sentencing," confirmed that "the race-of-victim influence was found at all stages of the criminal justice system process." In the period between 1930 and the 1971 *Furman* decision, blacks constituted over 50 percent of those executed for a capital crime, proportionally five times that of their numbers in the general American population; see Gross and Mauro, *Death and Discrimination*, 17.

46. David Margolick, "In Land of Death Penalty, Accusations of Racial Bias," *New York Times*, 10 July 1991, A1, A7.

47. "Death Penalty Sentencing," 7.

48. "Punishments are cruel when they involve torture or a lingering death; but the

punishment of death is not cruel, within the meaning of that word as used in the Constitution. It implies there something inhuman and barbarous, something more than the mere extinguishing of life." *In re Kemmler,* 136 U.S. 436 (1890) at 447.

49. *The Compact Edition of the Oxford English Dictionary,* 4th ed., s.v. "cruel."

50. *O'Neil v. Vermont,* 144 U.S. 323 (1892) at 340.

51. *Furman* at 332....

52. See Walter Benjamin, "Critique of Violence," *Reflections,* ed. Peter Demetz, trans. Edmund Jephcott (New York: Harcourt Brace Jovanovich, 1978), 277–300, and Jacques Derrida, "Force of Law: The Mystical Foundation of Authority," *Cardozo Law Review* 11 (5–6 July–August 1990): 920–1045.

53. *Furman* at 303.

54. Michael McConnell, "The Religious Clauses of the First Amendment: Where Is the Supreme Court Heading?" *Catholic Lawyer* 32 (summer 1989): 187–202, 197.

55. *Lemon v. Kurtzen,* 403 U.S. 602 (1971) at 612–13.

56. "Short of those expressly productive of a benevolent neutrality which will permit religious exercise to exist without sponsorship and without interference." *Walz v. Tax Commission,* 397 U.S. 664 (1970) at 669.

57. S. Thelwall, trans., "On Idolatry," *The Anti-Nicene Fathers—Translations of the Writings of the Fathers down to A.D. 325: Latin Christianity: Its Founders, Tertullian,* ed. Alexander Roberts and James Donaldson (Grand Rapids, Mich.: Eerdmans, 1968), 3:61–76, 61.

58. Donald G. Jones and Russell E. Richey, eds., *American Civil Religion* (New York: Harper & Row, 1974), and Robert Bellah and Phillip E. Hammond, eds., *Varieties of Civil Religion* (San Francisco: Harper & Row, 1980).

59. See n. 22 herein.

60. *Walz* at 669.

61. Harry Potter, *Hanging in Judgment: Religion and the Death Penalty in England* (New York: Continuum, 1993), 160.

62. Ibid. Emphasis added.

63. *Parliamentary Debates,* House of Lords (27 April 1948), 5th Series, vol. 155, cols. 426–27, as cited in Potter, *Hanging in Judgment,* 147.

64. Elizabeth D. Purdam and J. Anthony Paredes, "Rituals of Death: Capital Punishment and Human Sacrifice," in *Facing the Death Penalty: Essays on a Cruel and Unusual Punishment,* ed. Michael L. Radelet (Philadelphia: Temple University, 1989), 139–55, 152.

PART SEVEN

THE ROLE OF RELIGION AND THE PRACTICES OF FAITH COMMUNITIES

[20]

Religious Orientation, Race, and Support for the Death Penalty

Robert L. Young

Introduction

By virtually any definition, religion involves a central concern with making sense of life and death. The American legal system, rooted in Judeo-Christian ethics, routinely confronts issues that test our basic assumptions about the meaning and sanctity of life and about the role of the State in shaping and sustaining such meanings. The exact nature of the State's role in the taking of life remains at or near the center of this controversy. Contemporary debates over capital punishment represent the continuation of a historically rich struggle in which verbal assaults have tended to focus on moral and philosophical concerns even as many of the more consequential battles have been waged in the political arena. Indeed, a rise in political activism among certain fundamentalist religious groups has forged an even closer link between the moral-philosophical and political dimensions of this issue.... [However,] researchers of public opinion have essentially ignored the role of religion in shaping attitudes toward capital punishment.

SOURCE: Robert L. Young, "Religious Orientation, Race and Support for the Death Penalty," *Journal for the Scientific Study of Religion* 31, no. 1 (1992). Reprinted by permission.

This research...was inspired largely by an experience I had several years ago as a consultant to the court-appointed defense in a capital murder case. During the course of the jury selection, I was struck with the number of venire members who cited the Bible in unsolicited justification of their position on capital punishment. In fact, the scriptures were cited almost equally by both supporters and opponents. This poses an interesting question for religious fundamentalists: With the Bible providing what is perceived to be unequivocal support for both sides of this debate (Bohm 1987), what is a sincere Christian fundamentalist to think? More generally, the central question of this research is: What is the role of individual religious orientations in shaping attitudes toward the death penalty?

Religion and Social Attitudes

The idea that religion is of major significance in American civil life has been expressed unequivocally by Lenski (1963:320), who concluded that "religion in various ways is constantly influencing the daily lives of the masses of men and women." Although the influence of religion on attitudes toward the death penalty has been largely ignored, numerous studies have linked religious variables to a host of other social attitudes.

Among the earliest and best known are the works of Allport (1954), Adorno et al. (1950), and others who showed that certain religious factors were associated with racial prejudice, ethnocentrism, and authoritarianism. Those initial findings were sufficiently provocative to have triggered a number of follow-up studies. For example, Allport (1966) and Allport and Ross (1967) found that such negative concomitants of religiosity applied only to those whose religious orientation is rooted in instrumental or utilitarian motives. Allport and Ross (1967) contrasted this extrinsic orientation [E] with the more intrinsically religious nature [I] of those who "live" their religion. They contended that the intrinsically religious are less prejudiced than are either the extrinsically or the "indiscriminately" religious. Although a number of studies have supported the Allport-Ross thesis (Maddock and Kenny 1972; Herek 1987; Ponton and Gorsuch 1988), others have shown that the relationship between I-E orientation and prejudice is much more complex and variable than previously assumed (Batson and Ventis 1982; Batson 1976; Batson and Flory 1990; McFarland 1989). Moreover, Kirkpatrick and Hood (1990) have persuasively criticized the simple I-E framework on both methodological and theoretical grounds.

The literature on the relationship of fundamentalism and related concepts (e.g., Batson's [1976] notion of "doctrinal orthodoxy") to prejudice is equally inconclusive. After a thorough review of the literature up to the early 1970s, Gorsuch and Aleshire (1974:281) argued that "the more intrinsically religious, nonfundamentalistic, and theologically discriminating," the more tolerant the individual. In a more recent review, however, Hood (1983) has contended that the consistency of such findings in early research was the result of a "pervasive bias" against fundamentalism. He is especially critical of those who have explained the relationship between fundamentalism and prejudice in terms of authoritarianism, citing the works of Hoge and Carroll (1973) and Gilmore (1969) as counter-evidence.

Perhaps the most reasonable conclusion to be drawn from the literature is that religious orientation is a highly complex phenomenon that supports a variety of seemingly contradictory attitudes and behaviors. This has been supported by McFarland (1989:333), for example, who has found that fundamentalism "cloaks a general closed minded, ethnocentric mindset," which supports a "general tendency to discriminate" while simultaneously producing a "contradictory tendency" toward non-discrimination, based on the biblical admonition that all are equal in God's eyes.

Indeed, it is the recognition of the complex and often seemingly contradictory nature of religious beliefs that informs the analysis presented here. Rather than relying on the somewhat questionable I-E distinction, or on a simple contrast between fundamentalists and others, this research has attempted to investigate the unique roles of certain key religious variables in determining support for or opposition to the death penalty. To that end, it is necessary to articulate clear conceptual distinctions between empirically related elements of religious life.

Fundamentalism, Evangelism, and the Death Penalty

Discussions of fundamentalism and evangelicalism often create more confusion than clarity. According to Kellstedt and Smidt (1991:259), "fundamentalism does not have a widely shared meaning among journalists, scholars, or the general public." Indeed, sociologists of religion have been inconsistent in their use of these terms, sometimes employing fundamentalism and evangelicalism interchangeably, and sometimes combining various elements of the two in order to describe a particular subgroup.

The term "fundamentalist" can be traced at least as far back as the publication of *The Fundamentals* in 1910. That very significant work promulgated a number of closely related doctrines that provided the intellectual thrust for the fundamentalist movement. Inasmuch as each of the four other primary doctrines discussed in *The Fundamentals* can be derived essentially from a literal interpretation of the scriptures, it is clear that the central tenet of this orientation is biblical literalism. However, many contemporary discussions of fundamentalism define the general orientation not only in terms of biblical literalism, but also to include born-again experiences and the tendency to proselytize

(Kellstedt and Smidt 1991). While these three factors might be positively correlated empirically, maintaining conceptual distinctions among them is critical to this research.

Evangelicalism and fundamentalism did indeed have common roots in the reaction of certain groups to what they perceived to be the perversions of the social gospel movement and the increased secularization of late nineteenth-century America (Johnstone 1975). Even today there is considerable empirical overlap, but a clarification of the difference between these two orientations will help us understand their impact on attitudes toward various social issues. Rather than the more general and ambiguous "evangelicalism," I will employ the term "evangelism" to denote specifically a proselytizing orientation. While the essence of *fundamentalism* can be found in a central or closely related set of beliefs, *evangelism* is essentially defined as an active effort to convert others to the faith. Although Christian fundamentalists tend to be evangelists, many evangelists are not fundamentalists (Kellstedt and Smidt 1991).

More importantly for this research, however, the two terms suggest conceptually distinct orientations toward secular issues. Fundamentalists tend to deny the possibility of moral relativity. Such absolutism, whether a cause or a consequence of fundamentalist beliefs, is likely to be associated with the perception of considerable evil in the world, for the morality of human action is not to be judged relative to social context.

This rejection of moral relativity might be one of the conceptual links between fundamentalism and political conservatism, a link that has been noted by a number of authors (Ammerman 1987; Peshkin 1986; Kellstedt and Smidt 1991). . . . It is clear that any analysis of the relationship between fundamentalism and death penalty attitudes (also empirically related to conservatism) should be carried out in such a way as to take political orientation also into consideration.

In contrast to fundamentalism, the evangelistic desire to convert, although in some cases rooted in absolutist beliefs, could be interpreted as an expression of compassion and concern for the souls of others. If so, such compassion might exert pressure in a more liberal direction with regard to certain social issues. . . . Thus we might expect support for the death penalty to be relatively low among those of an evangelistic orientation. Indeed, there is a certain logic to an evangelistic preference for life imprisonment over the death penalty, since the latter puts the lost soul beyond the reach of those who might be able to lead him or her to a state of grace.

Alternatively, evangelism might reflect a selfish need to ensure one's own salvation through conformity to biblical and clerical directives. . . .

Fundamentalism would seem to provide less ambiguous support for a punitive orientation. If there is a cognitive link between fundamentalism and support for extreme forms of punishment, it might be found in the ideology of individualism (Roberts 1990:267). With their decentralized organizational structure and emphasis on individual salvation, fundamentalist denominations might encourage a tendency to hold individuals responsible for their crimes rather than blaming situational circumstances. Indeed, Lupfer et al. (1988) have provided evidence that fundamentalists are more inclined than others to favor personal over environmental attributions, even when the evidence does not support such attributions. Their data, however, suggest that this tendency could be an indirect manifestation of greater authoritarianism among fundamentalists. Moreover, Wrightsman's (1964) data have shown that fundamentalist college students score low on the trustworthiness dimension of his "Philosophies of Human Nature Scale." Finally, in at least one other related study, Vinney et al. (1988) found no link between the belief in free will, a correlate of fundamentalism, and either the rationale or the magnitude of punishment. Thus, while there is a theoretical logic to the notion that fundamentalism produces a more punitive orientation, the empirical evidence is less than compelling.

However, if we assume fundamentalists conform to the positions of their leaders, there is clear evidence that support for capital punishment should be relatively high among members of fundamentalist churches. Numerous statements of support for the death penalty by prominent fundamentalist leaders can be found in such publications as the *Fundamentalist Journal* (e.g., Falwell 1982). Such support is also reflected in the attitudes of fundamentalist seminary students, whom Hunter (1984) found to be significantly more supportive of capital punishment than were students at either evangelical colleges or public universities.

Thus logic, and to some extent empirical research, both suggest that the empirically correlated orientations of evangelism and fundamentalism represent countervailing influences on death penalty attitudes. To the extent that fundamentalists tend to hold the individual solely responsible for his or her actions, they are likely to be more punitive than others. Moreover, those who attend church regularly are likely to hear such punitiveness legitimated from the pulpit. When controls for fundamentalist beliefs and church attendance are introduced, however, evangelicals might be less inclined than others to support the death penalty.

Devotionalism and the Death Penalty

For many individuals, fundamentalist or evangelistic orientations are the result of being socialized into a particular religious subculture. Race, region of the country, and social class significantly influence one's religious affiliation. However, the extent to which religion influences attitudes and behaviors depends largely upon the importance of religion in the daily life of the individual. Those for whom religion is not salient should not be expected to harbor social attitudes consistent with their religious beliefs.

Devotionalism is a clear indication of the salience of religion in daily life. Regular prayer, Bible reading, and attendance at worship services indicate more than a situational commitment to religion. Thus any differences between the effects of fundamentalism and evangelism on support for capital punishment should be most prominent among those who are most devoted to their religion.

Race, Religion, and the Death Penalty

It is common knowledge that support for capital punishment varies substantially by race. For a variety of reasons, whites are much more likely than blacks to support the death penalty (Young 1991). Moreover, the centrality and unique character of religion in Afro-American versus white American culture have been well documented by, e.g., Frazier (1974) and Sernett (1975). . . .

More recently, the importance of religion in Afro-American life was revealed during the civil rights movement of the 1950s and '60s. Not only did black ministers provide leadership to the movement, but the church itself was often the focal point of organizational efforts. Indeed, the role of black religion in civil affairs has been an accepted and important element in Afro-American social and political life. Although Euro-American religion has often involved itself indirectly in political and social issues, it has not often played such a central role. Thus, as a result of both historical and contemporary factors, we might expect religion to affect the social and political attitudes of black and white Americans somewhat differently.

Methods

Data and Analysis

The data for this study were taken from the 1988 General Social Survey (Davis and Smith 1989). The full probability sample consisted of 1,481 English-speaking persons 18 years of age or older. The loss of a few cases due to missing data and the elimination of members of other racial groups from the sample resulted in a final sample of 1,078 whites and 150 blacks. Respondents consisted of Protestants, Catholics, Jews, and those who expressed no religious preference. Other religious groups were excluded because (1) they were so few in number, and (2) it was assumed that many of the core questions would not be relevant for them.

Because the dependent variable is dichotomous, models were tested through the use of logistic regression analysis (Haberman 1978; Pindyck and Rubinfeld 1981) with the BMDP statistical software program (Dixon 1985). Logit models may be interpreted in much the same way as the results of an ordinary least-squares analysis: The coefficients represent the relationship of each independent variable with the dependent variable, minus the effects of other variables in the model. The most notable exception to the OLS analogy is that in logistic regression what is modelled, in an additive form, is the natural log of the odds of the dependent variable. The distribution of the ratios of the coefficients to their standard errors is asymptotically normal.

Variables

Literal biblical interpretation, evangelism, and the experience of being "born again" have been discussed by various authors as elements of a fundamentalist and/or evangelical orientation. As suggested above, although these three variables are empirically correlated, they appear in this analysis as separate variables. Fundamentalist church affiliation was coded from respondents' answers to the following questions: (1) What is your religious preference? and (2) What specific denomination is that, if any? (Smith 1986). "Literal interpreters" were defined as those who believed that "the Bible is the actual word of God and is to be taken literally, word for word" (Davis and Smith 1989:168). Evangelists were defined as those who answered "yes" to the question "Have you ever tried to encourage someone to believe in Jesus Christ or to accept Jesus Christ as his or her savior?" (406). The REBORN variable was defined by a positive response to the question "Would you say you have been 'born again' or have had a 'born again' experience—that is, a turning point in your life when you committed yourself to Christ?" (406). Finally, devotionalism was measured by questions regarding how often the respondent 1) attended religious services, 2) prayed, and 3) read the Bible at home. Although all of the religion variables were intercorrelated, the largest single bivariate correlation, between REBORN and EVANGELISM, was .58. Correlations among the three DEVOTIONALISM items ranged from .40 to .42.

AGE, SEX, and EDUCATION (high school or less versus beyond high school) were included as control variables since each has been shown in previous studies to correlate with race and with support for the death penalty. The CONSERVATISM variable (defined according to the respondent's location of self on a seven-point scale from extremely liberal to extremely conservative) was also included as a control because of its positive correlation with the dependent variable and with a number of the religious variables.

Finally, REGION of residence (other versus South) was included because of the possibility of its interaction with race. Although recent survey data have indicated similar levels of support for capital punishment across regions, the unique history of the South with regard to both legal and illegal executions of blacks might make southern blacks especially averse to the death penalty. The use of region of residences, as opposed to region of socialization, was based on Stump's (1984) finding that religious commitment is related to region of current residence rather than to region of origin.

Results

Table 1 contains the results of the additive logistic regression model. As expected, whites and males were more supportive of capital punishment than were blacks and females. Although age, education, and region of residence did not affect level of support, conservatism had a significant positive influence. Of the five religious variables, having had a "born again" experience was the only one not related to death penalty support. Membership in a fundamentalist church and belief in biblical literalism increased support, while evangelism was associated with reduced support.

Although devotionalism was significantly related to opposition to the death penalty, it was also expected to have an interactive influence. As an indicator of the salience of religion in the everyday life of the individual, level of devotionalism was expected to affect the extent to which the other religious variables influenced support for capital punishment. In order to probe this idea, I dichotomized the sample according to level of devotionalism. The results of that analysis, though not reported here, suggested that devotionalism interacts only with evangelism, decreasing support for the death penalty primarily among evangelists who scored high on devotionalism. The appropriate interaction term, therefore, was included in the final interaction model.

The primary set of expected interactions involved the influence of race on the relationship between the religious variables and the dependent variables. As a preliminary step toward identifying the relevant interactions for the final model, separate models were run for blacks and whites (Table 2). An examination of the variable means reveals substantial differences in the overall religious orientations of the two groups. The most obvious interactions suggested by Table 2 are the joint impacts of (1) race and membership in a fundamentalist church, and (2) race and devotionalism. Also suggested are possible interac-

Table I

Additive Model of Support for the Death Penalty

Indep. Variable	Coefficient	Std. Error	p-value	Var. Mean
Race	−.7301	.1007	<.01	.122
Sex	−.2039	.0754	<.01	.564
Age	.0015	.0043	.73	44.8
Education	−.0151	.0768	.84	.425
Region	.0111	.0794	.89	.346
Conservatism	.2201	.0809	<.01	.348
Fund. Church	.1742	.0915	.06	.349
Literalism	.1964	.0871	.02	.345
Reborn	−.0220	.0972	.82	.371
Devotionalism	−.2125	.0849	.01	.366
Evangelism	−.2028	.0898	.02	.468

tions between race and evangelism, and, least probably, between race and literal biblical interpretation.

The full interaction model appears in Table 3. This formal specification of the relationships, suggested both by theoretical considerations and by the initial empirical analysis discussed above, presents a fairly clear picture. It is obvious from this analysis that the role of religion in shaping attitudes toward the death penalty is quite different for blacks and whites. In general, evangelism is associated with relatively less support, although its impact is strongest among blacks. In fact, among all the subgroups identified in this study, opposition to capital punishment was strongest among black evangelists. As expected, a fundamentalist orientation toward the Bible was associated with relatively strong support for the death penalty, and this influence held for both blacks and whites.

In contrast, attendance at fundamentalist churches and devotionalism led to different attitudes for the two races. Attending fundamentalist churches increased support only among whites, while devotionalism decreased support only among whites. Finally, although the results seen in Table 3 are equivocal on this point, they suggest that the tendency of evangelists to oppose the death penalty is largely restricted to those who take their religion seriously enough to sustain regular devotional practices.

Of course, it is quite likely that a number of the religious variables are also associated with political conservatism and various social status variables. Thus it is important to note that all these relationships held even when the influences of political conservatism age, education, sex, and region of residence were considered.

Table 2

Model for Support for the Death Penalty by Race

SAMPLE	IND. VARIABLE	COEFF.	STD. ERROR	p-VALUE	VAR. MEAN
White					
	Sex	−.1777	.0833	.03	.554
	Age	.0058	.0048	.23	45.4
	Education	−.0459	.0849	.59	.430
	Region	.0403	.0905	.66	.346
	Conservatism	.2895	.0909	<.01	.367
	Fund. Church	.2672	.1065	.01	.300
	Literalism	.1480	.0994	.14	.201
	Reborn	−.0397	.1114	.72	.342
	Devotionalism	−.3149	.0958	<.01	.347
	Evangelism	−.1242	.1002	.22	.439
Black					
	Sex	−.2664	.1965	.17	.633
	Age	−.0235	.0117	.05	40.8
	Education	.0240	.2001	.90	.397
	Region	−.2106	.1903	.27	.337
	Conservatism	−.1375	.2232	.53	.212
	Fund. Church	−.2302	.2144	.28	.702
	Literalism	.4378	.2052	.04	.318
	Reborn	.0623	.2228	.78	.573
	Devotionalism	.1981	.2019	.33	.510
	Evangelism	−.7256	.2368	<.01	.675

Table 3

Interaction Model of Support for the Death Penalty

IND. VARIABLE	COEFF.	STD. ERROR	p-VALUE
Race	−.5509	.1199	<.01
Education	−.0094	.0778	.90
Region	−.0061	.0805	.94
Conservatism	−.2245	.0821	<.01
Fund. Church	.0007	.1164	.99
Literalism	.2651	.1083	.01
Reborn	−.0085	.0998	.93
Devotionalism	.0667	.1105	.55
Evangelism	−.4248	.1239	<.01
Race X Fund. Church	−.2875	.1142	.01
Race X Literal	.0984	.1063	.35
Race X Devotionalism	.2182	.1056	.04
Race X Evangelism	−.2657	.1153	.02
Devotion X Evangelism	−.1395	.0843	.10

Conclusions

The results of this study reveal a relatively clear and concise image of the role of religious orientation in influencing attitudes toward the death penalty. Of all the religious variables in the final model, evangelism showed the single largest impact on the dependent variable. This finding supports an interpretation of evangelism as a manifestation of (or perhaps a demand for) compassion and concern for the fate of others. That such concern for prisoners is especially evident among black Americans is probably related to their tendency to make situational rather than personal attributions, and to the relative skepticism with which they view the American criminal justice system (Young 1991).

The association of fundamentalism with high levels of support for the death penalty was also not surprising. The absolutism of a fundamentalist orientation appears to eliminate some of the uncertainty which others experience in considering the appropriateness of this punishment. Whether this association is a function of higher levels of authoritarianism, as some have suggested, or is the result of specific attributional tendencies of fundamentalists, is impossible to determine from this study. What does seem clear, however, is that support for the death penalty is likely to be increased by the belief in individual free will and responsibility that characterizes fundamentalism.

It is also important to note that these inclinations are apparently nurtured only in *white* fundamentalist churches, since affiliation with fundamentalist churches had no significant influence on the death penalty attitudes of blacks. In black churches, the individualism associated with white Protestantism might be tempered by a more collectivist orientation that is deeply rooted in Afro-American history. In fact, the *recent* emphasis among white fundamentalists on collective action as a way of promoting their vision of a just society contrasts with a *long-standing* concern for exactly that among America's black churches (Sernett 1975).

The results of this study also suggest the need for a theoretical clarification of certain concepts in the sociology of religion. Until this is accomplished, the empirical association between such variables as fundamentalism and evangelism should not blind us to the necessity of maintaining clear conceptual distinctions. The melding of such distinctions into convenient monolithic images denies the inherent complexity of religion as both a psychological and a social force.

References

Adorno, T. W., Else Frankel-Brunswik, Daniel J. Levinson, and R. Nevitt Sanford
    1950. *The Authoritarian Personality.* New York: Harper and Brothers.

Allport, Gordon W.
  1954. *The Nature of Prejudice.* Cambridge, Mass.: Addison-Wesley.
  1966. "The Religious Context of Prejudice." *Journal for the Scientific Study of Religion* 5(3): 447–57 (fall).
Allport, Gordon W., and Michael Ross
  1967. "Personal religious orientation and prejudice." *Journal of Personality and Social Psychology* 5(4): 432–43 (April).
Ammerman, Nancy
  1987. *Bible Believers: Fundamentalists in the Modern World.* New Brunswick: Rutgers University Press.
Batson, C. Daniel
  1976. "Religion as Prosocial: Agent or Double Agent?" *Journal for the Scientific Study of Religion* 15(1): 29–45 (March).
Batson, C. Daniel, and W. Larry Ventis
  1982. *The Religious Experience.* New York: Oxford University Press.
Batson, C. Daniel, and Janine Dyck Flory
  1990. "Goal-Relevant Cognitions Associated with Helping by Individuals High on Intrinsic, End Religion." *Journal for the Scientific Study of Religion* 29(3): 346–60 (September).
Bohm, Robert M.
  1987. "American Death Penalty Attitudes: A Critical Examination of Recent Evidence." *Criminal Justice and Behavior* 14(3): 380–96 (September).
Davis, James Allan, and Tom W. Smith
  1989. *General Social Surveys, 1972–1989.* [Machine-readable data file]. Principal investigator, James A. Davis; director and co-principal investigator, Tom W. Smith. NORC ed. Chicago: National Opinion Research Center, producer, 1989; Storrs, Conn.: The Roper Center for Public Opinion Research, University of Connecticut, distributor. 1 data file (24,893 logical records) and 1 codebook (861 p.).
Dixon, W. J., ed.
  1985. *BMDP Statistical Software.* Berkeley: University of California Press.
Falwell, Jerry
  1982. "Capital Punishment for Capital Crimes." *Fundamentalist Journal* 1(3): 8–9 (March).
Finamore, Frank, and James M. Carlson
  1987. "Religiosity, Belief in a Just World, and Crime Control Attitudes." *Psychological Reports* 61(1): 135–38 (August).
Frazier, E. Franklin
  1974. *The Negro Church in America.* New York: Schocken Books.
    The Fundamentals: A Testimony to the Truth, vols. 1–12. Chicago: Testimony Publishing Co. [c. 1910].
Gilmore, Susan K.
  1969. "Personality Differences between High and Low Dogmatism

Groups of Pentecostal Believers." *Journal for the Scientific Study of Religion* 8(1): 161–64 (spring).

Gorsuch, Richard L., and Daniel Aleshire
  1974. "Christian Faith and Ethnic Prejudice: A Review and Interpretation of Research." *Journal for the Scientific Study of Religion* 13(3): 281–307 (September).

Haberman, Shelby J.
  1978. *Analysis of Qualitative Data.* New York: Academic Press.

Herek, Gregory M.
  1987. "Religious Orientation and Prejudice: A Comparison of Racial and Sexual Attitudes." *Personality and Social Psychology Bulletin* 13(1): 34–44 (March).

Hoge, Dean R., and Jackson W. Carroll.
  1973. "Religiosity and Prejudice in Northern Southern Churches." *Journal for the Scientific Study of Religion* 12(2): 181–97 (June).

Hood, Ralph W. Jr.
  1983. "Social Psychology and Religious Fundamentalism." In *Rural Psychology,* edited by Alan W. Childs and Gary B. Milton, 169–98.

Hunter, James Davidson
  1984. "Religion and Political Civility: The Coming Generation of American Evangelicals." *Journal for the Scientific Study of Religion* 23(4): 364–80 (December).

Johnstone, Ronald L.
  1975. *Religion and Society in Interaction.* Englewood Cliffs, N.J.: Prentice-Hall.

Kauffman, Donald T., ed.
  1985. *Baker's Concise Dictionary of Religion.* Grand Rapids, Mich.: Baker Book House.

Kellstedt, Lyman, and Corwin Smidt
  1991. "Measuring Fundamentalism: An Analysis of Different Operational Strategies." *Journal for the Scientific Study of Religion.* 30(3): 259–78 (September).

Kirkpatrick, Lee A., and Ralph W. Hood Jr.
  1990. "Intrinsic-Extrinsic Religious Orientation: The Boon or Bane of Contemporary Psychology of Religion?" *Journal for the Scientific Study of Religion* 29(4): 442–62 (December).

Lenski, Gerhard
  1963. *The Religious Factor.* Garden City, N.Y.: Anchor Books.

Lupfer, Michael B., Patricia L. Hopkins, and Patricia Kelly
  1988. "An Exploration of the Attributional Styles of Christian Fundamentalists and of Authoritarians." *Journal for the Scientific Study of Religion* 27(3): 389–98.

Maddock, Richard C., and Charles T. Kenny
  1972. "Philosophies of Human Nature and Personal Religious Orienta-

tion." *Journal for the Scientific Study of Religion* 11(3): 277–81 (September).

McFarland, Sam G.

1989. "Religious Orientations and the Targets of Discrimination." *Journal for the Scientific Study of Religion* 28(3): 324–36 (September).

Peshkin, Alan

1986. *God's Choice: The Total World of a Fundamentalist Christian School.* Chicago: University of Chicago Press.

Pindyck, Robert S., and Daniel L. Rubinfield

1981. *Econometric Models and Economic Forecasts.* New York: McGraw-Hill.

Ponton, Marcel O., and Richard L. Gorsuch

1988. "Prejudice and Religion among Venezuelans." *Journal for the Scientific Study of Religion* 27(2): 260–71 (June).

Roberts, Keith A.

1990. *Religion in Sociological Perspective.* Belmont, Calif.: Wadsworth.

Sernett, Milton C.

1975. *Black Religion and American Evangelicalism.* Metuchen, N.J.: Scarecrow Press and the American Theological Library Association.

Smith, Tom W.

1986. "Classifying Protestant Denominations." GSS Technical Report No. 67. Chicago: NORC.

1990. "Classifying Protestant Denominations." *Review of Religious Research* 31(3): 225–45 (March).

Stump, Roger W.

1984. "Regional Migration and Religion Commitment in the U.S.A." *Journal for the Scientific Study of Religion* 23(3): 292–303 (September).

Viney, Wayne, Paula Parker-Martin, and Sandra D. H. Dotten

1988. "Beliefs in Free Will and Determinism and Lack of Relation to Punishment Rationale and Magnitude." *Journal of General Psychology* 115(1): 15–23 (January).

Wrightsman, Lawrence S.

1964. "Measurement of Philosophies of Human Nature." *Psychological Reports* 14(3): 743–51 (June).

Young, Robert L.

1991. "Race, Conceptions of Crime and Justice, and Support for the Death Penalty." *Social Psychology Quarterly* 54(1): 67–75 (March).

Zeller, Richard A., and Edward G. Carmines

1980. *Measurement in the Social Sciences: The Link between Theory and Data.* New York: Cambridge University Press.

[21]

How Renewal in Church Practices Can Transform the Death Penalty Debate

Michael L. Westmoreland-White

TOO OFTEN, CHRISTIANS SEEKING to influence public policy find an apparent deaf ear among legislators, jurists, and other policy makers. This may seem especially to be the case with the issue of capital punishment. The majority of official church statements on this issue, and most of the leaders of mainline denominations who have spoken publicly on capital punishment, have been decidedly against the practice.[1] Yet legislators continue to enact new laws requiring the death penalty, and governors continue to ignore religious leaders' pleas for clemency and to execute convicted felons. One reason for this lack of impact seems to be a perception by policy makers that church leaders and official statements do not reflect the opinions of the rank-and-file church members. Rightly or wrongly, the impression is given in much of Christian public policy advocacy that church leaders are out of touch with their constituencies.

Further, the shape of much of Christian public policy advocacy seems to be little different from that of other interest-group politics. The churches act as if civil government is responsible for transforming the culture to reflect the in-

SOURCE: Michael L. Westmoreland-White, "Capital Punishment and the Practices of the Church: How Renewal in Church Practices Can Transform the Death Penalty Debate." This essay is an expansion of part of a Crossroads Monograph, *Capital Punishment and U.S. Christians: A Public Policy Proposal for Divided Churches,* forthcoming from Evangelicals for Social Action.

breaking reign of God by following the moral pronouncements of church leaders. The fundamental mission of the church in the world to anticipate the life characterized by that reign is shifted to the locus of civil government.[2]

This is not to say that Christians should not engage in public policy advocacy, either as individuals or as churches. On the contrary, the Christian witness to the state is a vital part of the prophetic dimension of its calling.[3] But if that witness is going to have its own integrity, rather than simply mirroring the interest-group politics of the rest of the population of liberal democracies, then it must grow out of and reflect the authentic life of the churches as they live out the gospel message.

Christian ethics deals in the first instance with the character and behavior of those who call Jesus "Lord" and claim to be disciples. As several writers have emphasized in recent years, the discipline of Christian ethics should focus first and foremost on the moral character and behavior of those communities called the church. Certainly Christians should seek (persuasively, not coercively) to influence society along lines more consistent with biblical norms. Yet unless Christians are first clear about their own identities as followers of Jesus Christ, they have no distinctive message to deliver to the world. Christians are to be an alternate society, engaged with the wider society rather than withdrawn from it, but engaged on terms peculiar to the gospel, rather than as one more interest group in a pluralistic democracy.[4] For this reason, I want to briefly consider how churches should respond to capital punishment in their internal practices, quite apart from recommending policy proposals and strategies for influencing civil government.

First, far more churches need to be involved in visitation ministries to jails and prisons, even to death rows. Despite the clear teaching of Jesus (e.g., Luke 4:16–21; Matt. 25:31–46), few Christians in this society know anyone in prison. We cannot hope to respond faithfully to issues of crime and punishment when we do not even make contact with those in jails and prisons. This is not a task to be left to prison chaplaincies or specialized ministries, since the implication of the parable of the sheep and the goats is that visiting those in prison is something "the righteous" as a whole should do. If such ministries were the norm in most congregations, we would go far in recovering the biblical identity of our churches.[5]

Further, our very presence might begin to influence the corrections and criminal justice systems in ways we cannot now foresee. After all, visitation practices often have profound influences on those doing the visiting. In 1986, I visited a prisoner in the Georgia state prison system. I was accompanying a friend who had established a relationship with this man by correspondence and had since visited him several times. The prisoner was serving a life sentence for murder. He had originally been sentenced to death, but his had been among those sentences commuted to life imprisonment in the early 1970s following the *Furman* decision. I talked openly with this man, a white man of medium height and build then in his early forties, and listened attentively to his story. As a young man, he had made some very bad choices and, through circumstances too lengthy to repeat here, had become involved in a plan to kill one of his two business partners and frame the other. The motives were both monetary greed and desire for the victim's wife, who, according to this man, masterminded the scheme but was never brought to trial. He carried out the plan, and was caught after the murder, tried, and convicted, having confessed his guilt during the trial. He freely admitted to his guilt and showed deep remorse. While in prison, he had become a Christian, had been a model prisoner, and had made several petitions for work that would earn money to be paid as restitution to the victim's family. The state of Georgia continued to turn down both his requests and petitions for parole. While I had been suspicious of the death penalty before this encounter, meeting this convicted murderer and visiting him a few times solidified my opposition. My new friend had experienced redemption that would not have been possible had he been executed. I now knew personally that, for all the problems with imprisonment as a form of punishment, it at least allowed for redemptive possibilities in the lives of criminals—possibilities that were cut off by the death penalty. This experience has shaped my approach to the death penalty in concrete ways. The testimonies of many others involved in prison visitation is similar.

Charles Colson, himself convicted of crime as part of Richard Nixon's staff and subsequently imprisoned, experienced a deep Christian conversion and founded Prison Fellowship, an evangelical ministry of prison visitation. In an interview with *Sojourners* magazine, testifying to the impact of carrying out the biblical admonition to visit those in prison, Colson said:

> I've come to know too many men in prison who I believe are there unfairly. . . . I've seen too much in the way of statistics that those chosen for execution come from minorities or poverty backgrounds—people who probably would not be there if they had been able to afford decent legal help, or if society fairly and equitably administered and enforced criminal justice laws. . . .
>
> Our churches are basically evangelical churches and church membership is basically white, middle- or middle-to-upper class, and they tend to . . . equate conservative theology with conservative politics. They will accept the simplistic notion "crack down on criminals and you're going to stop crime," and they believe that the ultimate crackdown is capital punishment. . . .
>
> It'll change. It's exactly like going into the prisons. The Christian has not thought of it. The Christian has had a culturally conditioned reaction. When he thinks it through biblically, I think most serious Christians . . . are open to changing their attitude.[6]

Second, we need to be in active solidarity with both the victims (and their families) and perpetrators (and their families) of violent crime. Solidarity, as I use the term here, does not imply condoning the crimes or excusing the perpetrators of responsibility, but remembering that their criminal actions do not exhaust their human identity. Christian churches ought to be among the first to seek out the families of both murder victims and murderers and minister to them, welcoming them into their community, praying with and for them, going with them to court and prison, and so forth.

The Victim Offender Reconciliation Program, created by the Mennonite Central Committee, is a worthy model for other Christian groups. Their experiences with the practice of solidarity show its transforming potential. The VORP process consists of a face-to-face encounter between victim and offender in cases that have entered the criminal justice process and where the offender has admitted to the offense. In these meetings, emphasis is on three elements: facts, feelings, and agreements. The meeting is facilitated and chaired by a trained mediator, preferably a community volunteer. Mennonites began the process, but soon involved many others in training as mediators. These third-party facilitators play an extremely important role in the process. They are trained not to impose their own interpretations or solutions. Meetings are conducted in an atmosphere that provides some structure, yet allows the participants to determine the outcomes. Both the victim and the offender get a chance to ask questions and tell their stories, including the impact of what has happened. Then they decide together what to do about the situation. Once they come to an agreement, they sign a written contract, often but not always involving financial restitution.[7] By remaining in solidarity with both victim and offender, the mediator is able to facilitate transformation. Unlike nonmediated restitution contracts, the VORP-mediated contracts are fulfilled at a high rate, above 80 percent. Both victims and offenders report high levels of satisfaction with the process, and the initial evidence is that the process does change offender behavior and lessen recidivism.[8] Here is an important model for the practice of solidarity, but this is not the only practice it exemplifies.

Another facet of the VORP process is its illustration of the importance of the mutual practices of repentance and forgiveness. Offenders must truly admit their guilt and take responsibility for their actions. Victims must confront both the offender and their own desire for revenge. Paul Redekop, director of mediation services in Winnipeg, Manitoba, tells of one case where Marge, a woman in her late twenties and nine months pregnant, went to a local bar with a friend. In a fit of anger at her companion, Marge threw a glass across the crowded barroom; the glass struck Edna, a woman in her forties and a stranger to Marge, knocking her unconscious and causing a large gash in her head. Marge was charged with assault with a deadly weapon, and eventually the case was referred to mediation.

At the meeting, Marge acknowledged responsibility for what she had done and expressed remorse for the harm she had caused. Edna described the experience at the hospital, where they had shaved her head and stitched the wound without anesthetic; it had been painful and humiliating. She had missed time from work, and she remained fearful about going out in public. She and her husband, who accompanied her to the meeting, had been very skeptical about the mediation session. During the session, however, the mediators helped the two women to recognize their mutual fears. While Edna was afraid of Marge, Marge was terrified of what was going to happen to her. Marge was also willing to make amends, and agreed to pay for Edna's lost wages. By the end of the session, the tone had changed dramatically. They were now talking directly to each other, apologizing, and joking about the incident. At the end, Edna promised to help Marge if there were any further problems with the charges against her. Marge had confessed and repented; Edna had confronted both Marge and her own fears and desire to retaliate. Through the mediation, Edna was enabled to practice forgiveness.[9]

I suggest also that Christians who own businesses ought to be hiring ex-convicts at a much higher rate than other businesses do. As Christians, we claim to believe that forgiveness, reconciliation, and a new life are possible for anyone. We ought to demonstrate this in our hiring, job-training, and supervision practices. This should be an explicit topic of discussion among churches as it recently has become in my own congregation, Jeff Street Baptist Community at Liberty, in Louisville, Kentucky. It can move beyond discussion through the prison visitation ministries, which might act (formally or informally) as job referral services for released convicts. The impact that this would have in lowering the recidivism rate among persons convicted and imprisoned for a crime is incalculable. Here, our "social action" would grow directly out of our own experience as forgiven people, reaffirmed every time the Lord's Supper is celebrated.

Our experience in this area at Jeff Street is only beginning and is hindered by the fact that most of our members are poor and do not own businesses. Nevertheless, we have managed to be very successful in finding jobs for members, neighbors in our inner-city community, and ex-convicts; in one case, this placement was vital to a sentence of probation rather than imprisonment.

We have discovered that self-righteousness is an extreme barrier to any compassionate action. Our congregation includes many recovering drug and alcohol addicts. They are aware of the need for grace in the form of forgiveness and the power to change. Worshiping with them has allowed others of us to be far more open in our prayer requests and our struggles. We have sometimes been enabled to risk great vulnerability by acknowledging our failures, sins, and inadequacies. I myself have been supported in prayer and solidarity, experiencing God's grace and forgiveness, through this congregation, when I had to admit to painful problems in my own family life. The experience of compassionate grace and forgiveness as part of the regular life of the congregation leads to a more compassionate, less self-righteous approach to issues of crime and punishment.

Christians should work to provide legal assistance to poor persons accused of murder and poor convicted murderers seeking appeals. All persons should be defended equally, instead of the rich having unfair legal advantages. This may involve donating money to the Legal Aid Society and writing our senators and representatives to restore the drastically reduced funding of Legal Aid. Yet even though private donations cannot replace the necessary public funds, churches should not hesitate to set up funding of their own. Unless we are willing to put up our own money, it is not likely that public officials will take our requests for tax-supported funding seriously. Public defenders' offices are usually staffed with very competent and dedicated attorneys who work hard at defending accused murderers, often harder than private attorneys doing court-ordered *pro bono* work. I know this from my own experience working as a bailiff in the Duval County Circuit Court in Jacksonville, Florida. However, public defenders have enormous caseloads, and very few investigators to assist them, whereas prosecutors have much smaller caseloads and an entire police force of investigators. If churches or denominations established groups of expert attorneys, specializing in death penalty cases, to be available for both initial trials and appeals, it could help to alleviate the burden borne by public defenders directly and would act as leverage in getting public defenders more funding and staff.

More controversially, I urge that Christian family members of homicide victims refuse to testify or cooperate with the police investigation until and unless prosecutors publicly, in a legally binding fashion, guarantee not to seek the death penalty if the accused is convicted. The Friends Committee to Abolish the Death Penalty has drawn up a "Declaration of Life" for individuals to sign and notarize and attach to their wills. This declaration states that, in the event the signer becomes a murder victim, he or she directs prosecutors not to seek the death penalty for the person convicted of the murder. The declaration urges family members to renounce revenge, and asks that the victim's wishes be read to the court in a trial or sentencing hearing of someone accused of the murder. The declaration makes clear that this is not a request to ignore the crime or fail to punish the perpetrator.[10] My wife and I have each signed such declarations and are circulating them among church members. Such a practice of refusing to seek revenge against murderers follows naturally from discipleship to the one who forgave his murderers from the cross, even as they jeered him at his unjust public execution.

Along these same lines, Christians should write editorials in newspapers and seek to influence public opinion against the death penalty. They should seek to educate the public to the realities discussed in these pages. This work of public education, so necessary if any repeal of capital punishment will ever become politically possible, will be more persuasive if church practices show consistency in these convictions.

More generally, these practices should not be separated from the work of churches to intervene in the processes leading to juvenile crime and the causes of crime more generally. I know of one congregation, Canaan Baptist Church of Christ in Harlem, New York, that has an effective program to eradicate the menace of drugs, not only by legislation and law enforcement, but by developing recovery programs for addicts and prevention programs for others. Similarly, Christians should seek to overcome the threat of the avalanche of gun violence by refusing to carry any weapons or have them in their homes. Such a pledge was developed by the Louisville Council on Peacemaking. It is one response to the 1996 enactment of a Kentucky law permitting the carrying of concealed weapons, a law passed despite opposition both from the churches and from every law enforcement agency in the state. Christians who desire to shoot handguns for sport should keep them locked up at registered gun clubs and refuse ever to have them in their homes or cars or on their persons. Hunters should take equally strict precautions with rifles and shotguns. All Christians should refuse to own guns "for protection," both because they do not fear those who can kill the body alone (Matt. 10:28) and because they know that handguns kill far more family members than hostile intruders—by a ratio of 20 to 1, according to Louisville police.

Here is L. Harold DeWolf's conclusion in an essay on the death penalty:

All the serious studies of crime in America indicate that while the *certainty* and *swiftness* of apprehension, conviction, and sentencing do have considerable deterrent effect, the *severity* of penalties has little to do with the frequency of homicides and "crime on the streets." With regularity the authoritative commissions appointed by recent Presidents to make recommendations concerning crime, civil disorders, or certain types of crime have returned similar reports. No matter whether appointed by President Kennedy, Johnson, or Nixon, when the commissions have secured the facts they have recommended mainly actions affecting the social milieu which breeds crime, not the increasing of penalties. Unfortunately, eliminating racism, economic injustice, or easy possession of guns is politically less popular than cultivating the myth that "cracking down on crime," especially killing the killers, will solve the problem.

In this instance, following the most humane impulses of Judaism and Christianity—and of our best secular traditions—will be the most promising policy for the protection of life and property. The pragmatically most hopeful, as well as the righteous, way to law and order in a democratic society is the way of social justice, humanity, and mercy. It is a long hard road, but there is no other way to the goal.[11]

I conclude that churches need to engage actively in crime-prevention and crime-reduction programs through active practices that combat racism, economic injustice, and easy possession of guns; that support police in their hard work of apprehending criminals; and that strengthen the sense of neighborhood. Louisville is well known, and rightly so, for its ecumenical neighborhood programs (Crescent Hill United Ministries, St. Matthews Area Ministries, Portland Community Center, and others) that help meet needs of families that otherwise could breed disorganization and crime, and that create a sense of cooperative neighborhood working together throughout the city. The sense of belonging to an organized neighborhood rather than to an anonymous city has dramatically reduced crime rates. Louisville's churches actively support these area ministries and thus make them possible and successful.

These practices are hardly exhaustive, and readers who are more creative may see many more dimensions left unmentioned. My overall point is that the churches' response to capital punishment, like their response to all "social problems," ought to focus first on the necessity of being the church, of following Christ concretely in their lives together and dispersed.

Notes

1. See J. Gordon Melton, *The Churches Speak on Capital Punishment* (Detroit: Gale Research, 1989).

2. This is the charge made forcefully by John Howard Yoder in calling contemporary Christian social ethics to be simply one more form of "Constantinianism," whereby the church becomes chaplain to the empire. John Howard Yoder, "The Constantinian Sources of Western Social Ethics," in *The Priestly Kingdom: Social Ethics as Gospel* (Notre Dame, Ind.: University of Notre Dame Press, 1984), 135–50. For one insider's frustrated account of just such an experience with a public policy agency of a mainline church in the United States, see Audrey R. Chapman, *Faith, Power, and Politics: Political Ministry in Mainline Churches* (New York: The Pilgrim Press, 1991).

3. See, e.g., John Howard Yoder, *The Christian Witness to the State*, Institute of Mennonite Studies, no. 3 (Newton, Kans.: Faith & Life Press, 1964).

4. The alternative to withdrawal, assimilation, or theocracy is articulated most clearly in the chapters by John Howard Yoder and Glen Stassen in the reconsideration of the ethics of H. Richard Niebuhr for contemporary U.S. churches. Glen H. Stassen, Diane M. Yeager, and John Howard Yoder, *Au-*

thentic Transformation: A New Vision of Christ and Culture (Nashville: Abingdon Press, 1996).

5. The historic peace churches (Mennonites, Brethren, and Friends) and the Roman Catholic Church have done the most in this area. African American congregations have above-average participation in such ministries.

6. "'Society Wants Blood': An Interview with Chuck Colson," *Sojourners* (July 1979): 14.

7. Howard Zehr, *Changing Lenses: A New Focus for Crime and Justice* (Scottdale, Pa.: Herald Press, 1990), 160–61.

8. Ibid., 164–65.

9. Howard Zehr, *Mediating the Victim/Offender Conflict: The Victim Offender Reconciliation Program* (Akron, Pa.: Mennonite Central Committee U.S., 1990), 24–25.

10. A copy of this declaration is attached as an appendix to the end of this article.

11. L. Harold DeWolf, "The Death Penalty: Cruel, Unusual, Unethical, and Futile," *Religion in Life* 42 (spring 1973): 40–41.

APPENDIX

A Declaration of Life

I, the undersigned, being of sound and disposing mind and memory, do hereby in the presence of witnesses make this Declaration of Life:

I believe the killing of one human being by another is morally wrong.

I believe it is morally wrong for any state or other governmental entity to take the life of a human being for any reason.

I believe that capital punishment is not a deterrent to crime and serves only the purpose of revenge.

THEREFORE, I hereby declare that should I die as a result of a violent crime, I request that the person or persons found guilty of homicide for my killing not be subject to or put in jeopardy of the death penalty under any circumstances, no matter how heinous their crime or how much I may have suffered. The death penalty would only increase my suffering.

I request that the Prosecutor or District Attorney (or State's Attorney or Commonwealth Attorney) having the jurisdiction of the person or persons alleged to have committed my homicide not file or prosecute an action for capital punishment as a result of my homicide.

I request that this Declaration be made admissible in any trial of any person charged with my homicide, and read and delivered to the jury. I also request the Court to allow this Declaration to be admissible as a statement of the victim at the sentencing of the person or persons charged and convicted of my homicide; and to pass sentence in accordance with my wishes.

I request that the Governor or other executive officer(s) grant pardon, clemency, or take whatever action is necessary to stay and prohibit the carrying out of the execution of any person or persons found guilty of my homicide.

This Declaration is NOT meant to be, and should not be taken as, a statement that the person or persons who have committed my homicide should go unpunished. They should be punished, but in a manner that breaks the cycle of violence rather than one that perpetuates it as does the death penalty.

I request that my family and friends take whatever actions are necessary to carry out the intent and purpose of this Declaration; and I further request them to take no action contrary to this Declaration.

I request that, should I die under the circumstances as set forth in the Declaration and the death penalty is requested, my family, friends, and personal representative deliver copies of this Declaration as follows: to the Prosecutor or District, State, or Commonwealth Attorney having jurisdiction over the person or persons charged with my homicide; to the Attorney representing the person or persons charged with my homicide; to the judge presiding over the case involving my homicide; for recording, to the Recorder of the County in which my homicide took place and to the Recorder of the County in which the person or persons charged with my homicide are to be tried; to all newspapers, radio, and television stations of general circulation in the County in which my homicide took place and the County in which the person or persons charged with my homicide are to be tried; and to any other person, persons, or entities my family, friends, or personal representatives deem appropriate in order to carry out my wishes as set forth herein.

I affirm under the pains and penalties for perjury that the above Declaration of Life is true.

WITNESS

_____

_____ printed name

DECLARANT

_____

_____ printed name

_____ Social Security Number

STATE OF_____

COUNTY OF_____

Before me, a Notary Public in and for said county and state, personally appeared the Declarant and acknowledged the execution of the foregoing instrument

this _____ day of _____ 19__.

WITNESS my hand and notarial seal.

_____

NOTARY PUBLIC

_____

Printed Name

My commission expires:_____

County of residence:_____.